MW01256377

THE ODEON

Also by Daniel Tobin

POETRY

Where the World Is Made (1999)

Double Life (2004)

The Narrows (2005)

Second Things (2008)

Belated Heavens (2010)

The Net (2014)

From Nothing (2016)

Blood Labors (2018)

The Mansions (2023)

CHAPBOOK

Glossarias I: From the Distances of Sleep (2025)

TRANSLATION

The Stone in the Air: A Suite of Forty Poems from the German of Paul Celan (2018)

CRITICISM

Passage to the Center: Imagination and the Sacred in the Poetry of Seamus Heaney (1999)

Awake in America: On Irish American Poetry (2011)

On Serious Earth: Poetry and Transcendence (2019)

EDITED COLLECTIONS

Light in Hand: Selected Early Poems of Lola Ridge (2007)

Poet's Work, Poet's Play: Essays on the Practice and the Art (2007, with Pimone Triplett)

The Book of Irish American Poetry: From the Eighteenth Century to the Present (2008)

To the Many: The Collected Early Works of Lola Ridge (2018)

THE ODEON

ESSAYS ON POETRY

Daniel Tobin

Louisiana State University Press

Baton Rouge

Published by Louisiana State University Press
lsupress.org

Designer: Barbara Neely Bourgoyne
Typeface: Calluna

Cover photograph: Unsplash/Jose Manuel Esp

Library of Congress Cataloging-in-Publication Data
Names: Tobin, Daniel, author
Title: The Odeon : essays on poetry / Daniel Tobin.
Description: Baton Rouge : Louisiana State University Press, 2025. |
    Includes bibliographical references and index.
Identifiers: LCCN 2025018328 (print) | LCCN 2025018329 (ebook) | ISBN
    978-0-8071-8470-7 (cloth) | ISBN 978-0-8071-8519-3 (paperback) | ISBN
    978-0-8071-8517-9 (epub) | ISBN 978-0-8071-8518-6 (pdf)
Subjects: LCSH: Poetry | LCGFT: Literary criticism | Essays
Classification: LCC PN1031 .T54 2025 (print) | LCC PN1031 (ebook) | DDC
    808.1—dc23/eng/20250507
LC record available at https://lccn.loc.gov/2025018328
LC ebook record available at https://lccn.loc.gov/2025018329

for Raul Rodriguez and Michael Palma, first teachers in the art

Contents

PREFACE ix

The Odeon, or, Singing and Sensibility 3

John Donne and the Odeon 18

What's Donne Isn't Done: On Ideas of Order and the
Machinery of Poetry 45

. . . .

Ancient Salt, American Grains: On the Poet as Scavenger 65

One Arc Synoptic: Plot, Poetry, and the Span of Consciousness 86

Forms after Forms: On Metamorphosis and Improvisation 128

. . . .

"Hello, I Must Be Going": The Poetry of Farewell 149

Writing for the Dead 168

Lamentation, Poetry, and the Double Life 198

ACKNOWLEDGMENTS 231

NOTES 233

WORKS CITED 241

INDEX 247

Preface

The essays that compose *The Odeon* were originally written for occasions, whether as lectures or presentations, or for publication in books and journals where they first appeared. The attentive reader will nonetheless find resonances and obsessions running through them, not unlike leitmotifs, however initially unplotted and unplanned. In all cases, to some degree, these essays have been revised and developed. The earliest of them was written some years ago; the most recent within a year or so of its publication here. In a substantial way, all of the essays delve into matters of craft and sensibility, poetry and reality, introduced in slightly more pointed fashion in my previous book of essays, *On Serious Earth: Poetry and Transcendence.* The essays of *The Odeon* collectively reflect the thinking of that earlier work and elaborate, I trust, its insights and preoccupations.

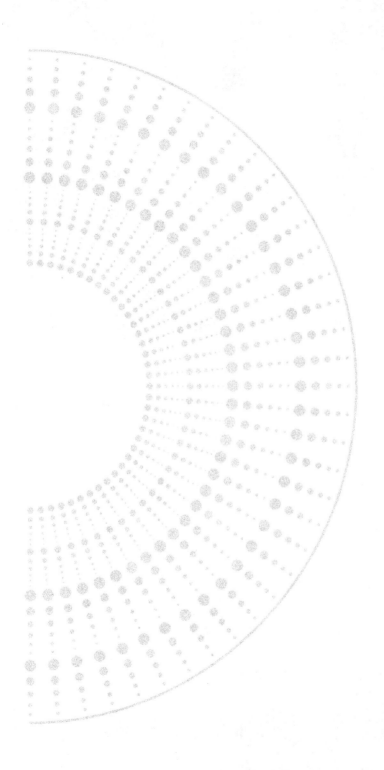

THE ODEON, OR,
SINGING AND SENSIBILITY

Talk about the marginality of poetry, of whether poetry matters, or of poets appearing on public broadcasting stations or reading inaugural poems carries little of real value unless it eventually turns to questions of intention for the art. I mean intention beyond public recognition and prevailing trends, the readiness of the audience and critical receptivity. I mean poetry's relation to some vision of reality and the degree to which the poet pursues that connection, however fitfully, adversely but intentionally in the work. Such an encompassing pursuit, one expects, grows only over time and with a deepening of a poet's dedication to the art. This kind of fully engaged imaginative enterprise becomes more difficult where there is nothing like any shared underlying nexus of agreement within "the Odeon" of practice as it fares in the present cultural moment. The name Odeon comes from the Greek *Oideion,* which means literally "the singing place," itself from the Greek verb *aeido,* "I sing." I love that built-in elision inside the word from public to private and back again, though in ancient Greece and Rome the citizenry built an Odeon for musical exercises and poetry competitions. Yet even in our own time, often on the margins, the origin of poetry in the singing "I" affirms its ghostlier demarcations in the deep registers beyond circumstance and status and state. Still, how can the "I" sing as richly as it might in a cacophony of contrary voices, equivocal choirs, or merely in a vacuum?

Some such question lies behind Mark Edmundson's challenging essay, "Poetry Slam: Or, The Decline of American Verse." For Edmundson, from the diminishment of Robert Lowell's dominance in the last century until our own eclectic present, American poetry has become timid in its purview, or so hermetic in its practice that it ventures little else beside the "creation of a voice."[1] When American poets do aspire to something more than the kind of voice that allows them to "thrive at court," the court of publication and perhaps passing regard, the results are "portentous without touching on any fundamental truth of human experience."[2] For Edmundson, three qualities are necessary for real achievement matching the highest standards of the poet's work: the gift, something to say, and ambition. From Edmundson's elucidation of what he sees as the current malaise in American poetry, it is, above all, the middle quality that is most lacking. There are poets gifted to greater or lesser degrees, and many poets whose careers or work exhibit ambition, but few (if any) for Edmundson have something to say that is not reticent or timid or perpetually hedging, or merely unreadable. Where is the hunger for "speaking in large terms?" he asks. Where, in short, is the poet who would engage the fullness of the historical moment?

For Edmundson, this latter question suggests most of all a poet who would speak for "the polis," such as it is today. There is a deep though perhaps overly indulgent desire in "Poetry Slam" for the persona of the traditionally public poet—a Lowell, a Yeats. Of course, Lowell turned inward in *Life Studies,* and Yeats wrote out of the dramatically charged ideal of poetry as a "personal utterance." For each, the public and the personal conjoined in the poetry to dynamic effect, and both were masters of the poem's architecture. Behind Edmundson's disappointment, his desire for the kind of public poet that stands up like a "hogweed" amidst the discrete fields of the American grain,[3] is the desire for poetry serious enough to pursue ultimacy—a vision of reality, a sensibility that, even in the present context, might embrace diversity without endorsing what one might call a "metaphysics" of dissimilarity. Poetry of that further ambition, that sensibility, requires, before all, the assumption that the poet's "rage for order" has an end equal to the intensity of that rage, however elusive or potentially inexpressible. It affirms in the power of its singing that there is indeed something to sing, something that must be sung. Think of Dante at the end of the *Paradiso:* the ultimate, indescribable limit forges the most intense pressure to invent, there, at the threshold of the final anagogical transfiguration, the world of complete insight, theologically speaking, beyond particulars and their passing relations. In short, to adapt a phrase from theological tradition, one might say that we have entered upon a Land of Unlikeness. The term "unlikeness" as I want to use it here has less to do with any claims about "fallen humanity" and everything to do with an underlying vision that sees the world and language as disintegrated, as inherently divergent from each other, from themselves, and from meaning.

"We must look for an order that orders indeed, but leaves reality, every iota of yours and mine intact—multitudinous, different, and free, but together at last," the critic William Lynch reflects in what has become a sadly neglected though classic book, *Christ and Apollo*.[4] This is analogical order, which is the foundation also of metaphor—language's inherent tensive binding together of unity and difference. Poetry at root is metaphor, and there can be no metaphor without analogy, for without the dynamics of analogy the world is islanded into discrete fragments that bear no relation to each other. The analogical, in short, articulates a state of "similarity-in-difference." Lynch, in turn, characterizes the dissociative model of reality and imagination as "equivocal." For Lynch, the equivocal defines "a mentality which believes that in the whole world of reality and being no two beings *are* in the same sense; everything is completely diverse from everything else."[5] In an equivocal world, we cannot extrapolate to any overarching universal, an idea of order that Lynch calls, at the other extreme, the "univocal." Both the univocal and the equivocal are reductive, he contends, since both elide the essential fact of reality's delicate balance in which the one and the many are held together in dynamic, analogical relation. As that starkly incisive and most world-renouncing of twentieth-century thinkers Simone Weil observed with exemplary concision: the function of language "is to express the relationship between things." Radical thought. In practice, regardless of deeply vested cultural conflicts, or disaccustomed ideas about reality and art, most poets assume the realist perspective as a working model. Regardless of attitudes toward tradition, we assume what we make *means,* however playfully or errantly. We recognize implicitly if not explicitly that to assume a thoroughgoing nominalism, to run precipitously down the path of atomized particulars, is to bind all things to their own isolate realities—poems, language, the world—everything and everyone inhabiting its own impermeable box of discrete existence. But to live, really live, as though we inhabited such impermeable boxes is, I believe, impossible; to write in such a way might just as well be a strategy for turning away, however potentially dazzling that strategy may be.

If the poet's vision of reality is implicit in the making of a poem, of the sensibility behind the poem, and of the poem's signature expression, then one may ask whether that vision can exert pressure on the poet from below? That seems, to me at least, inevitable. There isn't one, but many prevailing visions, though if there were one, that one underlying assumption might be that we live in a world devoid of universals, organized by mechanism—the world conceived of as an "aggregation of parts," mechanistic, merely assuming the appearance of a whole, an entirely equivocal world. This seems so despite the fact that physics, much less metaphysics, implicates consciousness in the very quantum fabric out of which the macro-world emerges—whatever consciousness is or might be beyond some aggregate mist we thinly feel to be the actual. As if to elaborate this point, quantum cosmologist Heinrich Päs in *The One* explores the physical underpinnings of our idea of the universe, the *universum*, "all things combined together into one," thereby seeking to embrace "the universe both as a fundamental unity . . . and as the diversity it appears to us to contain."[6] As a scientist pervasively conversant both theoretically and experimentally with the cutting edge of quantum mechanics, Päs argues convincingly against the positivism and reductionism that have largely defined physics until relatively recently, and therefore against the inherent equivocations of Heisenberg's and Bohr's "Copenhagen Interpretation" of quantum reality that epistemologically cordons off the infinitely small from the infinitely vast, the quantum world from "the classical world" of daily experience, gravity, and billions of stars within trillions of galaxies. Through the properties of entanglement (the inextricable and fundamentally relational "connectedness" of all things in the physical universe) and decoherence (the inevitable limitation of perspective incumbent upon any consciousness defined, as it must be, within space-time), Päs aims to re-frame physics in view of what he calls a "monist" conception of the universe as the compendiously unitary "wave-function" that potentially resolves theoretical conundrums that have proved conceptually resistant, despite the astounding experimental and practical success of quantum theory. Moreover, he makes his case in conversation with Eastern and Western philosophical traditions, and traditionally native perspectives, with the intent to counterpoint what he regards as the inhibitive and at times destructive trends shaping both religion and science. Though both individuals appear to inhabit very different intellectual and epistemological traditions, Lynch and Päs share a commitment across their relative frames of reference to pull us back from a world misconceived and fractured into parts without access to, and without even a conception of, a Whole.

Of course, my own concern is poetry, and it is informed by a poet's sensibility, and my own penchant for such physical and metaphysical matters as Lynch and Päs elaborate in their works undoubtedly and self-reflexively reveals something of my own. "Overall is beyond me," A. R. Ammons declares in "Corson's Inlet," as if to expose his own decoherent vision, combined of course with his roundly analogical insistence on the verity of the anagogical One that sustains the "world line" of his every walk and poem. Despite such convergences of thought and imagination across fields of inquiry and expression, one nonetheless finds a plethora of contemporary poems that apply language in a manner that reflects some vision of life as a mere aggregate of patterns that accrue but do not shape into a whole—poems that are, one might say, less than the sum of their parts. One might say, in fact, that they exhibit a particularly emphatic application of "the mimetic fallacy."[7] The world does not add up, is meaningless, and therefore the poem need not add up, and may simply ride on its surface play of evanescence—associative, dissociative, it doesn't much matter. Such poems, one might say, confuse dynamics with architecture. On the other hand, there are poems that crimp the dynamics of making with an overbearing architectonic impulse bound to some constricted notion of form: the poet who writes "in form," I would say, rather than "with" form, as though a poem's structure were merely a vessel in which to pour subject matter. Rather than capturing a complex emotion within form's motion, its vital architecture, such poems smooth and simplify the irreducible edges. To pursue a poem's formal needs, traditional or otherwise, is to regard form as a map that, by the end of the journey, has turned into a new territory. Such poems exemplify in Seamus Heaney's words "a ratification of the impulse toward transcendence."[8] Irrespective of any underlying or overarching physics or metaphysics, I believe Heaney's declaration stands as a concise and useful definition of the unacknowledged assumption underwriting the poet's work.

Heaney's "impulse toward transcendence" need not, therefore, necessarily carry any explicit religious import. On the other hand, in quite a different context, Gwendolyn Brooks's poem "The Sermon on the Warpland" raises questions of religious ultimacy directly in the epigraph, "the fact that we are black is our ultimate reality." The poem as sermon suggests obvious religious content but, more than religious inference, Brooks's epigraph explicitly transposes her self-evident religious frame into a political context. The poet retools the impulse toward transcendence to counter the pressures of historical reality. Any otherworldly overtones have been re-framed by a sadly and brutally all-too-worldly context. At the same time, sermons are given by individuals who presumably have access by dint of training and knowledge to inspiration that might move people and that might speak to and for others what has been left unspoken, unjustly in this case, and that is precisely how the sermon may offer some redress. One might say that the poem as sermon seeks to enlarge the singing place, the Odeon, for other voices. Certainly, Brooks's poem "Boy Breaking Glass" treats that theme and its social context head-on from its opening lines:

Whose broken window is a cry of art
(success, that winks aware
as elegance, as a treasonable faith)
is raw: is sonic: is old-eyed première.
Our beautiful flaw and terrible ornament.
Our barbarous and metal little man.

"Boy Breaking Glass" is nothing less than a brilliant critique in verse of socially and racially enforced silence, a refusal of admittance to the Odeon, to the singing place, the curtailment of the human need for artistic expression. To abort that impulse, however, is to create its antithesis, so Brooks's argument goes, and the poem invests its expression with the jagged inevitability of that logic. The abrupt opening, the interruption of Brooks's first sentence by the parenthetical remark, the wrenching syntax, the sentence fragments that follow, the sudden overheard voice as from the inarticulate core of the boy's mind finding voice—all perform the very fragmentation enacted by the "metal little man's" exertion of what creativity he can reliably "create," as the lines that follow indicate: "a desecration." As the poem progresses, we find aggregated other shards of perception, other voices, one echoing "the night and cargoes" of the middle passage, another perhaps from one of the boats: "Each to his grief, each to / his loneliness and fidgety revenge." "The only sanity is a cup of tea. / The music is in minors." "Each one other / is having different weather." Brooks's method here is allusive, seemingly dis-associative—equivocal. The poem's strategy is one of a disruptive collage. What prevents the poem from being a facile imitation of the fragmentation it confronts and therefore prevents it from committing the mimetic fallacy? It is where the poem goes, how it enlarges the apparent cacophony of its movements into song—a song as inculcating of the need for transcendence as it is atonal in its orchestration:

"It was you, it was you who threw away my name!
And this is everything I have for me."

Who has not Congress, lobster, love, luau,
the Regency Room, the Statue of Liberty,
runs. A sloppy amalgamation.
A mistake.
A cliff.
A hymn, a snare, and an exceeding sun.

Brooks's boy is a victim of the univocality of racism—his name thrown away. "Boy Breaking Glass" ends with an accusation, and finally with a list that runs the gamut sonically and socially as the boy runs. It is the poem's sonic arrangement that carries the reader along its jagged, consonantal progress—c, l, r, m, and s sounds dominate, leading to the explosive last line in which the contraries, hymn, snare, are transcended by the final image of "an exceeding sun." What does that exceeding sun signify—trouble ahead, an oncoming heat wave? Is it a gesture toward the boy's potential somehow realized in the future? I do not think one can paraphrase the poem's end the way I paraphrased its argument above. The poem exceeds its own final enduring figure—it opens outward at light speed toward some unfathomable fullness of creative largesse, irreducibly neutral, the very supersession of the poem's fraught and terrible ornament, its desecrated analogue. The disenfranchised boy made "a sloppy amalgamation" by his lot in life but the poem is not. Here the poet, in Eliot's phrase, has "amalgamated" the dynamic disparities of social class, race, and violence inside the poem's complex architecture. "Boy Breaking Glass" refuses to accept the world as a mere aggregate of parts and circumstance. Its sense of justice will not allow for such a response. Instead, Brooks amalgamates an answer that converts the experience of being silenced into the dynamic whole that is the poem's contrarian and consummate singing.

What action does a poem take, being itself the product of a consciousness that would follow the poet's solitary trade to wherever it leads artistically? What does the "I" sing for in the singing place? For Gwendolyn Brooks, a poem's contemplative action ought to transcend its artistic integrity and the poet's ambition, though obviously the work discounts neither. Brooks pitches her art toward worldly action without descending to propaganda. Nonetheless, there are circumstances of social injustice that inform "Boy Breaking Glass." Poetry, and certain poems especially, can galvanize another kind of expressly contemplative action—on consciousness itself. One such poem is Brigit Pegeen Kelly's "Song." Kelly's poem tells the story of a goat brutally killed by two boys, and of the girl who owned the goat and loved it as her pet. It is a simple premise, almost an allegory, rife with the potential for sentimentality, that cardinal sin against emotional truth. Yet, in Kelly's hands, the story unfolds with all the aura and cadence of the truly visionary:

> Listen: there was a goat's head hanging by ropes in a tree.
> At night it hung there and sang. And those who heard it
> Felt a hurt in their hearts and thought they were hearing
> The song of a night bird. They sat up in their beds, and then
> They lay back down again. In the night wind, the goat's head
> Swayed back and forth, and from far off it shone faintly
> The way the moonlight shone on the train track miles away
> Beside which the goat's headless body lay. Some boys
> Had hacked its head off. It was harder work than they had imagined. . . .
> And then ran off into the darkness that seems to hide everything.

The poem's first word is a directive demanded by an omniscient speaker, though still an intimate apostrophe to the reader. It is impossible not to hear in Kelly's directive something akin in urgency and gravity to the Ancient Mariner coming upon the wedding guest who, having encountered the stranger, "cannot choose but hear." "Song" sings its narrative with a voice emerging out of the blankness of the page as if out of the far recesses of consciousness itself, the way one of Hildegaard von Bingen's visions might have emerged from the migrainous dance of light as from out of the anagogical world of spiritual realities. A goat's head hanging, singing, swaying, is not necessarily a "type" of crucifixion, not yet at least. Only later does the struggling goat cry like a man, and still later is the boys' desecration confirmed a "sacrifice," albeit a "silly" one. How subtly but startlingly and ingeniously Kelly's poem moves with cinematic intensity down the page and, as it does, moves backwards in time, the verbs shifting from present tense, present participle, to past tense: Listen, hanging, swayed. It is the goat's death song—its song-in-death—that the poem follows back to the killing scene. Like a midwestern magical realist nightmare, "Song" lowers us ever more deeply into a world where ordinary reality and otherworldly visions are coterminous, and where private harm commingles with public commonweal. It is our world become again figuratively alive to the spirit. In this vitally charged world, the essential, eternal relations between things—all the scattered parts, the violent sunderings—reveal themselves:

> The head hung in the tree. The body lay by the tracks
> The head called to the body. The body to the head.
> They missed each other. The missing grew large between them,
> Until it pulled the heart right out of the body, until
> The drawn heart flew toward the head, flew as a bird flies
> Back to its cage and the familiar perch from which it trills.
> Then the heart sang in the head, softly at first and then louder. . . .

In quantum experiments, the experimenter fires a particle of light through a screen such that it splits into two. Still, those two particles are nonetheless bound together forever despite being flung to opposite zones in time and space. The term for this phenomenon is "spooky action at a distance," and that is exactly what Kelly imagines between the goat's head and the goat's heart, now fabulously at the macrocosmic level of the everyday. The poet envisions this deep connection across scales despite the world's nominal fragmentation, and figures this elusive connectedness-in-difference into the being of the poem.

"Song" is a single strophe with a cadence that runs, typically, seven beats per line. Highly structured in its narrative, the poem's the first twenty lines focus on the goat and its song. The next twenty-nine lines focus on the little girl and the backstory of the boys' meaningless violation, their joke, her trauma, the townspeople seeking the culprits. The final fifteen lines focus on the spiritual repercussions for the violators—and not only for the animal and the little girl, but for life itself. Not unlike the pointless act of shooting the albatross in "The Rime of the Ancient Mariner," the repercussions of violence alter the nexus of relationships at a cosmic level. The poem's final turn comes with the stark repetition of its initial directive: "But listen," and then "here is the point." It is immensely daring for a poem to state so baldly its point and purpose, but "Song" from the outset is just such an immensely daring poem, which is why it compels. The singing stops when the goat's heart is reunited with its head, but not for the boys who thought they had finished the job and washed the blood from their hands:

> What they didn't know
> Was that the goat's head would go on singing, just for them,
> Long after the ropes were down, and that they would learn to listen
> Pail after pail, stroke after patient stroke. They would
> Wake in the night thinking they heard the wind in the trees
> Or a night bird, but their hearts beating harder. There
> Would be a whistle, a hum, a high murmur, and, at last, a song,
> The low song a lost boy sings remembering his mother's call.
> Not a cruel song, no, no, not cruel at all. This song
> Is sweet. It is sweet. The heart dies of this sweetness.

It is too easy to say that what Kelly evokes here is simply conscience rising in the boys' minds long after their "silly sacrifice" found completion. No, what the boys hear is not a moral comeuppance sonically tuned, but a mystical siren's song that kills the cruel heart out of love, the very love that binds head to heart and holds all things in analogical communion. Does the heart die as prelude to a *metanoia*, a change of heart? Kelly's poem does not say, but leaves us in the brutal sweet mystery of that empty place—a harrowing measured against our own, anagogical unknowing.

Neither Brooks's "Boy Breaking Glass" nor Kelly's "Song" overtly gestures toward the kind of self-announcing bardic aesthetic Mark Edmundson implies is currently lacking in American poetry. Yet, surely, each poem in its way touches on a fundamental truth of human experience. That truth I would venture is an analogical truth, inevitably and ineluctably relational in nature, a likeness not a univocal identification. Though Brooks's boy breaks glass, there is nothing equivocal in that shattering. Though Kelly's murdered goat sings, it embodies all our songs of suffering by being first of all, and unrepeatably, its own. There is no nominalist assumption behind any of these poems. Neither the boy nor the goat exists in name only for the poets. They are real insofar as they exemplify through their uniqueness the universality that requires their unrepeatable existence, a universality arrived at, paradoxically, only through difference, in difference, the full measure of which inevitably transcends representation by being anagogical. Language carries us to the brink of the invisible, leads us up, as the word *anagogic* enacts at its root, into mystery. Perhaps, one might speculate, the analogical is nothing other than a kind of syntax of the metaphysical. The word *logos* with its teleological purposefulness embeds itself in the word: the unequivocal given condition that rides us onward in meaning-making relation to one another and to what exceeds us, bearing us not to one univocal end but to many promised, purposeful ends that nonetheless constellate in unity—an unfinishable infinitude, the ultimate run-on sentence. I digress. By the ends of their poems, Brooks and Kelly both make superb music; each commands metaphors, each exhibits remarkable lyric and narrative gifts, and each, surely, has "something to say," as Mark Edmundson requires, though perhaps in a manner distinct from the way he defines that requirement. Both poems join power of expression to thematic gravitas, and both Brooks and Kelly are ambitious, foremost for the work.

Poems like "Boy Breaking Glass" and "Song" depend on a vision of reality and an artistic commitment to that vision, regardless of audience, precisely because they take a stand for human consciousness and the expression of human consciousness against a world violently cut off from the idea of a deeper, analogical unity. In both cases, the song one wants to hear in the Odeon is a song of atonement, redress, of singing out of and on behalf of the silenced, whether a thwarted boy or a beheaded goat, and each a figure for the world entire, disheartened and dismembered at the spiritual core. Both figures reaffirm in their own idiom the analogical imagination retaining its force and scope.

If "Boy Breaking Glass" and "Song" imply a connection to such humanly necessary matters beyond whatever social and religious commentaries they might negotiate in their artful way, then Ellen Bryant Voigt's poem "Song and Story" makes the spiritual role of the poet's work explicit. In doing so, Voigt's poem identifies the poet's role as irreducibly and enduringly human and therefore a matter of the poet's ultimate concern—"ultimate concern" being theologian Paul Tillich's succinct definition for the word "faith." "Song and Story" begins bluntly and brutally with a young girl strapped in a mechanical crib, unconscious, with a "glottal tube" taped into her face. There is no motion, only the "flutter of her heart" recorded on a monitor, a flutter that "steadies into a row of waves" every time her mother sings. The poem's opening lines are syntactically curt, end-stopped, though we still hear the recognizable backbeat of Voigt's masterfully supple blank verse. In the ninth line, when the mother starts to sing, the poem suddenly modulates its tone and music into a new cadence. That cadence is unmistakably ritual speech, ritual action; the row of waves become "song of the sea, song of the scythe" and so the poem delivers us from brute time, passing time, into mythic time: "old woman by the well, picking up stones / old woman by the well, picking up stones." The poem's shift in tone, its refrain that will be repeated two more times with slight variation and with the same ritualized cadence, does something else as well. It carries the hard world of the poem over from profane time through mythic time into ritual time, sacred time, from *Chronos* into *Kairos*, from time measured by number to time experienced as meaning.[9] So the waves of the sick child's heartbeat transfigure into ocean waves, and we become transported into the song of the sea:

> When Orpheus, beating rhythm with a spear
> against the deck of the armed ship, sang
> to steady the oars, he borrowed an old measure:
> broadax striking oak, oak singing back,
> the churn, the pump, the shuttle sweeping the warp
> like the waves against the shore they were pulling toward.

Orpheus, of course, is the primordial poet of Greek myth, the son of Memory (Mnemosyne), whose song can make the very stones turn and listen. Voigt's poem moves us as through a sweeping warp in space and time to another claustrophobic scene of men bound closely together, at war, and the call and response of this old measure makes bearable the oldest of stories, our human story: "They were living a story—the story of desire." Regardless of the outcome, having lived their version of the singular narrative, the song will carry them back to the "wave-licked, smooth initial shore." On that shore the masculine music of broadax striking oak declines to the feminine music of domestic endurance: "song of the locust, song of the broom // old woman in the field binding wheat / old woman by the fire, grinding corn."

In its first two strophes and its ritual refrain, "Song and Story" captures the essence of human existence—life in jeopardy, life unfolding as it will out of the necessities of desire, life enduring beyond loss and longing. In the third strophe, Voigt's poem brings us the poet, Orpheus, preparing his song "for the overlords of hell / to break the hearts they didn't know they had." As in Brigit Pegeen Kelly's poem, "Song and Story" brings us to an encounter with death, the final barrier and gulf that the song, the poem, would impossibly bridge. This song, poetry, so Voigt's poem assures us, is "not the music of pain." On the contrary, like the child motionless in her crib, like the mother bearing witness to her child's pain and her own, like the men at war, "pain" the poem declares, "has no music":

> pain is not a song: it is a story . . .
> It starts, *Eurydice was taken from the fields.*
> She did not sing—you cannot sing in hell—
> but in that viscous dark she could hear
> her lover singing on the path, the song
> flung like a rope into the crater of hell,
> song of the sickle, song of the hive

In its final turn, then, the poem circles back, but in its passage the singular scene of pain and compassion with which it began now suggests with an almost archetypal significance. Beyond the archetypal, however, we might better understand this jointure of discrete events as analogical, for in their very discreteness the two scenes enlarge each other. They mutually participate in the making of meaning, surpluses of meaning. The part, this sickness, perhaps this death, is nothing less than the whole, all suffering, all deaths without ceasing to be this one, this death. The poet does not equivocate about what the singer, the poet, must do to be optimally, paradigmatically, the poet:

> The one who can sing sings to the one who can't,
> who waits in the pit, like Procne among the slaves,
> as the gods decide how all such stories end,
> the story woven into the marriage gown,
> or scratched with a stick in the dust around the well,
> or written in blood on the box on the stucco wall—

Voigt's allusion to the story of Procne and Philomel, the latter of whom suffered rape and atrocity at the hands of Procne's husband, Tereus, underscores the poem's vision of disruptive continuity between story and song. Story is inevitable, is of time, and therefore reenacts our desire, our suffering, and ultimately our mutability. Its sacral truth originates in its ability to represent profane life, life that passes away. Song, bound to story, subtends it the way the sacred subtends the profane, the way the immaterial subtends the material, the way the spiritual subtends the physical—or that is the unspoken assumption of the poet's faith. How does the poem know this truth well enough to portray it? Voigt's "Song and Story" enforces a nonnegotiable directive upon the listener, and underscores the urgency of that directive with an abrupt disturbance of line-length and cadence:

> look at the wall:
> the song, rising and falling, sings in the heartbeat,
> sings in the seasons, sings in the daily round—
> even at night, deep in the murmuring wood—
> listen—one bird, full-throated, calls to another,
> *little sister,* frantic little sparrow under the eaves.

Look. Listen. It is hard to imagine a poem ending with a more definitive command. It is all around us, among us, deep in the murmuring wood echoing Dante's *selva oscura* where everything that ever was, is, or will be calls out its own self-song to another in relation, it must be in relation beyond the demarcations. In Ellen Bryant Voigt's "Song and Story," the singing place, the Odeon, becomes wholly transparent to a vision of reality underscored by *Kairos,* temporality in all of its grief and suffering nonetheless governed by irreducible meaning. The poet's work—the "I" who would sing—must do so for others, so Voigt's poem reaffirms in our later disbelieving time the poet's sacred obligation. What the poet would sing in the singing place is the one song in and through the many—not one univocal story, but the enduring under-song of superabundance through which, in the daily round, all things come to be and are with each other in the making, intimately linked in their individual being. Is there anything more urgently needed to be sung?

"Boy Breaking Glass," "Song," and "Song and Story" manifest the kind of vision and urgency that I long to see more of, where poets come together to sing, both physically and virtually—the Odeon of our moment in the art beyond the courts of profession and trends. Each poem displays the utmost ambition, each has something urgent to say, each is brilliantly crafted. When I look at handwritten drafts of poems penned by poets famous or not, the ragged handwriting, scratched out words, lines, and stanzas, I think of the particular hand, the ink and paper, that meeting of objects and the unique consciousness shaping something out of it all, as though something unprecedented and utterly immaterial were entering into material life. The Internet grows like a biological system, investing itself with an architecture, a hierarchy that emerges gradually from the dynamics of participants on line. Only the slightest number of clicks separates each one from everyone, the hits strengthening some sites more than others—a kind of shared accrual of value, a survival of the fittest, everyone islanded, no one an island (or everyone) in its ever-emergent topology. One prominent scholar decries the timidity and inwardness of contemporary American poetry, though even the most public poem originates in the inwardness of the poet, the inwardness of the poet facing outward, backward, and forward. It is the poet turning inside out outside in, in the language, worldly, broadly analogical even in these latter days—and meaning so profligate it exceeds us even as it valorizes our words. Praise the unlikely in our Land of Unlikeness, how it surprisingly returns a likeness, and the survival of that likeness in our differences singing still in the Odeon.

JOHN DONNE AND THE ODEON

NET

Today, because I am sufficiently connected here in my book-glutted home in Boston, I have decided to make my little room an everywhere. As it so happens, I am hovering now above an area of greater London known as Mitcham that four hundred years ago was an outlying village backwater away from the teeming intrigue and bustle of King James's city and his court. One click, another, and another, and I am a virtual parachutist riding the virtual air down to a knotty maze of suburban streets that look neatly groomed, their names rising amidst the topology along with the names of businesses and landmarks—Body Zest, Merton Pre-School, Seven Island Pond. Another click and I have donned a golden terra-suit to incarnate myself on Donne Place.

Out of the Map Man's eyes I see four attractive homes, two-family, stucco and brick, though none of them ostentatious or opulent. This is what passes for an upper middle-class suburb in one of the great world cities of the twenty-first-century West—no trace of the cottage where John Donne moved with his family after years of estrangement from his father-in-law, Sir George More, who was so incensed by the poet's elopement with his daughter, Anne, he had his unlawful son-in-law thrown briefly into the Fleet Street prison. Donne, as he wrote to Sir George, had "undone" his daughter in a manner that could not be "undone" and, as such, in a triple entendre, Donne had become "undone" himself. Though Donne was released, it took a long time to undo the personal and professional damage. The couple's reconciliation with Sir George came five years after their secret marriage in 1601, effectively destroying Donne's professional life, such that he relied on charity until Sir George "agreed to give the couple an income of £80 per year," as John Heath Stubbs recounts in his magisterial biography, *John Donne: The Reformed Soul*.[1] Donne referred to the cottage in Mitcham as his "prison," "dungeon," "his hospital" where he kept a first floor study, his "poor Library" that at times filled with "raw vapors . . . from the cellar below."[2] He would live in Mitcham for some six years, during which time he composed his two "Anniversaries," among other masterworks, before moving to Drury Lane and London's inner sanctum, before Anne died in childbirth with their twelfth child (only seven of whom survived), before he gave up the ambitions of court and acceded after years of refusing to become an Anglican divine and, eventually, famously, the Dean of St. Paul's Cathedral, where his likeness in stone, draped in his death shroud, can be viewed today.

Donne's world-line, as a contemporary physicist might call it, that messy knitting together of the personal life and the wider prospects of time and space, cuts in and through his own historical circumstance and keeps on going:

> For of meridians and parallels,
> Man hath weaved out a net, and this net thrown
> Upon the heavens, and now they are his own.

These lines from Donne's "An Anatomy of the World, The First Anniversary" not only speak to the centrality of topology in Donne's vision, they elaborate his profound intellectual and imaginative engagement with the rapidly transforming world of his time. They also telegraph across five centuries to the breakneck transformations of our own moment, and to the place of poetry in a world that appears more atomized even as it is woven together ever more tightly by nets of association that Donne with his visionary wit could not have wholly imagined, but which his work in its own time and idiom foreknew. No man is an island, Donne famously wrote in his *Devotions upon Emergent Occasions.* What could be more emergent than the occasion of our own lives here and now, where a solitary person living in a condominium in Boston can travel virtually in seconds to a site more than three thousand miles away simply by typing "Mitcham" and "Donne" on a search engine? Man hath weaved out a net, yes, and the earth in a manner has become more strangely, though perhaps not more truly, our own.

If anything, from this vantage the world has become small, an island, flat, built and ever-more premised on connectivity. While this may be the case in superficial terms, it is almost self-evident that the presumably deeper bonds connecting people and peoples have lost any deeper cultural affiliation. The binding language of traditional protocols, to borrow from contemporary "net-speak," appears to be working at cross-purposes. From Donne's time, and before, what Owen Barfield called "the background picture" of the human being "as a microcosm within the macrocosm" has been lost.[3] The island, so to speak, has become decentralized, which is a marvelous way to establish exponential "data" exchange but perhaps not so efficacious for obtaining anything akin to a shared vision, if such a thing were possible now. We live, conversely, in a *disjecta membra,* as Barfield claimed, and that is only more emphatically the case in the twenty-first century, in our "post" modern milieu. We live, in short, with local exceptions, in a dissociated world held together by fragile links of utility and self-promotion underpinned by laws of mutual advantage—a materialist ethos and cosmos that cannot but influence cultural representations and, hence, art. Poetry is no exception. This may not be the state of "mental chaos" T. S. Eliot envisioned would ensue once "our traditions" had completely exploded like the Hindenburg,[4] but it may well resonate accurately with Marilynne Robinson's reflection that such a state contributes to "the exclusion of felt life from the varieties of thought and art."[5] For Robinson as for Barfield, the prevailing materialist worldview has established itself very nearly to the exclusion of any counter "interpretation of the facts of nature."[6] It has become "the only possible method" and therefore precludes out of hand any reference to what might be even loosely understood as a metaphysical stance toward life and art. Reading Donne, or any poet so inclined, would appear to be antiquarian in such a climate, unless there is more to the human place and material reality than an accidental network of matter and energy, without purpose, without teleology, without end.

Ted Hughes once declared that a poet's sensibility is shaped ultimately by their idea of God, which of course would include the idea of God's nonexistence. Seamus Heaney, despite his own reticence in religious matters, declared that "poetry is a ratification of the impulse toward transcendence."[7] From the standpoint of their own exceptional accomplishments, both poets are echoing T. S. Eliot, though neither embraces Eliot's high-flown orthodoxy. In "The Metaphysical Poets" Eliot affirms the central importance of reading the Metaphysicals and Donne in particular, and he affirms reading them with confidence in their relevance for the practice of the art irrespective of a particular historical moment: "When a poet's mind is perfectly equipped for its work, it is constantly amalgamating disparate experience; the ordinary man's experience is chaotic, irregular, fragmentary. The latter falls in love and reads Spinoza, and these two experiences have nothing to do with each other, or with the noise of the typewriters or the smell of cooking; in the mind of the poet these experiences are always forming new wholes."[8] Admittedly, these lines have become so often quoted as to be considered reducible to Eliot's singular sensibility, his own fraught biography. Then again, Yeats's ideal that poetry should hold in single thought "reality and justice," and Stevens's "blessed rage for order," and Frost's "momentary stay against confusion" would suggest that there is something to the idea that the poet's work optimally binds together disparities and creates dynamic unities. What would be the purpose of Adrienne Rich's "Diving into the Wreck" if not to bring back from the deep reaches something—a poem—with universal significance beyond merely political and cultural redress? Poets like Rich intend to shake the established order to create a more encompassing and just order. They do so in order to transform the given conditions—to, in a word, *transcend* them.

In Eliot's estimation Donne typifies the poet's ability to bring disparate aspects of reality into comprehending vision: the ideal poet "telescopes associations." "Connectivity" is a word used today to describe the internet's capacity for linking the vastly evolving global network of singular digital users of technology, though Donne's imaginative "connectivity" is what Eliot so admires. Likewise, Eliot praises Donne's "mechanism of sensibility, which could devour any kind of experience."[9] It is interesting, and not a little prescient, to use a word like "mechanism" to describe Donne's genius, his proclivity to see into and uncover hidden unities, hidden likenesses, precisely through the experience of difference—as if the multiplicity of things revealed a deeper organizing principle that held everything in dynamic relation. The "mechanism of sensibility," of his sensibility, was to see those hidden connections. Yet, perhaps surprisingly given the growing preponderance of the world perceived as mechanism over recent centuries, Eliot likewise saw the omnivorous capacity of imagination to find connections somehow more commensurate with the poetry of Donne's time than his own—or ours, one might extrapolate. To borrow Eliot's famous phrase, a "dissociation of sensibility" settled into Western culture since the seventeenth century, coterminous with the rise of positivism and reductionism, both of which assert reality does not track to higher orders of being and meaning. The kind of imaginative "connectivity" that telescopes associations signals a more fundamental misfiring, as if the sub-circuits of our understanding were actually, and essentially, disconnected. We perceive only an illusion of connection. The associations are really dissociations. There are only parts, and the parts do not make a Whole. Or, one might say, there is no centripetal force, only centrifugal, and we are in fact, as Nietzsche mused, falling in all directions at once. Metaphysics, in such a scenario, becomes a nonsensical term, since there is nothing above the materials themselves, no *meta* above the *physical.* Our dissociation of sensibility expresses a dissociative model of reality. As such, as language becomes more technically refined feeling becomes ever more crudely expressed and embodied—that, at least, is Eliot's conclusion. But it is only the immediate outcome. Inevitably the assumption that language makes meaning, or discovers meaning, disintegrates. We are left with a world of consuming self-reference.

Extrapolating from Eliot's vision of a world in which thought is severed from feeling, William Lynch in *Christ and Apollo* notably characterizes the dissociative model of reality as "equivocal." The term "equivocal" defines "a mentality which believes that in the whole world in reality and being no two beings *are* in the same sense; everything is completely diverse from everything else."[10] The figure of the Land of Unlikeness with its long theological pedigree finds a modern incarnation, contra the claims of globalism, in our proclivity for dis-integration: to see language devoid of ultimate claims to meaning, a Babel of irreconcilable points of view, and the tendency for diversity to be severed from the deeper and more pervasively recognized fundament of inclusion. We abide in a region of "dissimilarity," to use Augustine's word for this bewildering state of affairs. It is a term that rings strangely contemporary despite the intervening sixteen hundred years from Augustine's age to our own. Against unlikeness, dissimilarity, I would emphasize the counter position—that ideally the poet's work and the greatest poems amalgamate disparate experience, hold together contraries, in the dynamic unity of the poem. At a time when "an emptiness is thought to have entered human experience with the recognition that an understanding of the physical world can develop and accelerate through disciplines of reasoning for which God is not a given,"[11] the poet's work continues nonetheless to rest on what one might call, with full awareness of the paradox, a *subtending* metaphysics. It rests on the often unstated and unrecognized assumption that one's efforts in the art require a premise of ordering that outstrips the world understood as the product of accident alone. Without that assumption there is only babble, Babel, and after Babel only an "anarchic multiplicity."[12] Yet, there is something in the net of our history, our traditions, our physical make-up, our time, and our consciousness, that continues to exert its pressure and continues to fuel poetry's vital directive to form new wholes, new connections across boundaries of sensibility and time and place.

PATTERN

In the spring of 1593, as John Heath Stubbs recounts,[13] one William Harrington was brought by the anti-Papist authorities under Queen Elizabeth to Tyburn Tree where he was tortured and executed. The executioner cut off his genitals before he disemboweled him slowly and burnt his intestines while the dying man watched. The crowd cheered, pleased to have a priest and traitor brought to justice. Harrington was a friend of John Donne's brother, Henry, who would himself die soon after in prison as a traitor to the crown. With a strong Catholic pedigree harkening back to Sir Thomas More, the Donne family lived under suspicion and, at times, in exile. Donne's ambitions and his conversion to the Church of England reflect both the tumultuous nature of the time and his own deeply conflicted personal life. It would appear Eliot's idealized image that Donne the poet "could feel his thought as immediately as the odor of a rose"[14] elides the crucible of how art gets made in often extreme circumstantial and psychically fraught conditions, however Eliot's surmise might speak accurately to the achievement on the page.

Though the vast majority of us are shielded from the immediate experience of brutality and butchery, none of us is any more than a click away from such horrors streamed into our minds at a screen's remove—bombings, beheadings, all the foment and terror of our own historical moment. Donne's time, moreover, not unlike our own, marks a transition in which revolutionary discoveries altered perceptions of reality, scientifically as well as geographically. For all the differences between Donne's world and ours there is a great continuity of human imagination confronting what Wallace Stevens called "the pressure of reality."[15] For Stevens, the pressure of reality "exists for individuals according to the circumstances of their lives or according to the characteristics of their minds," and it ultimately determines "the artistic character of an era."[16] How does one respond to this pressure? "It is a violence from within that protects us from a violence without," Stevens concluded. "It is the imagination pressing back against the pressure of reality."[17]

John Donne's "The Canonization" vividly exemplifies how a great poet's characteristic effort of imagination can indeed press back against reality with the result that the poem's artistry establishes a new and irrefutable "amalgamation" of the world and the work. The poem was written in the spring of 1602 when Donne was awaiting judgment over his secret marriage to Anne More.[18] The barely restrained rage of the opening apostrophe places the reader by proxy in the role of John Donne's and Anne Donne's enemies, and that rage unfolds progressively in an ever more outrageous sequence of taunts:

> For God's sake hold your tongue, and let me love,
>> Or chide my palsy, or my gout,
> My five grey hairs, or ruined fortune, flout,
>> With wealth your state, your mind with arts improve,
>>> Take you a course, get you a place,
>>> Observe his Honour, or his Grace,
> Or the King's real, or his stampèd face
>> Contemplate; what you will, approve,
>> So you will let me love.

"The Canonization" gathers the force of its energy in an act of self-dramatizing speech that calls us up short and presents a series of mocking alternatives to the violent imposition of reality's will that so plagues the speaker. The series begins self-referentially by focusing on the poet's body and his worldly state, but turns in the fourth line, where the shortcomings of his unnamed enemies are targeted for edification in economics, the arts—or any course of study for that matter—before still more immoderately demanding that they go meditate on the King's face. Here is poetry willing to approach treason as well as risk blasphemy.

The essence of Donne's brilliance in this opening stanza, as throughout the poem and in all of his greatest works, is his ability to bind dramatic speech,

syntax, and structure into a single dynamic form. That Donne's "The Canonization" rides vibrantly along as spoken word is self-evident from the start:
"For God's sake," a phrase that is at once idiomatic and carries inside itself
theological implications that the poem toys with as it unfolds. At the same
time, this stanza's single sentence moves through its right-branching clauses
in a manner that progressively shifts and enlarges its perspective and intensifies the urgency of the affront the poet feels. The poem enforces its dramatic
vitality and its syntactical complexity within a highly elaborate stanza that
epitomizes the importance of structure for creating imaginative pressure—the
very pressure by which the poem, with a barely contained violence of its own,
answers back. Donne's stanza alternates iambic pentameter lines with tetrameter lines and ends with a final trimeter line. It does so by rhyming *abbacccaa*.
"The Canonization" stanza, in short, unifies the expansive with the intensive.
Donne's structural intensity is particularly noticeable in the three "c" rhyming
words, lines 5–7 in each stanza. The compression of these three rhyming lines
creates an intensive core to the stanza structure. To create still more compression and intensity in the first stanza and those that follow, Donne end-stops
nearly every line. In turn, the final trimeter line in its relative brevity carries
the force of a summation.

At the same time as the first stanza moves through its vocal, syntactical,
and structural paces, it embodies the overall pattern of a circle, a very tight circle, off-rhymed but doubly rhymed, and, following the imprint of the first, the
first and last line of every stanza end with the word "love." In short, Donne's
stanza inscribes an arc of thought and feeling such that one ends where one
had begun, but one does so having undergone a passage that involves a simul-
taneous sharpening and enlargement of perception as well as the expansion
and intensification of felt knowledge. The four succeeding stanzas of "The
Canonization" repeat this pattern and elaborate its compass of effects and
implication the way fractal patterns repeat even as they evolve into more elaborate versions of themselves.

The five questions that carry through the first two-thirds of the second
stanza modulate the near taunts of the first into a string of hyperboles that
in turn mock the conventional imagery—sailing ships, floods of tears—of
Petrarchan love poetry. By its end the poem establishes the lovers in an alternate reality apart from the reality of soldiers and litigious men—in other words

the violent and self-advancing powers of the world. Having been a soldier and having studied law, Donne knew whereof he spoke, and he marshals his experience into the poem's developing argument. The question "Who's injured by my love?" shifts the tone from the aggressively aggrieved to that of a clever litigator, and the rest of the stanza elaborates that shift in tone and perspective. It is the third stanza, however, where Donne encodes most intensively the poem's core conceit, its imaginative DNA. The stanza begins with a directive, "Call us," and this call invites a kind of primal naming suggestive of a more substantial calling, commingling in one stroke the double sense of invocation and vocation in both the religious and poetic senses of those terms. Love makes them such, for love itself is the truest maker, the truest poet. Now, in a string of leaps that dovetail the litigator's logic with the poet's imaginative powers, the poem enacts the very metamorphosis by which art seeks to best the pressure of reality through an act of transfiguration:

> Call her one, me another fly,
> We're tapers too, and at our own cost die,
> And we in us find the eagle and the dove.
> The phoenix riddle hath more wit
> By us: we two, being one, are it.
> So, to one neutral thing both sexes fit.
> We die and rise the same, and prove
> Mysterious by this love.

Fly, candle, eagle, dove, phoenix—Donne's string of metaphors moving from the lowliest to the figural to the mythic elaborates the physical union of the lovers. It does so, however, through a barely encoded metaphysics in which mythology elides to theology, the dying and rising phoenix to the dying and rising, unnamed God in whose presiding pattern the lovers also die and rise. "To die" in Elizabethan parlance was code for sexual intercourse, and Donne is surely playing on this pun throughout this stanza and at the start of the next. Yet it is precisely this down and dirty wit in Donne's poetry that enables him to fit together the sexual and the metaphysical, the materially low and the spiritually high. The stanza constitutes a veritable knot of blunt statement, metaphorical slippage, and wild allusion that is as reverent in its muted theological assumptions as it is irreverent in its brashness. The declaration, "we two, being one, are it" could just as easily be spoken by the Father, son, and Spirit of the Holy Trinity, without of course the sexual inuendo. Theologically speaking, the stanza embeds this reading when the lovers are bedded in the manner in which Donne beds them, as they die and rise, and rise simultaneously into mystery. Here, the ultimate metaphysical mystery of Love (if one is so inclined) becomes recapitulated in the physical mystery Donne evokes as the vehicle of the lovers' transfiguration, and that recapitulation is perfectly orthodox. God, after all, has become incarnate for the orthodox Christian. Donne's wit is far more than light-minded cleverness; it is a capacity that exhibits the height of human invention and models an amplitude native to the human condition at its most vividly realized.

Of course, Donne's conjoining of apparent opposites—sex and spirit, sacred and profane—is precisely what Samuel Johnson objected to so famously and vigorously. The "metaphysick style," Johnson declared, originates in the kind of wit that combines "dissimilar images," discovers "occult resemblances in things apparently unlike" and through which, summarily, "the most heterogeneous ideas are yoked by violence together; nature and art are ransacked for illustrations, comparisons, and allusions."[19] Donne's "The Canonization" exults in such imaginative violence, and does so for the very reason Stevens identified four centuries later: reality exerts enormous pressure on the poet as on any person, but in the poet's case reality's violent imposition finds its answer in the transfiguring force of imagination. "The Canonization" is audacious in its enactment of the poet's presumption to trump the powers of dire circumstance. The last two stanzas of Donne's poem perform exactly this office:

We can die by it, if not live by love,
    And if unfit for tombs and hearse
Our legend be, it will be fit for verse . . .

Here to die *is* to die, the lovers having died already for each other's pleasure and self- completion, and thus they rise into poetry, that well-wrought urn—surely one of the most famous metaphors for art that we have, thanks to John Donne and Cleanth Brooks by way of John Keats. It is crucial that in Donne's vision the urn "becomes the greatest ashes." Here again we discover Donne's genius for telescoping surpluses of meaning (rather than elisions thereof) into a single word or image. The urn, the poem, as a memorial makes death, the hardest of reality's hard edges, more becoming, less its ugly self. Beyond this, the urn literally transforms itself into that which it contains, and as such what is contained becomes the urn, the poem. Art, Donne affirms, has transfigured even death by swallowing it whole. The poem enacts a metamorphosis by which phoenix and Christ are but two figures in a still more fundamental pattern that the poem embodies. From this vantage, the smallest urn equals a half-acre tomb and the lovers' metaphysical "canonization" via their physical communion promises something more than a mere subversion of religious categories.

The poem's final invocation, spoken by the very powers of reality that plagued the lovers in life, bears witness to their dual sainthood. A poem that begins in enraged apostrophe by the aggrieved ends in an earnest apology by the powers whose injustice martyred them. This final move of the poem draws back from asserting an idea of poetry premised on some belated conception of art for art's sake. Donne's poem ultimately gestures from its rarified vantage back to the world, for in its final invocation the whole world's soul contracts into the glasses of the lovers' eyes as they look at each other. It is a stunningly vital image of perfect relation. That this contraction is "driven" into the lovers' eyes itself suggests violence at something akin to the cosmic level, like a star going supernova. Donne's poem, however, reverses the polarities of even this black hole, had the poet known of such cosmic realities. Rather, the world which is a fractured corpus of countries, towns, and courts has in the lovers' eyes become two, and those two become one through their responsive gaze. That mutual gaze is "peace," at once a worldly and otherworldly ideal. "We two, being one, are it." And it, here, is not only the mythic phoenix, or any figure theological or otherwise, but "it" is the aching world entire. "The Canonization" enacts the pattern of an initially unforeseen redemption at every level of scale, above and below, intensively and extensively, in flesh and spirit, in microcosm as in macrocosm, all progressively embodied by the poem. Is it all hyperbole? Of course, though if it is nothing but hyperbole where does that leave the world and poetry?

FIGURE

Between Donne's at once subversive and lofty argument on behalf of poetry in "The Canonization" and Stevens's premise that art must assume the role of religion since the notion of God itself is nothing other than "the supreme poetic idea"[20] there appears to be a vast gulf. In his essay "Symbol as Revelation," Yeats concurs in spirit with Stevens: "How can the arts overcome the slow dying of men's hearts that we call the progress of the world and lay their hands upon men's heartstrings again without becoming the garment of religion as in old times?"[21] Donne took the garment of religion as a given; indeed, he eventually donned the garment of an Anglican priest despite his youthful wild nights. As John Heath Stubbs astutely observes, Donne's whole life composes a quest for "the right eternity" and hence the right worldly expression of that eternity.[22] Contrary to Yeats and Stevens, Eliot regards art as a poor substitute for religion, and one must believe Donne would agree with his view. By further contrast, the next starkly visible station on the long journey away from anything like Donne's brilliantly engineered communion arrives when W. H. Auden in his famous elegy for Yeats declares "poetry makes nothing happen." It is hard, finally, not to hear in the last lines of Philip Larkin's "An Arundel Tomb" a tired echo of Donne's own invocation affirming poetry's triumph over reality and death. Witnessing the lovers on this tomb—neither urn nor half-acre—the begrudgingly resolute, skeptical Larkin concludes:

> Only an attitude remains:
>
> Time has transfigured them into
> Untruth. The stone fidelity
> They hardly meant has come to be
> Their final blazon, and to prove
> Our almost-instinct almost true:
> What will survive of us is love.

That Larkin steals Donne's off-rhyme "prove / love" from "The Canonization" is a profound gesture of respect and imaginative commerce engendered over three and a half centuries, even as he begs to differ from Donne's triumphal conclusion. Larkin's transfiguration is the inverse of Donne's—the world is the physical world, death wins, and to think otherwise is at best to hedge your bet. Religion in the end for Larkin becomes "that vast, moth-eaten musical brocade / created to pretend we never die," as he famously declares in "Aubade." Still, the unspoken assumption underlying Larkin's dissent, and even his sad resignation, is that he would not have it so. It is this "almost-instinct" on the poet's part that, in fact, enables the concourse between himself and his bygone, gratefully less "dissociated" forebear. Larkin writes under the assumption that poems mean, language means, and both are reflective of the world and not merely their own adumbrated reality, even if death does hold the trump card. "Work," as he wisely but grudgingly states at the end of the unsparing "Aubade," nonetheless needs to be done.

Larkin's echo of Donne notwithstanding, the world in which Donne lived was at least as violent and unjust as our own, even if our scale of violence and the speed with which we can apprehend its effects defies comparison and, at times, our injustices find more subtle and amenable expression. Nevertheless, the old-time garment of religion, somewhat vaster and not quite so institutionally moth-eaten as it might seemingly appear today, afforded Donne something more than Larkin's musical brocade. It afforded him a matrix of emblems, figures, typologies and, most vitally, a supreme idea, incorruptible, however corrupt the world was, however corrupt human institutions became: that God had become present as a human being not only as an Actor in history but in the body of the world. Donne was no fool. He saw the world for what it was, saw its violence, its injustices, experienced them, compromised with them, committed his own, and feared for worse to come. Nonetheless, the real presence of God incarnate, the ultimate mystery of the Divine double life (indeed, a treble life) such as Dante could barely begin to figure at the end of the *Paradiso,* provided for Donne an incomparable template for human possibility.

The medieval imprint of the imitation of Christ, pursued so that one might encounter the image of Christ in the individual soul sustained as it was through a vital contemplative tradition, remained strong in Donne's time despite the fracturing of European Christianity, despite, as well, the mounting dominance of science in shaping humanity's vision of its place in the universe. Louis Martz, the greatest scholar of seventeenth-century English poetry, convincingly and definitively shows that the metaphysical style of Donne and his contemporaries George Herbert and Henry Vaughan, among others, finds its imprint in methods of meditation still current at the time.[23] For Donne in particular the *Spiritual Exercises* of St. Ignatius of Loyola afforded a practice conducive to the making of poetry, despite the fact that he wrote a tract, the *Pseudo-Martyr,* excoriating the Jesuits, in which St. Ignatius himself appears prominently in Hell beside Satan.[24] The Ignatian method requires a powerful exercising of the imagination through acts of "interior dramatization" in which one visualizes scenes from the life of Christ as though one were literally present. As Martz summarizes, the aim of meditation "is to apprehend the reality and meaning of the presence of God with every faculty" under human command.[25] As he further underscores: "meditation points toward poetry in its use of images, in its technique of arousing the passionate affections of the will." In the case of such poets as Donne, the meditative poem "represents the convergence of two arts upon a single object."[26] There is something of Stanislavski's method of triggering "sense memory" in the Ignatian method as well as in Donne's poetry. One can see also how Martz rightly links this same approach to the self-dramatizing poetics of W. B. Yeats and to Wallace Stevens's "poem of the mind in the act of finding / What will suffice." The same urge to write a poetry that joins the mind to the sense of felt embodiment underwrites the poems of Emily Dickinson—"My life it stood – / a Loaded Gun"—and countless other poets, whether concerned explicitly with matters of religion and metaphysics or matters wholly of worldly experience.

There is something deep in the Western intellectual tradition that binds meditation and poetry to a vision of language that is nothing short of incarnational in the broadest sense. Typology, the tradition of reading historical events and mythic figures as "types" of one another (America as a "New Jerusalem," as "a shining city on a hill'), has its roots in biblical exegesis. Jonah's liberation from the whale becomes a type of Christ's resurrection in the view of the gospels. Reading typologically, however, does not mean the pre-figuring event loses its particular significance. Rather, "there is a mutuality of forces for insight operating between the two events. Each is borrowing light from the other."[27] Similarly, in Donne's "The Canonization," the phoenix "figures" as a type of Christ, dying and rising the same, like the lovers who themselves become conjoined figures of Christ likewise dying and rising in flesh and then in spirit. Figure, from the Latin *figura,* has its origins in predictive typology—the

Old Testament read to foreshadow the New. Yet, figuration of this kind need not be unidirectional or bound to the privileging of one dispensation over another. Figuration involves complication. Figures by their nature ramify, creating surpluses of meaning. Wordsworth's evocation of the Power of Imagination as he crosses the Alps in Book Fifteen of "The Prelude" represents a shift in the orientation of typology and figuration from the historical to the natural. As the poet's senses become filled with the overwhelming presence of nature all things become "fellow-travelers" and every heightened perception from "woods decaying," to "the blasts of waterfalls," to the "winds thwarting winds," to the rocks muttering "close upon our ears" become analogous to:

> . . . workings of one mind, the features
> Of the same face, blossoms upon one tree;
> Characters of the great Apocalypse,
> The types and symbols of Eternity,
> Of first, and last, and midst, and without end.

In short, Wordsworth seizes upon the fundamentally relational dynamics of typology and figuration, of symbol-making, of tuning one's imagination to the emblematic nature of reality. Nothing is islanded apart from any other thing. All things exist at once as themselves and All-in-All: first, last, midst, and without end. Though later in the century Gerard Manley Hopkins can describe the flight of a windhover and see in it the action of "Christ our Lord," his recognition of the relation between these two apparently distinct actions owes everything to the premise that language binds us to the world, just as the world is bound to language. Language and reality together enact a fordable distance. Out of this binding assumption emerges a vision of the really Real, forged of course through Hopkins's Catholic faith but at the same time entirely his own:

> As kingfishers catch fire, dragonflies draw flame;
> As tumbled over rim in roundy wells
> Stones ring; like each tucked string tells, each hung bell's
> Bow swung finds tongue to fling our broad its name;
> Each mortal thing does one thing and the same:

Deals out that being indoors each one dwells;
    Selves—goes itself; *myself* it speaks and spells,
Crying *What I do is me: for that I came.*

I say more: the just man justices;
    Keeps grace: that keeps all his goings graces;
Acts in God's eye what in God's eye he is—
    Christ—for Christ plays in ten thousand places,
Lovely in limbs, and lovely in eyes not his
    To the Father through the features of men's faces.

"Deals out that being indoors each one dwells; / Selves—goes itself; *myself* it speaks and spells... Acts in God's eye what in God's eye he is": What Hopkins's great sonnet exemplifies so utterly is the work of the analogical imagination which, in addition to any theological relevance or foundation, remains a necessary condition for the poet's work, assuming of course the poet has more than language games in mind. As William Lynch reflects, "We must look for an order that orders indeed, but leaves reality, every iota of yours and mine intact—multitudinous, different, and free, but together at last."[28] This is analogical order, which is the foundation also of metaphor. And language, one might venture here, is inherently metaphorical. Poetry at root is metaphor, and there can be no metaphor without the assumption of analogy, for without the dynamics of analogy the world is islanded into discrete fragments that bear no relation to each other, or to language. David Tracy observes in *The Analogical Imagination* that analogy fundamentally articulates a state of "similarity-in-difference,"[29] and, as Stephen Fields further reminds us, language's analogical condition "serves as bridge uniting infinite and finite."[30] In the work of poems like "The Canonization" and "As Kingfishers Catch Fire, Dragonflies Draw Flame," metaphor performs the alchemy of transforming itself into mimesis,[31] such that the lamp of the poem's imaginative dynamics articulates itself into a mirror of reality, the figure of a world and not just a single poem.

Similarly, in *Faith, Hope and Poetry,* Matthew Guite helpfully locates the origins of this kind of analogical seeing in what he calls "the old culture" that had "inherited the notion that the two great books we are given to read are the Word and the Works of God," the Bible and the book of nature, and both according to Guite are "polysemous"—they are inherently figural, relational, given to symbolic or emblematic readings.[32] Hopkins, something like a belated resident of the passing culture though current with the intellectual climate of his day, sees Christ playing in ten thousand places, lovely in eyes not his. Hopkins's world is polysemous; it is charged with "the grandeur of God" that flames out "like shining from shook foil." The parts of the world are more than themselves while remaining nothing other than what they are. Their *haecity*, to use Duns Scotus's term—the "thisness" of any thing's being, its unrepeatable uniqueness—is precisely what allows that thing to exist in relation, in full participation, with all other things through the one of which it is a part: "The one is not a dead, monotonous fact; it only becomes itself by articulating itself into many jointings and members, and it has not become itself until, in its advance, it has created the last member, the last jointing to itself."[33]

What is good for the order of reality is good also for the order of the work. It is the loss or elision of this polysemous, analogical dimension of reality that marks the great transition into the modern and postmodern world. This transition, moreover, can be characterized as the product of nominalism's prevailing succession over realism in how one conceives reality. The disagreement between realism and nominalism in medieval philosophy turns on the fundamental difference in how one understands the resemblances of things. For the realist, there are two categories of the real—the particular and the universal. We see patterns, relationships, resemblances, because everything not only exists as its particular reality; it exists also with reference to the universal. The lamp is red. In that sentence "redness" constitutes a universal category. Other things are red besides the lamp such that a variety of particulars share the universal attribute redness. Herein rests the philosophical basis for imagination's analogical nature. That the perception of redness is a relative physical condition is irrelevant to the conception of reality underpinning the argument.

For the nominalist, however, there are no universal categories. Particulars have qualities that reflect only our own representational powers—how we think of things, the structures of human thinking, culture, language. There is no universally binding pattern; they manifest, to use Wallace Stevens's words, only "the precious portents of our own powers."[34] Now we are in what is generally viewed as the postmodern milieu where, as Owen Barfield observed in *Saving the Appearances,* our representations have become our idols.[35] We cannot extrapolate to any underlying much less overarching universal, what Lynch called a "univocal" order of reality.[36] Both the univocal and the equivocal are reductive, since both elide the essential fact of reality's analogical nature, that delicate balance of vision in which the one and the many hold together—bridge together—in dynamic, analogical relation through an interwoven architecture binding together All-in-All. Or, as that most starkly incisive and world-renouncing of twentieth-century thinkers, Simone Weil, observed with exemplary concision: the function of language "is to express the relationship between things."[37] In our time the equivocal has become univocal in its singular claims for how and what the world is. In poetic practice, regardless of all the deeply vested cultural conflicts, or the disaccustomed ideas about reality and art, most poets assume the realist perspective, however unacknowledged, as a working model. We assume what we make means, whether only playfully or errantly. We recognize implicitly if not explicitly that to assume a thoroughgoing nominalism, to run precipitously down the path of atomized particulars, is to bind all things to their own isolate realities—poems, language, the world—everything and everyone inhabiting its own impermeable box of discrete existence, a world governed by an irreducible and pervasive unlikeness.

Yet to live as though we inhabited such impermeable boxes in a world of totalized unlikeness is impossible. "There world is everything that is the case," Wittgenstein famously wrote in his *Tractatus,* but even Wittgenstein sought escape in his thinking from the view that locks each thing, and language itself, in its respective case. Like a philosopher, a poet need not call on the traditional emblems and figures of faith to locate powers of analogy and imagination within the wider compass of particulars bound ineluctably to universals. Take for example Mark Strand's "A Piece of the Storm":

From the shadow of domes in the city of domes,
A snowflake, a blizzard of one, weightless, entered your room
And made its way to the arm of the chair where you, looking up
From your book, saw it the moment it landed.
That's all there was to it. No more than a solemn waking
To brevity, to the lifting and falling away of attention, swiftly,
A time between times, a flowerless funeral. . . .

Through its vivid cadences, its descriptive powers, and its attentive movement of mind, Strand's "A Piece of the Storm" captures brilliantly the reality of one particular thing, however transient, in a world of things bound by the necessity of reality to the universal. It does so in space, in its one little room in the city of domes, and it does so in time with the prospect of some eventual return, not unlike an eternal return. Christ is not playing in ten thousand places, there are no types and symbols of first and last and midst and without end, but there is the blizzard of one, which cannot be the one without being a part of the many, nor can there be the many unless there is indubitably the one. It must be so into the future until the idea of the future comes to feel like an aspect of eternity—the sky, as the poem's ending states, "has an opening.." And so, in its "time between times," Strand's poem resonates profoundly with those of a meditative tradition shaped by an analogical imagination that only seems of another time because we have become less adept at reading the signs, because the signs themselves have fallen from their worldly, as well as their otherworldly, readiness into the separate domains of our dissociated sensibilities: that is, into of the merely signified[38] where language succumbs to difference without any unifying end and without meaning—one unlikeness calling emptily to all the wholly other others and doing so endlessly.

KNOT

"Midwinter spring is its own season / Sempiternal though sodden towards sundown,/ Suspended in time, between pole and tropic" —so "Little Gidding" places the reader at the beginning of the last of Eliot's *Four Quartets.* Like Strand's "A Piece of the Storm," his meditative caesura offers the vision of a time between times. That vision is the time and space of the poem itself— the well-wrought urn of the poem as unassailable artifact, not impermeable. Poems are intertextual: they partake of their moment in history, of the evolution of culture and ideas, and of course they derive in part from the poet's experience. However, it is wrong to say that poets are merely processors of their times through their work as some literary theories would have us believe. Poems are made things, hopefully at least well if not greatly made, and the discoveries and choices poets make to make poems shape the poems they make. To pit such mutually accommodating views against each other has been one of the longstanding betrayals of the academic study of literature. From another perspective, poetry has become less and less about the impact of reality on the poem, or the poet's work as maker in relation to the world, and more about a spectrum of orientation that runs the gamut from self-expression to identity politics to the idea of the poem as nothing more than a nexus of signifiers. Ron Silliman affirms the latter view succinctly when he observes "a resurrection of the realist or pre-modern paradigm can only represent our despair at our own impact on the world, [and] any retro-modern reunification of the sign merely reduplicates this backward-facing utopianism in a different guise."[39] Ironically, Silliman's statement is a statement of faith rather than objective truth since, according to his own lights, there is no bedrock of meaning. One might call such a vision a forward-facing utopianism into an endless hall of mirrors mirroring nothing. In this view, the poetry of polysemous reality, at once worldly and linguistic, has been "blown apart."[40]

Charles Bernstein builds on Silliman's shattering of polysemous reality when he observes that that the influx of immigrants from the late nineteenth century forward has so "radically subverted the language environment" in America that what he calls etymologic English—symbolic and connotative English—has been supplanted by associational English, which he defines as "a lateral glissade into mishearing," emphasizing "sound rather than root connections."[41] In either case the poem rides along the shallows rather than finding in and through language ranges of thought and feeling that exceed the limits of the literal. If there are surpluses in the poem, they are composed of such surface currents as might have caught the poet's eye "disturbing the dust on a bowl of rose leaves" to no knowable purpose. Nonetheless, it would seem not entirely unreasonable, if not essential, to hold that poets can still pursue without fear of nostalgia the kind of deeply rooted poetics that Donne practiced, and with no slight to the pressing impact of reality in our time, culturally, intellectually, artistically. To do so, poets should pursue what John Barth called astutely "the writer's investiture in as many aspects of the text as possible with emblematic significance."[42] That Barth, a novelist with a distinctly post-modern sensibility, abides and abets such practice is, I believe, a significant directive for poets. It is a directive that complements Eliot's doctrine of poetic amalgamation. Barth and Eliot, strange bedfellows though they may be, both aim to wrestle order from disorder by intention and artistic means or, as William Lynch again astutely observes, "dissociation is not helped by anything but true association, and we have always to question when we have the latter."[43]

Donne, some four hundred years ago, certainly practiced the kind of thoroughgoing artistry for which Barth's word "investiture" feels uniquely apt, the kind of associative practice necessary for a twenty-first-century poet as for a seventeenth-century poet, despite the obvious developments in practice and expansions in culture and tradition. All of Donne's poems and certainly his greatest have this quality, but perhaps none more quintessentially so than his Holy Sonnet 14. Donne's Holy Sonnets were composed between 1609 and 1617 and cover the period in his life where the rakish "Jack" Donne of his youth—womanizer, ambitious courtier, soldier—slowly and painfully began to recede in favor of John Donne the great religious poet, thinker, and preacher. Of course, Donne invests even his lustiest poems with the metaphysical as well as the physical, as we saw in "The Canonization." His renunciation of "Jack" was complete by the time of Anne's death in 1617, which very nearly brought Donne himself to suicide.[44] The Holy Sonnets as a sequence indeed track the path of his *conversio,* or conversion, to use a word from the contemplative tradition that infuses their imagery and their arc. They are deeply invested with the meditative practice so influential in Donne's day. That practice reaches the height of poetic application in the Holy Sonnets and especially in number 14. The depth and pervasiveness of Donne's emblematic investiture can be seen, principally, in his use of meter, his use of metaphor, his diction, his structure, his figuration, and his syntax.

Like "The Canonization," Holy Sonnet 14 is an apostrophe dramatically articulated, now to God and not to the poet's worldly enemies. In fact, the sonnet establishes the intensity of Donne's tone and perspective by reversing the polarity of the rage he expresses in the earlier poem. Now the poet turns on the self as the focus of his rage. The sonnet's conceit of the soul as "usurped town" transmogrifies the "countries, towns, courts" of "The Canonization," those very things that plead for a pattern of enduring love, now come to stand before us as the corrupted property of the soul separated by its own actions from God, the Source of its being. The stakes could not be higher for the soul or the poet dramatically rendering the soul's desperate cry. One feels that urgency of emotion irrespective of one's own religious leanings in the rhythm of the first four lines:

Batter my heart, three-person'd God, for you
As yet but knock, breathe, shine, and seek to mend;
That I may rise, and stand, o'erthrow me, and bend
Your force to break, blow, burn, and make me new.

Emotional content should be felt primarily in a poem's rhythm, and that is nowhere truer than in these crucial opening lines. The investiture here is so metrically vivid that as an exercise one might change a single foot and, in effect, ruin the poem. One can, for example, in a thought experiment verging on pure perversion, envision a nightmare poetry workshop where the well-intentioned but socially constricted group finds the first word of Donne's poem offensive. It requires a synonym, they suggest, something less volatile—"molest" or, the even softer, "unlock." Either word, of course, will ruin the poem by removing the physicality of "batter" which expresses the speaker's emotional state with uncompromising passion. The real matter, however, is that the first foot of the poem has been altered from trochaic to iambic. This reversal of metrical polarity effectively alters the rhythm of nearly every foot and all four lines that follow. "Molest my heart three-person'd God, for you" changes Donne's impassioned speech to the metronomic clap-trap of a robot with a personality disorder. Donne's trochaic initial foot, combined of course with the physical and tonal energies of the word "batter," has the effect of "springing" the rhythm of the first line and the lines that follow. The syllables *heart three-per* all carry stresses with Donne's trochaic opening, as do the syllables "knock, breathe, shine" and finally "break, blow, burn"—a pattern of three stresses in a row that tune the poem to the three-person'd God and to God's begged-for action upon the soul by the soul that is in thrall to all that is not God. Change the first trochee and you change the entire electrical charge and temperature of the poem. There is an iambic backbeat to these lines as to the whole poem, but this single initial move conditions the lines for maximum dramatic expression, maximum intensity. The disruptive force of "O'erthrow me" in the third line, after the caesura, gains still greater energy because of it, and the torque one feels in the enjambment "and bend / your force" carries an even more vital charge. Why? It is because the metrical urgency of the word "batter" flicks a kind of switch that engages the poem's emotional warp-drive.

One could track Donne's complex metrical scheme throughout the rest of Holy Sonnet 14—for example the pattern of trochaic substitutions in the front foot of certain lines—but suffice it to say that Donne's investiture in this area has supercharged the poem with passionate speech. What about his use of metaphor and simile? The poem's entire conceit of the soul as captive to its own passions and thus to God's enemy, of the soul therefore as gendered and female, originates in a long contemplative tradition practiced by both men and women that harkens back to the biblical Song of Songs. The metaphoric pattern, somewhat altered, also has non-Christian associations. Gods descending from on high to rape women is standard fare in Ovid, though Donne's vividly physical rendering of the pattern in this poem remains spiritually inflected. Yet it is no less intense for being so. In fact, the violence of the soul's petition to be ravished, to be subsumed in spiritual ecstasy, in mystical union, increases its strangeness and its power because of those disruptively antithetical echoes that lie outside the tradition of Western contemplation.

Donne's diction adds to the effect, as with the word "labor" in line six which puns the labors of birth. For the speaker to "labor to admit" God into the womb of the soul would be, in another reversal, for God to give birth to the soul in its potential fullness, which can only be in and through the action of God. Thus, the word "labor" here bespeaks the dual action of the human soul coming to fullness in God by God's action in and through the soul. "Viceroy" is another such word. Reason as "viceroy" places that crucial power of the soul in the forefront of the soul's army of defenders, but as "viceroy" it is also "the king of vice" and therefore is the very power that enables the enemy to besiege the soul in captivity. It is, one might say, the enemy itself. Finally, according to the poem the soul's labors to admit God come to "no end." Here, as with his secret marriage, Donne has undone himself through the anagram of bringing his own spiritual liberation to naught through the limitations of reason and the will. Donne on his own comes to no end, his name and hence his true self scrambled into a spiritual negation, a coded randomness without teleology, without purpose. Only by surrender to God will Donne be fully Donne, fully completed having reached identity in every sense, his end ongoing in eternal life.

The formal arc of Donne's Holy Sonnet 14 develops through the conceit of the soul's captivity and ends in the soul's desire for a new imprisonment in God which is, paradoxically, its ecstatic fulfillment, from the Greek *ecstasis,* to "move out," to go forth. Structurally the sonnet joins a Petrarchan octet to a Shakespearean sestet, the former affiliated with courtly love poetry and the latter enabling the sonnet to end on the strong rhetorical closure of the final couplet. Even in his structure Donne yolks together contraries, or at least differently inflected formal variations. In a sense, everything Donne marshals to express his condition as well as the nexus of his intellectual and emotional life contributes to the entire poem as metaphor, as the poet's figural expression, which in this case happens to be the fleshy and spiritual reality of all humankind. Nothing could be more emblematic. It is important to recognize that the three-personed God to whom the speaker addresses his plea is also figural. More accurately, Donne addresses himself to his ultimate reality at the threshold where the analogical transmogrifies into the anagogical—the "world of complete insight," where "the inner life of the Trinitarian God" reveals itself "as the total communication of self by different Persons to one another"[45]—in short, the very ground of the analogical order of reality, its dynamically personal architecture and foundation. Donne believed in this Trinitarian God, the embodiment of an eternal difference-in-unity, unity-in-difference, and applies that vision of ultimate reality to develop the figural, the analogical vitality of his poems.

In Holy Sonnet 16, for example, he evokes the Son's "jointure in the knotty Trinity." Notably, the word "knot" appears in line eleven of Holy Sonnet 14 just before the poem makes its final turn: "Divorce me, untie or break that knot again." The full meaning of Donne's sense is elusive, unless one recognizes other instances where the figure of the "knot" appears in his poetry. For example, in "The Ecstasy" Donne writes:

> As our blood labours to beget
>   Spirits as like souls as it can,
> Because such fingers need to knit
>   That subtle knot which makes us man,
>
> So must pure lovers' souls descend
>   T'affections, and to faculties
> Which sense may reach and apprehend,
>   Else a great prince in prison lies.

In these lines human identity is intimately and essentially tied to the figure of the knot. Moreover, in "The Ecstasy" Donne uses the very same language of labor and imprisonment we find in Holy Sonnet 14 to articulate the necessity for carnal love—to what purpose? To beget spirits. All human life for Donne, as for Keats, is a vale of soul-making. In "The Progress of the Soul" Donne invokes God again as the "knot of all causes" that binds all evolving reality, "the commissary of Destiny," to the one ultimate reality which is God alone. That God to whom Donne in longing calls out is "three-person'd," "knotty." In that very knottiness resides the "subtle knot" of God's own image in human beings, the imprint of God's own multiple singularity, God's singular multiplicity at the crux of which, theologically, is the Son.

The Son is also poetically the crux in Donne's Holy Sonnet 14, and the crux of the matter gains full figural expression syntactically in the poem's final dramatic gesture, its final outcry:

> Divorce me, untie or break that knot again;
> Take me to you, imprison me, for I,
> Except you enthrall me, never shall be free,
> Nor ever chaste, except you ravish me.

For the Divine Image to be restored to Donne, as to anyone, the very knot that makes us human—a created thing—must be undone. That is why the poem turns on the speaker's impassioned plea to be "ravished" even unto nothingness. Theologically, such ravishment has its fullest expression in the figure of Christ on the cross, Christ who joins in his very being the knot of divinity and humanity through the incarnation. Donne expresses this reality, and his desire to be wholly inhabited by the figure of Christ, in the syntactical chiasmus that ends the poem: "for I / Except you enthrall me, never shall be free, / Nor ever chaste, except you ravish me." The term chiasmus means "to cross," and so as the sonnet comes to its end Donne makes the sign of the cross in the very language by which he seeks to cross into the fullness of his human spiritual potential. Christ's cross becomes knotted with his own life in that ecstasy.

John Donne liked to compose on horseback,[46] and one can see and hear that skillful handling of the reins in the intricacy of his pacing as well as in the emotional and intellectual leaps he takes in Holy Sonnet 14—his effort to transcend the barriers, not the least of which are flesh and spirit. The image of the poet composing on horseback is an analogue for the activity of the poet's mind at work amalgamating disparities. In following his mind and heart, the whole person having been brought into activity in his work, Donne accesses depths of meaning that enrich the poem immensely. Nonetheless, one does not need to know an entire cultural nexus to feel the poem's impact or understand its terms in that immediacy. All of the technical dynamics of Holy Sonnet 14 have transfigured those sources into its own unique necessity. Bernstein might well regard Holy Sonnet 14 as a prime example of "etymologic poetry," the very kind that, in his view, is being supplanted by the associative poem,[47] the poem that by design surfs the shallows, or hunts and gathers among the purely occasional. What Bernstein misses in this too-neat opposition, his divestment of opposing ideas, is that the etymological is inherently associative, and deeply so. The gravitas of Donne's poem hits us because of the associative leaps it makes through its guiding conceit, its structural innovation, its syntactical complexity—true association mindfully and artfully accomplished with utmost emotional force.

Not surprisingly, Holy Sonnet 14 also associates with Donne's other poems through its figural imagination and its diction. The poem, in its capacity to range associatively and deeply in its compositional make-up, gives the lie to the idea that associative poetics is somehow a relatively new phenomenon. The immigrant populations Bernstein cites to make his point—that the associative in poetry (at least in America over the past hundred and fifty years) has evolved through mishearing—assumes that these populations brought nothing with them (apparently) except their lack of listening skills. On the contrary, whole paradigms of life were carried across from countless locales as much in each individual's consciousness as in travel bags. Such ways of life and thinking never existed in wholesale isolation—it is delusional to think so—but evolved in patterns of crisscrossing webs of historical and geographical encounter at once material and, one dares to say, spiritual. Our very DNA is not only rooted it is routed, at once etymological and associative in its origins and its history, harkening back to African savannahs and back further to other iterations of hominid life as well as the shaping forces of the planet and the physical universe itself. Our individual lives are composed of associations, encoded with etymologies—nexuses of relation rife for metaphor, rife for analogy, rife for transfiguration. Poems are no different. However seemingly dissociative an associative poem may be, it must have the ultimate goal of meaning, as Carl Phillips has observed, lest, being nothing more than babble, like the city of Babel it fails to last.[48] The challenge is to make every new mutation, every new metamorphosis, something that contributes vitally to the body of the poem and, ideally, to the body of the wider tradition. Such investiture requires more than Bernstein's "lateral glissando" on the playfully littered littoral of the moment. It requires a purpose of meaningfulness and depth by the most incisive and capacious means possible. It requires, to adapt a phrase from a poem by the late Jewish-American poet, Stanley Kunitz, the risk of looking beyond the litter for the prospect of living in "the layers."

WHAT'S DONNE ISN'T DONE

On Ideas of Order and the Machinery of Poetry

Oh! Blessed rage for order, pale Ramon,
The maker's rage to order words of the sea,
Words of the fragrant portals, dimly-starred,
And of ourselves and of our origins,
In ghostlier demarcations, keener sounds.

We are driving down the Llyn peninsula in North Wales on our pilgrimage
to Aberdaron. We intend to pay our respects to the memory and work of the
other great Welsh poet whose surname is Thomas, the somewhat less famous
of the two, but no less remarkable however contrary temperamentally. R. S.
Thomas served for many years as clergyman of the Church of Wales in this
remote village. As we descend the hill along the narrow roadway, a stretch
of moiling ocean opens into view beside a thin strand. Above the village St.
Hywyn's double nave appears to preside modestly and benignly, like a shear-
water at rest on a rocky verge, unmoving. For those who know the poetry
of R. S. Thomas there is something at once deeply grounded, layered, and
nonetheless ethereal in the sensibility, at once retrospective and prospective,
at once mindful of the reaches that came before, of the urgencies of its time,
and of the reaches that stretch out ahead and that can be glimpsed at best
darkly through the imperfect glass of a searching mind. There is also rage in
the work, blessed rage, of the kind Wallace Stevens definitively conjured in
"The Idea of Order at Key West." Thomas, like Stevens's unnamed vocalist at
the edge of the human, also sang beyond the genius of the sea, though for him
religion still offered compelling protocols for the life and the imagination. We
took a long time wandering in and out of the church, looking out over the
shingle beach with its one great stone washed ashore, micron by micron over

eons, then walked further up the thickly hedged road, before heading down again to the village and the one sparsely populated hotel for a meal.

The traditional way to posit an idea of order is to regard it as some long-lost unity of being that once was resident in a Golden Age or an Eden, or maybe in an Unmoved Mover or Watchmaker God—a God distant and removed, however ingenious, a supreme being but a being nonetheless among lesser beings. That, however, is not the traditional understanding of God established biblically, which is a God who in God's very transcendence posits immanence: God is at once beyond being and the source of all being—I AM THAT I AM, the Uncreated without which there is no creation. When in his poem "The Ecstasy" John Donne muses "blood labours to beget / Spirits" he is suggesting, at the very least, that whatever might have been lost of ideal Reality will be recoverable for each life, if only as a seemingly impossible possibility. The theology embedded in Donne's poetry is liminal from this standpoint—we are fallen creatures, but we are here to labor and beget ourselves and each other out of our fallen state by aligning our labors with God's. That singular labor is love. One poem nearer to our own time that places itself on this threshold and turns with a backward look toward the ideal in the face of violence is Robert Hayden's "Monet's Waterlilies." The poem begins "today," in a no less fraught moment in history, with the news from Selma and Saigon. Hayden's poem juxtaposes all the human turmoil evoked by just those names with "the serene great picture" that the poet loves, and returns to see again and again as an enduring vision of something beyond the brutalities and injustices of history, yet somehow present through art:

> Here space and time exist in light
> the eye like the eye of faith believes
>   The seen, the known
> dissolve in iridescence, become
> illusive flesh of light
>   that was not, was, forever is.

Surely, had he been living in Hayden's time, Donne himself would have recognized immediately Hayden's own genius for evoking an order of reality that offers something beyond solace—an idea or prospect of eternity. Indeed, by the poem's end the reader encounters "the shadow of its joy." Donne's particular religious perspective, enlarged by the throes of history, I believe, would have found no impediment in Hayden's Bahá'í faith, as heterodox as Donne was in certain aspects of his thinking, and as perspicacious of the future. He would have recognized an art that nonetheless sought to center itself in some trans-figuring vision, without neglecting the brutal exigencies of life. And what could be more a yoking together of the heterogeneous than time and eternity in Hayden's "illusive flesh of light / that was not, was, forever is?" Stamping the theme with her incomparable genius, Emily Dickinson in "This World is not Conclusion" takes a more austere and radical stand on the subject:

This World is not Conclusion
A Species stands beyond –
Invisible, as Music –
But positive, as Sound –
It beckons, and it baffles –
Philosophy, don't know –
And through a Riddle, at the last –
Sagacity, must go –
To guess it, puzzles scholars –
To gain it, Men have borne
Contempt of Generations
And Crucifixion, shown –
Faith slips—and laughs, and rallies –
Blushes, if any see –
Plucks at a twig of Evidence –
And asks a Vane, the way –
Much Gesture, from the Pulpit –
Strong Hallelujahs roll –
Narcotics cannot stop the Tooth
That nibbles at the soul –

Dickinson's great poem denies any stock encounter with an "idea of order" that renders religion, as it is practiced, a mere narcotic. Hers is an order that baffles as it beckons, one that could easily bring one into the volatile orbit of the world's contempt. Christ on the cross for Dickinson is hardly a reassuring figure. *Imitatio Christi* means being crucified oneself—so much for sexualized religious ecstasy. Of course, being an uncompromising genius attuned to the intellectual concerns of her day (despite the limitations conferred on her by gender in her society), she likewise adapts the language of Darwinian evolution for her own purposes. Dickinson's Species that "stands beyond" is invisible, more suggestive of something akin to Donne's spirits the blood labors to beget than the wholly materialist animal, governed by physical mechanism, the survival of the fittest. The world is not conclusion, but God is not found in twigs of evidence, in pre-established figures of the sacred—bread, wine; God is a Tooth and, in a reversal of the Eucharistic meal, God eats you, slowly, perhaps in what Donne called elsewhere "the commissary of Destiny." If the goal in death is to obtain a "spiritual body" then the passage to such transfiguration is no easy path to glory.

What John Donne only hints at in "The Ecstasy," what Hayden seeks to see past in "Monet's Waterlilies," and what Dickinson establishes in "This World is not Conclusion" in a manner that subverts the categorical thinking of religion and science equally, is an idea of order that privileges prospect over retrospect, emergence over Golden Ages and Edens. It is an idea that certainly stirred R. S. Thomas, looking out as he often did from his resident perch above Aberdaron into the North Sea's expansive offing. His poem "Emerging" speculates brilliantly on the matter. The poem begins with the assertion that it is "better to wait" for God on some "peninsula of the spirit" where "he will happen by once in a while" if one is patient enough. From there, the poem parses the demands of the heart, with all of its patience, and the mind ever-skeptical "of the anthropomorphisms of the fancy," acknowledging only that God must be "put together / like a poem or a composition in music." God, it seems to Thomas, only "conforms to art," whereas the generations have "watched in vain" for the anthropomorphic deity that "leans down / out of the air" with an extended hand. That promontory "is bare." What Thomas affirms, in contrast, is a vision of matter and spirit that confounds the binaries typical of human thought:

> We are beginning to see
> now it is matter is the scaffolding
> of spirit: that the poem emerges

from the morphemes and phonemes: that
as form in sculpture is the pris
of the hard rock, so in every life
it is the plain facts and natural happenings
that conceal God and reveal him to us
little by little under the mind's tooling.

Compared to Donne's elaborate conceit-making and structural orchestration, Thomas's "Emerging" looks bare, sculpted as it is to the mind's honed
edge of unadorned realization—a kind of Giacometti visage fashioned out of
words. Dickinson, I believe, would approve of Thomas's refusal of anthropomorphisms, his regard for them as fancy, including perhaps even a three-
person'd God. In Donne, blood labors to beget spirits; in Thomas we need to
look deeper still—into matter itself, and the very components of language. All
things emerge, like art, through scales of reality into greater reality, bearing up
those materials of which they are composed. Emergence trumps divergence,
the real trumps the nominal. Nothing is residual for Thomas. The "plain facts
and natural happenings" will bear this out. The God of "Emerging" is not a
Watchmaker God, the demiurgic god of the Deists, a latter day "supreme being" standing behind if not beside all other beings, not what theologian David
Bentley Hart calls the false god of "some stubborn tacit anthropomorphism
that is in fact diametrically at odds with the God of classical theism"[1]—not to
mention the ultimate reality communicated in the "perennial philosophies" of
all great faiths. God, rather, is "put together" in an analogous way to a work of
art, the embodiment of all beauty, as emergent paradoxically as physical reality
and sentience—as immanence—because it is our consciousness of God "under
the mind's tooling" that emerges while the Being of God as Ground of Being
endures revelatory in its very transcendence.[2] "Emerging" appears to articulate
what I've called a subtending metaphysics.[3] At the same time, Hart would caution against overstating the case, for immanence cannot stand on its own via-
bly and meaningfully, but must find its own sustaining actuality "analogically"
within the divine transcendence, which is always greater because it is eternal.
Immanence, emergence, is merely one manifestation of the divine superabundance that always exceeds, even as it embodies all contingent reality.

Still, it is not the poet's job to "prove" the existence of God or to confirm or disconfirm doctrine. Dante's journey in the middle of life through Hell, Purgatory, and on into Heaven substantially reflects the faith of his time through the prism of Thomism. The poem is invested at every possible level with that vision. It is itself, obviously, not a proof of the really Real underlying or beyond our life in the senses. Donne speculates in his poem "The Canonization" of lovers "proving" their love, Shakespeare's love needs to be "proved" in Sonnet 116, and Larkin almost but not quite "proves" love's survival after death in his great latter-day poem of almost eternal endurance, "An Arundel Tomb." R. S. Thomas's direct appeal to theories of emergence obviously is not proof of any theory. Yet, it is compelling because Thomas makes it so in the poem's attentive and surprising arc of the mind wrestling with one idea of the ultimate manifesting itself from below, not above. The same is true of Dickinson's "This World is not Conclusion." It is more than a little interesting that in our time the idea of order as process, as emergence—rather than statically removed, the Unmoved Mover—has gained considerable traction across fields of thought. Drawing on neuroscience, many philosophers view consciousness as an emergent phenomenon in a way that matches Thomas's vision of God in his poem "Emerging." At the same time, a version of the idea of emergence at the heart of Thomas's poem goes back to the heresy of the Italian theologian Socinus in the sixth century. Socinus believed that God was neither omnipotent nor omniscient but rather grew in "godliness" with the development of the universe. Thomas places something like that conception of God in the mind, in the consciousness. God is slowly revealed through "the mind's tooling." The view also resonates strongly with Teilhard de Chardin's process-driven "divine milieu," where evolution carries forward the teleological code of Christ emergent in material reality within its mechanisms until all physical reality achieves what Teilhard calls the "Omega Point": the point where physics and metaphysics come into perfect alignment like a kind of cosmic spirit level. From an entirely scientific perspective, the physicist Freeman Dyson wholly embraces the Socinian view of God in process when he declares: "I do not make any clear distinction between mind and God. God is what the mind becomes when it has passed beyond the scale of our comprehension."[4] At the same time, such a view suggests that an *emergent* God, like *emergent* consciousness, merely defines our own finite and therefore inevitably limited perceptions, temporally skewed as they are and must be. If time partakes in any way of ultimate reality, it is logically only because the eternal sustains the temporal, and subsumes it. In short, though aligning his metaphysics with contemporary physics, Dyson implicitly affirms the anagogic level of meaning, the level of complete insight, as an advent of our evolution. "The analogical imagination—that 'outmoded' metaphysical explanation for all that exists"—re-emerges as the definition of a world defined by unity-in-difference.[5]

There is a site on the internet where someone claims to prove that Google manifests many of the traditional attributes of God, most notably omniscience. Though I doubt the incipient divinity of the Google search engine, it's remarkable that the Net itself is an emergent system, or as one expert in statistical mechanics reflects: "While entirely of human design, the emerging network appears to have more in common with a cell or an ecological system than with a Swiss watch."[6] The apparently random nature of the Net exhibits "non-random topology," which only means that its evolving pattern of connections challenges physicists "to unearth the signatures of order from the apparent chaos of millions of nodes and links."[7] Though it grows exponentially without recourse to scale—and is therefore "scale free" like organic and ecological systems—what statisticians call "power-law distributions" arise naturally, and these laws invest the Net with properties leading to "the appearance of hierarchy."[8] In short, within the Net, scale manifests out of scale-free randomness, order grows out of a seeming chaos of decentralized associations and, remarkably, this phenomenon mirrors the more tangible manifestations of physical reality. The result in this emergent prioritization of links and domains is "a small world" with only a relatively few clicks separating anyone from anyone else at any given time. This small-world phenomenon reflects more or less the close ties of ancestry revealed in the gene pool—approximately six degrees of separation. Apparently, no man is an island, even when one is alone in one's room clicking away at web sites. What the Net exhibits through the application of its protocols, the terms that make the Net a cooperative system, what enables it to be a nexus founded on orderly emergence, entails a combination of dynamics and architecture that evolves in vital communion. Dynamics and architecture: the very attributes required for making an Internet, a universe, an emergent God, a creation, certainly a poem.

Perhaps not far removed from such apparently divergent reflections is the by now well-worn idea of order that a poem is a machine made of words. That statement has become commonplace since William Carlos Williams summarized his manifesto for poetry during the first half of the twentieth century. The Objectivist poetics of Williams and Zukofsky, like the next generation Projective poetics of Charles Olson, share an essentially futurist vision with many painters and sculptors emerging during the same period. That futurist vision is in many ways the imaginative byproduct of an Industrial Revolution bound to the ideal of progress that—it is not too much to say—created a fetish of the machine. The mind-warping implications of the quantum world we now inhabit, even at our scale of remove, have far and away revolutionized our conception of the machine such that chips the size of atoms can store more information than the Library of Congress and the ancient Library of Alexandria combined. It is not surprising that we have internalized this fetish for the future: we regard ourselves as machines, the conscious part of a cosmos evolving in a vast system of mechanisms. At least that is the case apparently, since we have yet to crack the code of unifying the infinitely small with the infinitely vast. Perhaps string theory will accomplish that miracle. At the same time, in its small world, the practice of poetry during the latter part of the twentieth century gravitated toward "organic form." The term embraces so-called free verse, and is large enough to include a wide range of poetic practice. What "organic form" generally admits is a strong mistrust of "fixed forms" and metrical composition, though Denise Levertov's richer definition suggests something broader and more inclusive. She understands organic form to be "based on an intuition of order, a form beyond forms, in which forms partake, and of which man's creative works are analogies, resemblances, natural allegories."[9] Such poetry, she affirms, is inherently "exploratory."

To orient one's own understanding of poetry and the world by Levertov's vantage is to invert the commonly mechanistic view of reality. If the Net, as is apparently the case, evolves in the manner of cellular or ecological systems, then our prevailing tendency to conceptualize reality according to the assumptions of a mechanistic universe—the Swiss watchmaker's universe of outdated Newtonian physics, or the universe of the Watchmaker God—needs radical revision. Charles Olson's "composition by field" leading to more experimental poetics finds an unlikely cue in this assumption. When we view the landscape of poetry from Levertov's equally resonant prospect, however, we find others in fact had already been there. In his *Biographia Literaria* Samuel

Taylor Coleridge elaborates the essential distinction between the modern and postmodern notions of organic form—the distinction between *natura naturans* and *natura naturata:* nature naturing, so to speak, and nature natured. *Natura naturans* is nothing other than Levertov's form beyond forms or, better, it is the principle of forming that underlies all formation. It is, in short, the dynamics of form-making when we consider form from a teleological perspective. *Natura naturata* is the plethora of forms things take, the "creative works" of which Levertov speaks. The concept bespeaks the architecture of forms as they have come to be, in the case of the poet's work the finished poem. Building on the thought of medieval philosopher Baruch Spinoza, Coleridge aligns the two modes, *natura naturans* and *natura naturata.* The purpose of nature naturing is to form that which has been natured. Losing sight of the former leads to a vision of the world divested into objects, mechanistic, static and, in the case of poetry, an idolization of the "fixed form." Losing sight of the latter leads to purposeless flow; it leads to the infinitely roiling energies of the quantum state devoid of any emergent properties. In the case of poetry, losing sight of architecture leads to shapelessness, the inability to arrive at closure or perhaps even to make sense. Dynamics requires architecture; architecture requires dynamics. Both require a greater purpose emerging out of potential's endlessly incipient play.

Most notably, for Coleridge, the same mutually transformative vision characterizes the human place through the power of the imagination. Like nature naturing, for Coleridge the primary imagination is dynamic and ever-present. As he states in the thirteenth chapter of his *Biographia Literaria,* the primary imagination is "a repetition in the finite mind of the eternal act of creation in the infinite I AM." The voice deep within us greater than ourselves is the echo of the Voice that speaks to Moses out of the burning bush—I AM THAT I AM : YHWH. Imagination manifests essentially the dynamics of the divine image in human form. The secondary imagination comes under the purview of the will, and differs for Coleridge only "in degree" and in "the mode of its operation." It is the application by which things such as poems are made. In Coleridge's view, as Malcolm Guite neatly states, the human mind "is not a ghost in the machine or a mist thrown up by the mere movement of matter," it is "correspondent to something else beyond itself, and beyond the cosmos it inhabits."[10] In Guite's view, one might say, the correspondent breeze of the

Romantics is the elusive but recognizable trace of the world's emergence to a divine state that in Hayden's words "was not, was, forever, is." Emergence is a concept required by creatures of time to express a Reality that always eludes us and therefore always calls us forward. For John Donne, in retrospect, the equivalent "signifier" encoding this divine / human correspondence is "wit." The "sight of God" is both the object and the "wit," Donne declares in his "Second Anniversary," which suggests the divine image is at once the motivating dynamic of existence and the ultimate architecture of its end, at once circumference and center; or as Dante figured at the end of the *Paradiso,* a circle squared, the principal paradigm of which is the Logos incarnated into physical form, which is also the very principle by which and through which all comes into being.

From Coleridge's time onward, so idealized a vision of the human place in the cosmos appears more and more remote, more and more compromised by the pressures of reality as lived and discerned on this limited scale of existence. The divine image, if invoked at all, appears better captured by the cutting words of Yeats's Crazy Jane to the Bishop:

> But Love has pitched his mansion in
> The place of excrement;
> For nothing can be sole or whole
> That has not been rent.

The seemingly heretical Crazy Jane alludes in these lines—surprisingly enough—to St. Augustine, who first observed that Christ, the Word-made-flesh, was born between urine and feces like everyone else. In saying exactly as much, Crazy Jane reveals that she is a more orthodox theologian and better student of Church history than the bishop who would have her live in "a heavenly mansion / Not in some foul sty." As a machine made of words, Yeats's "Crazy Jane Talks with the Bishop" is very much a strictly "formal" poem: strong on structure, composed in three six-line stanzas, the long "i" sounds rhyming through the first two stanzas between alternating unrhymed lines, and the rhyme in the third stanza taking up the sonic "n" resonance from the previous stanzas to arrive at its raging conclusion. For all its carefully constructed architecture and steady iambic tetrameters, indeed through those very attributes, the poem's dynamics are ferocious. What is at stake is how one lives in the fallen world, though beyond that the poem offers nothing less than a vision of reality, however unremittingly austere. Yeats is adamant for both: for expressing the "foul rag and bone shop of the heart," and for "Unity of Being." To have the heart's dynamics, or those of the mind for that matter, without the desire for some comprehending vision is to curtail a poem's range and impact. Yeats's is an inherently analogical vision despite his "unchristened" heart, as Seamus Heaney once called it.

Nearer to our own historical moment, one hears something of Yeats's ferocity in Andrew Hudgins's "Piss Christ." It is a poem written with a similarly piercing awareness of historical and theological insight, likewise hovering between belief and transgression:

> If we did not know it was cow's blood and urine,
> if we did not know that Serrano had for weeks
> hoarded his urine in a plastic vat,
> if we did know the cross was gimcrack plastic,
> we would assume it was too beautiful.
> We would assume it was the resurrection,
> glory, Christ transformed to light by light . . .

Through the strong anaphora of its opening lines "Piss Christ" seeks to subvert the assumption of the artist's apparent heresy. We know already that Andres Serrano's infamous artwork "Piss Christ" caused a firestorm, such that the National Endowment for the Arts in the United States came under scrutiny—and funding cuts—due to what was hailed as a sensational transgression against taste and religious values. Hudgins repositions our vantage, and he does so by foregrounding the reader's "not knowing" or "un-knowing" over what we think we know. If only it were true that we could change our perception, our presumption of physical reality, and not just a work of art, so dramatically. By appealing to our "unknowing," rather than our ignorance, Hudgins draws on a long history of apophatic thinking, of contemplative practice that finds the divine in darkness rather than in light. The remarkable arc of this first sentence, so apparently matter-of-fact, a straightforward ekphrastic response, is that it begins in the mire of physicality and evolves wondrously into resurrection and light before giving us the reason: "because the blood and urine burn like a halo, / and light, as always, light makes it beautiful." The internal repetition of the word "light" twice carries forward the pattern of anaphora established earlier, and as such Hudgins's rhetorical entry modulates into something closer to ritual, the way an oasis might appear in a desert out of rippling waves rising out of the sands. Ironically, we are lowered by the strophe-long sentence and Hudgins's ten-to-twelve-syllable loosely iambic line into the vat, and simultaneously raised up by the same movement into the light of resurrection.

Having moved the reader with cinematic elegance through the artistic and theological subject and substance of the poem, Hudgins in the second strophe offers something akin to an exegesis of Serrano's self-polluted icon. Hudgins and Crazy Jane embrace the same theology, and it is nothing other than orthodox. That theology requires nothing less than the profoundest change to our stock assumptions about what is sacred and what is profane. The celebrant has been transmogrified into the apologist, and both tones are necessary to the poem:

> We are born between the urine and the feces,
> Augustine says, and so was Christ, if there was a Christ,
> skidding into this world as we do
> on a tide of blood and urine. Blood, feces, urine—
> the fallen world is made of what we make.
> He peed, ejaculated, shat, wept, bled—
> bled under Pontius Pilate, and I assume
> the mutilated god, the criminal,
> humiliated god, voided himself
> on the cross, and blood and urine smeared his legs—
> the Piss Christ thrown in glowing blood, the whole
> and irreducible point of his descent:
> God plunged in human waste, and radiant.

This second strophe re-frames the poem's ritual use of the "base" materials of our material existence, now rendered in all their vivid materiality. Christ, "if there was a Christ," is wholly human right down to the fluids. Especially blood.

Hudgins is no closet Gnostic as was, evidently, Senator Jesse Helms, who so fervently condemned Serrano's art. In a brilliant verb choice, Christ "skids" into this world like all of us, like an accident in the process of happening. The process of happening: in Christ, "if there was a Christ," God enters into the process of happening to be "mutilated," "humiliated" as a mutable human being composed of mutable matter—both of those words emerging in the poem as sonic echoes of Pontius Pilate. Now Hudgins's other verbs shift from the slightly comical "skidding" to the theologically profound "voided" and "thrown." Both have the same depth of significance associatively and figuratively as Donne's use of the word "knot" in his "The Progress of the Soul," the knot of all causes." To void one's self is unavoidable at the moment of death, but the voiding the poem has in mind also alludes to the earliest known Christian statement of faith in St. Paul's Letter to the Philippians 2: 5-11, as well as an entire tradition of theological speculation. In Philippians, the Greek word denoting Christ's essential nature is *kenosis,* self-emptying. Christ through the incarnation is emptied into the fallen world and, in turn, through the crucifixion the source of the world's fallen nature has been voided, that is, redeemed: "the whole / and irreducible point of his descent." The word *kenosis* is itself a metaphor, a figure, referring to the emptying of a cask or vessel, and is linked in St. Paul's early creed to the figure of the servant who is bonded to repay a debt, an existence-altering redemption. God's self-emptying, his voiding of divinity into the humanity of Christ is the point. That point is really two points, Alpha and Omega, which become one in the figure of Christ. In the beginning is the end, in the end the beginning. God in Christ, "if there was a Christ," empties God's very Being into the body of the world. Christ, "if there was a Christ," is thrown here as we have been thrown, as the whole of everything is thrown into chance, into the limitless associations, into the profane matrix, the land of unlikeness, and everything thrown, therefore, likewise, into the sacred net, the Likeness of divine relation that sustains and embodies all things. This is the case, such paradoxical figurations would have it, whether we are fallen from an ideal origin or emergent toward some unfathomable *pleroma.*

"If there was a Christ" is in many ways the pivotal phrase in Hudgins's poem, for it articulates succinctly the prevailing skepticism that would have been anathema certainly in Donne's time, and it does so even for a poet like Hudgins who is obsessed with religious matters. At the same time, the poem's theologically robust and visionary ending belies the poet's ironic contingency clause, his theological hedge. If there wasn't a Christ there should have been, the poem implies, for without Christ, the Logos, the Word, or an equivalent figure, we are nothing more than the voidable, expendable matter of ourselves— piss is piss, shit is shit, blood is blood, all unredeemable—unable to be transfigured either by God or artist or politician or poet. In the land of unlikeness where the associations that make the world do not add up and dissimilarity finally reigns supreme, unredeemed, there can be no summation and no real art, for there can be no basis for meaning. Babel is babble, the only artistic currency.

From the standpoint of his implicit, if not explicit, religious optimism, Robert Hayden endorsed the underlying likeness of things, and that is precisely what enabled him to write the poems he wrote and to embrace the vision of a positive destiny for America. Hayden's Bahá'i faith overtly shapes his poetry.[11] Hudgins's Christian faith, or his wryly transgressive version of it, bears the same shaping power. There are, of course, many other poets for whom some deeply felt religious impetus exerts similar influence. But does one really need to appeal to the emblematic in one's poetry, to the expressly figural, to align one's work with some underlying idea of order? Mark Jarman raises this question in his thirteenth "Unholy Sonnet:"

> Drunk on the Umbrian hills at dusk and drunk
> On one pink cloud that stood beside the moon,
> Drunk on the moon, a marble smile, and drunk,
> Two young Americans, on one another,
> Far from home and wanting this forever—
> Who needed God?

Who needed God? The answer to Jarman's question is: they didn't, at least not consciously. And nor, perhaps, does anyone in such a perfectly ideal setting, those young bodies unencumbered by disease, hunger, age, blessed with good bread and good wine, inhabiting their own sacrament of two on that Umbrian hillside: latter-day lovers who desire nothing of Donne's earth-transfiguring pattern of love. In this sonnet, a rueful homage to Donne, time itself and so, inevitably, memory and consciousness press the question:

And why do I ask now?
Because I'm older and think God stirs
In details that keep bringing back that time,
Details that are just as vivid now—
Our bodies, bread, a sharp Umbrian wine.

Here, the emblems of faith have been divested of their sacramental significance and the details of life, remembered meaningfully, become sacraments
efficacious of God's presence. This *volta* from the overt emblem to the detail
is empowering. It is no great matter that Jarman transposes body, bread, and
wine—the constituent elements of the Eucharist—into profane proxies. In this
reverse transubstantiation they become the real presence of God incarnated
into memory. Is this, in fact, sacred or profane? The question is irrelevant in a
world consecrated by God through God's own self-emptying presence.

In both "The Canonization" and in his Holy Sonnet 14, John Donne's
theological metaphors live in the layers of tradition even as they lay siege
to the traditional firewall between sacred and profane. If the Divine Image
present in the world as established by the Incarnation destabilizes that neat
separation, then the equally traditional and orthodox understanding of God's
kenosis as the machine of incarnation—the necessary product of God's divine
economy—has the impact of placing as much sacral emphasis on the seemingly innocuous detail as the high-flown figure. God emptied into the world's
encompassing net of relations is the answering and completing pattern to the
pattern begged by the world "from above" in Donne's "The Canonization."
One might say that the process of *kenosis* establishes a pattern of love that
enables the pattern to gain validity from below, an answering emergence that
has ethical implications and not only creative ones. Christ himself, "if there
was a Christ," spent far more time with the cast-offs of society who needed
to be healed than with the well-heeled who often cast them off. Together
the two patterns are really one pattern, intended to be signified by the word
"Incarnation."

Yet, the world is nothing if not worldly. The late Michael Donaghy offers
a stirring essentially contemporary secular riff on such matters in a manner
that echoes Donne's own witty inventiveness. In the case of "More Machines"
metaphysics blurs into physics, and vice-versa. "More Machines" begins with

the equivalent of a "thought experiment" posed to determine the physical nature of a body in motion, only the body in motion is love itself, and love as in Donne's poem must embody and express a pattern:

> The clock of love? A smallish round affair
> That fits in the palm. A handy prop
> Like any of these: compare
> The pebble, the pearl, and the water drop.
> They're all well made. But only one will prove
> A fitting timepiece for our love.

Here, we find the rhyme "prove / love" now at the poem's outset instead of its end as in Philip Larkin's "An Arundel Tomb," and echoing likewise both Donne's "The Canonization" and Shakespeare's Sonnet 116. Donaghy intends to place his poem squarely in their company. Donne's "The Canonization" is a particularly complex feat of metaphorical, structural, and metaphysical engineering, no less than Shakespeare's Sonnet 116, and Donaghy does not back away from the challenge. The physical timepieces—pebble, pearl and water drop—introduce three metaphors into the poem, each of which is tested by the poet's imagination for its adequacy as a pattern suitable to express the reality of love. In short, the poet is self-reflexively dry-running his metaphors in the body of the poem as the poem proceeds, and he is doing so within a stanza structure that alternates *abab* before landing on a definitive couplet, *cc*. While the first stanza introduces the thought experiment, the second questions the adequacy of the pebble, and does so by entering the pebble's consciousness if, that is, a pebble could have consciousness. From the pebble's point of view, all of existence unfolds almost at hyper-speed: the sun is "a meteor," the day is "a strobe"; and yet "its machinery moves imperceptibly / Like the stars on continental drift." Because the pebble moves at an almost impossibly slow rate of speed, it paradoxically perceives reality moving at impossibly rapid speeds. Yet the pebble is not, the poet concludes, adequate for timing human love since, as the poem tells us, "it never *stops*." Donaghy's wit is sharp, and here that wit implicitly contends with Donne's idealized lovers. Implicit, too, is the notion that Donne's figures are no longer adequate to express love in a pattern suitable to a time that has become thoroughly desacralized.

Donaghy begins to test the second metaphor—the water drop—by quietly destabilizing the poem's structure and enjambing the second stanza into the third. That enjambment performs the action of the water drop descending. It also modulates the speaker's voice into that of a lab technician. The drop "falls from the spigot during a summer storm / A distance of three feet." At the medial caesura the speaker poses a question: "What does it see?" Water drops do not see, of course, and so the pseudo-scientific speaker reveals his pose. With each move the poem makes, Donaghy subverts its speaker's apparent rational remove with perceptions and questions that would be non sequiturs, in a world parceled into separate realities. What does the water drop see? Reality as stasis: "lightning fixed forever on a hot slate sky," "birds fixed in an eternal V." At the same time, unlike the seemingly stationary pebble, the drop's very movement allows it to fall so fast "it knows no growth or changes." Movement has become stasis, stasis becomes movement—the inverse of the pebble's reality, which leads to the inverse paradox. What does the water drop measure? "A quick dog fuck," the speaker tells us in an observation neither scientific nor expectedly poetic in its tone. Thus, the waterdrop "serves the beast as the stone serves God." We can see now that the poem's metaphorical testing, its succession of simultaneously physical and metaphorical thought experiments and hyperbolic use of relativity theory, has come to the crux. It is a vision of reality at cross-purposes. Now the poem proposes its final metaphor, its own true figure for the pattern of love:

> But our love doesn't hold with natural law.
> Accept this small glass planet then, a shard
> Grown smooth inside an oyster's craw.
> Like us, it learns to opalesce
> In darkness, in cold depths, in timelessness.

In the end, Donaghy's poem turns neither to any iteration of a Watchmaker God, nor to natural law, but to a version of the metaphysical worldview of microcosm and macrocosm, of the part in the whole, the whole in the part. The pearl is "a small glass planet." As a figure, it is at once analogically pearl and planet, planet and pearl. Microcosm manifests macrocosm. Despite the scale difference, in the figure, microcosm has become coextensive with macrocosm, just as time has become coterminous with eternity, as Plato dreamed—time, moving image of eternity. Donaghy's pearl is not *like* the planet, it *is* the planet without ever ceasing to be itself—entirely analogical. Appropriately, without any express appeal to theological considerations, the pearl of "More Machines" offers a pattern of love evolving over time, "learning," and doing so in the darkness and cold depths of its familiar milieu—emergent from below. In its final turn the poem shifts gears from metaphor to simile, "Like us," as it turns its focus from the figure of the pearl to the life of the lovers. From self-reflexive conceit-making we enter life. Donaghy's "More Machines," like all great poems conceived of, metaphorically, as machines, opens to the life emergent beyond its own aesthetic mechanisms. The milieu of the lovers' formation, like that of the pearl, is ultimately a version of "timelessness," a version of heaven here, another "midwinter spring in its own season" to borrow from Eliot's "Little Gidding," and thereby evolving in mutual, anagogical, participation. It is Michael Donaghy's belated variant of John Donne's "knot, of all causes," a mutation, so to speak, for a more secular and, as if it were possible, even more fractious time. Without any direct appeal to some Divine Image, the pearl of Michael Donaghy's "More Machines" illuminates the promise of a prospect not entirely knowable but available to the mind of the poet, and to anyone with eyes to see, imaginatively. That in itself, one might say, is a pearl of great price.

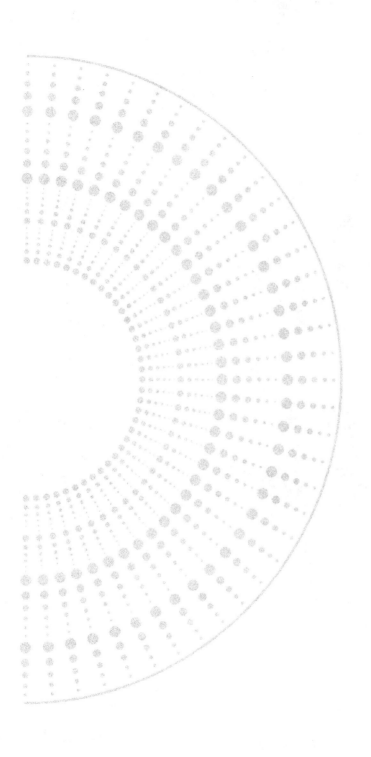

ANCIENT SALT, AMERICAN GRAINS

On the Poet as Scavenger

Since Ralph Waldo Emerson in "The Poet" declared that America needed to begin mining its own poetic resources instead of deriving the raw materials and methods of its art from England, and Walt Whitman heeded Emerson's call and largely reinvented American poetry in his own expansive image, poetry in America has succeeded in building an indigenous tradition on the foundation of Emerson's and Whitman's essentially futurist vision of the poetic imagination. America is an "open road," and the democratic and geographical vistas it surveys require an equally open art. In contrast, it is tempting to invoke Emily Dickinson as the avatar of a contrary poetic, one that while being distinctly American nonetheless preserves its formal and, in particular, its metrical ties to the past. That, at least, is New Formalist Timothy Steele's claim in *Missing Measures.* In his scenario, Whitman, Eliot, Pound, Williams, Olson, and their contemporary inheritors compose a dominant experimental lineage alongside that of Dickinson, Robinson, Frost, Bogan, Wilbur, Hecht, and the newer practitioners of the earlier dispensation of meter and form.

If American poetry's double inheritance seems overly pat and polarized in this particular narrative, one need only turn to the special American issue of the European journal *Metre* for confirmation of the rift from both sides of the chasm. "American poetry, as such, began with two geniuses" who cut "the Anglo-nostalgic umbilical tube with impertinence, impenitence," so Calvin Bedient writes. In his sweeping condemnation "a lot of current American poetry is . . . not American, but still English."[1] Michael Donaghy, the celebrated expatriate American poet who moved to London, countered Bedient's claim by denouncing the "two party system" of American poetry. Far from muzzling Dickinson's explosive silences under Whitman's impertinent yawp, Donaghy places her work centrally within a metaphysical tradition going back to Herbert and Donne.[2] Another salvo finds Robert Mezey answering what he calls

Diane Wakoski's "foolish rant" that she heard the devil in the poetry of John Hollander, as well as her endorsement of the simplistic notions that rhyme and meter underwrite political conservatism and that Robert Frost is "a bad European influence."[3] For Mezey, Diane Wakoski doesn't have "the faintest idea what she is talking about," and as such she represents the Zeitgeist "in one of its cruder and more mindless aspects."[4] Though I agree with Mezey in his condemnation of Wakoski's glib remarks, in such exchanges, legitimate questions of technique, aesthetic orientation, tradition, and period style devolve into the seeming skittishness of a *Saturday Night Live* routine: *"Robert, you impotent prig." "Diane, you ignorant slut."* Yet, it seems to me a poet inevitably writes at least in part out of the faith that genuinely good poetry—and certainly great poetry—transcends even the limits of its maker's stylistic assumptions as one of the necessary conditions for its being able to last beyond its own narrow historical moment. Out of the quarrel with others one makes rhetoric, so Yeats claimed, and out of the quarrel with self, poetry. To what extent can American poets shift the locus of the conflict between the "closed" forms of traditional poetics and the "open" forms of a long-established *avant-garde* from the contentious realm of rhetoric to the combustible arena of the individual imagination?

As if implicitly to answer this question, Robert Hass in his essay "Listening and Making" shifts the conflict between closed and open form to a productive though similar binary opposition. In poetry, Hass observes, "repetition makes us feel secure and variation makes us feel free."[5] In this formula, the *metron* or "measure" with its natural insistence on the closed system of reiterated feet becomes a vehicle for speech when it is freed, so to speak, by variation. Though one might argue that mere variation at best creates a limited opening for speech within the strict framework of meter, it might also be answered that nonmetrical poetry depends on the metrical system as a ghost in the poetic machine. Free verse is variation writ large, hardly playing tennis without the net (to recall Frost's pithy condemnation), since the net is skirting the iamb. As Hass observes, "freedom from pattern offers us at first an openness, a field of identity, room to move."[6] At the same time, however, "it contains the threat of chaos, rudderlessness, vacuity." Or, one may add, the mere flatness of much contemporary poetry. In contrast, for Hass, the "reverse face" or shadow side of repetition is claustrophobia, a kind of neurotic nostalgia for the safety of the metrical system. One can hear such nostalgia when Timothy Steele claims, excessively it seems to me, that the free verse poems of Pound and Eliot in both their more experimental and less strident manifestations, "undermine the norm [of measure] itself."[7] Steele's stance here is nostalgic because the perfect iamb is an abstraction, and as such the norm is not the grid or temporal lattice of measure but the poet's living speech—heightened, dramatized—by its transfiguration into the poem. The norm in the sense I intend is Shakespeare: "When in disgrace with fortune and men's eyes." The last two feet of the opening line of this famous sonnet are pushed toward iambic by the metrical expectation, though "men's eyes" by any account of the line's spoken quality is a spondaic foot. In short, the iambic regularity of the line is brought under the rule of the voice through syntax, which—thankfully—avoids making the iamb a metronome. Of course, it would be wrong to discount Steele's more incisive claim that at its best "conventional versification accommodates personally distinctive rhythm,"[8] and indeed Shakespeare's line exemplifies Steele's claim perfectly.

In modern poetry surely the paradigmatic example of this indisputable truth is the poetry of William Butler Yeats. Yeats, it goes without saying, is a poet for whom the closure of meter and form is emphatically necessary, and his antipathy to more open modes (not to mention his politics) would be strident enough in our day to incite Diane Wakoski's anti-conservative tirades. Here is his classic statement on the matter: "All that is personal soon rots. . . . If I wrote of personal love or sorrow in free verse, or any rhythm that left it unchanged, I would be full of self-contempt because of my egotism and indiscretion, and foresee the boredom of the reader. I must choose a traditional stanza, even what I alter must seem traditional. . . . Talk to me of originality and I will turn on you with rage. I am a crowd. I am a lonely man. I am nothing. Ancient salt is best packing."[9]

Isolated in this way, I imagine that to many contemporary American practitioners of the poet's art for whom the norm is free verse and not meter (inheritors of a confessional aesthetic and inhabitants of a climate that often praises and rewards a poet's message and affiliation—what Yeats called "the literature of the point of view"—over the mastery of their medium) Yeats's observations on craft could hardly seem more antiquated and curmudgeonly. "American poets learn your trade," he might say. Indeed, Yeats's way of working flies in the face of the American poetic ideal as framed by the Whitman tradition of openness and the worship of originality. His own rage for order, "to hammer his thoughts into unity," more often required him to fashion his traditional stanzas out of loose paragraphs and fragments—the very stuff of some modern and postmodern poetry: heaps of broken images, fragments shored against ruins. From the vantage of a century of experimentation, and the triumph of free verse as a mode seemingly consubstantial with the American idiom, it would seem that Yeats's need to pack the personal in the "ancient salt" of traditional form bears little if any relevance to writing, as William Carlos Williams suggested, in the American grain. Or, if it does, it would seem to place itself within the context of a polemical aside, nostalgic in its understanding of the art and contrary to the real force and scope of the American experience.

Yeats's appeal to the ancient salt of tradition represents the technical application of his Platonic ideal. Though, as he remarks, "a poet writes always of his personal life," at the same time "he is never the bundle of accident and incoherence that sits down to breakfast; he has been reborn as an idea, something intended, complete."[10] The closure Yeats seeks is not only technical and historical but, as implied here, metaphysical. The formal qualities of compression and closure that Yeats requires of his art are the artistic manifestations of ethical and ultimately spiritual needs. But Yeats by his own lights also cries in Plato's teeth. The desire to be reborn into a Platonic idea complete and intended, and therefore secure in the safe but claustrophobic neatness of the poem, is countered in the work by the answering gravity of the heart's foul rag and bone shop—the very accidence he seeks to escape. Plato's launch into formal idealism is rebutted by Aristotle's plunge into accident, into the disruptive but freeing processes of life. For Yeats, vivid speech is the embodiment of this counterforce within the poem: "It was a long time before I had made a music to my liking; I began to make it when I discovered some twenty years ago that I must seek, not as Wordsworth thought, words in common use, but a powerful and passionate syntax for passionate subject matter."[11]

Though Yeats further states that he compels himself "to accept these traditional metres that have developed in the language," the measure of his lines never reifies into the mere mechanics of verse as though they were the imitation of some ideal form; rather, measure in Yeats's poetry realizes a personal though distinctive rhythm through the way passionate syntax fuses with the *metron,* creating rhythm, combining itself with other textures of sound:

> That is no country for old men. The young
> In one another's arms, birds in the trees
> —Those dying generations—at their song,
> The salmon-falls, the mackerel-crowded seas,
> Fish, flesh, or fowl, commend all summer long
> Whatever is begotten, born, and dies.
> Caught in that sensual music all neglect
> Monuments of unageing intellect.

Thematically these famous opening lines from "Sailing to Byzantium" embody the fundamental tension in Yeats's work, the conflict between flesh and spirit, the Platonic idea and the Aristotelian attention to process. Thematically Plato has the upper hand, for Yeats clearly favors the monumental endurance of art over the passing pleasures of the dying generations. By the end of the poem, he transmutes himself into a golden bird, abstracted from life but nonetheless able to bear witness to it. He has become the ideal, transfigured from mere accidence. However, if we look even momentarily at the dynamic rhythm of Yeats's lines—rhythm created by the pressure of his syntax—we realize that in fact the sensual music of the poet's own impossible longing passionately shapes his declamation of the ideal. To my ear only three of these eight lines—3, 4, and 6—can be read as purely iambic, and all of them evoke some attribute of the passing fleshly world rather than the ideal realm of art. The second line is also iambic with a trochaic substitution in the fourth position, and likewise evokes the passing world with its doomed lovers. In lines 1, 5, 7, and 8, however, Yeats's syntax alters the percussive iamb according to the designs of the speaker's passion, his disgust with age, his muted jealousy of the young, his anger at impending death, his raging need for an eternity intuited paradoxically by the intellect alone. The greatest departure from the iambic backbeat occurs in the fifth line where the rhythm becomes positively sprung, the added stresses—"Fish, flesh, or fowl, commend all summer long"—combined with the textures of the three initial fricatives modulating into the quieter, liquid double "m"s and "l"s communicate the poet's almost speechless combination of fury and longing. The result of this yoking of meter and syntax here is energy, tension, intensity, while the last three feet of the stanza's final line return the poem to an iambic equilibrium. Scoring into the poem Yeats's unrelieved quarrel between flesh and spirit, this interplay between traditional meter and passionate syntax continues throughout the poem with tonal variations until it reaches its final equilibrium in the last line with the straight iambic pentameter of "of what is past, or passing, or to come."

One could have continued the analysis, enjoining Yeats's management of enjambment, caesura, and octava rima, but the essential point is that in a great poet like Yeats the seemingly closed system of meter and form becomes a vehicle in which passion is freed into the poem. "How can we know the dancer from the dance?" Yeats asks at the end of "Among School Children," knowing well that even improvisational dance requires a sense of form in order to liberate emotion. Nevertheless, given the American tradition of formal experimentation, do poets working in traditional meter and form comprise only a minor company within the American mainstream? Is the ancient salt really anathema to the American grain? The aesthetic claims that prompt such questions seem strained, and are finally a matter of polemics instead of practice. Neither Robinson, nor Frost, nor Wilbur, nor Nemerov, nor Hecht—regardless of what one might think of their poetry—are English poets because they write in traditional meter and form. No more are David Jones and Basil Bunting American poets because they followed the example of Pound in a British context that has remained closer to the grain of an indigenous tradition in which meter and form figure largely. Richard Wilbur's formalism, in turn, suggests nothing new except that it is a squarely American incarnation of historically longstanding traditions. Not unlike Yeats, at his best he appeals to ceremony without devolving into the ceremonious. And, of course, the formalism in English language poetry is in fact multinational. Sonnets traveled from Italy to England during the Renaissance. Sestinas and villanelles came into the language from the French. Pantoums are a Malaysian form. Ghazals, a newly vibrant form in contemporary American poetry through the work of Agha Shahid Ali, find their origin in Persian and Urdu culture. It is simply absurd to say that nonmetrical poetry is the only legitimate mode for American poets, and that to work otherwise is to engage in a marginal art, or at worst an un-American activity. Pound, the most vigorous advocate of the free verse revolution ("Compose in sequence of the musical phrase, not in sequence of metronome") was a Fascist. There is no inherent correlation between politics and style, and indeed the most liberal art can become dogmatic under the pressure of polemics.

Putting aside such prejudices, it is possible to explore for example how Yeats's ideas about passionate syntax might reverberate in an American context with Frost's theory of sentence sounds. "A dramatic necessity," Frost observed, "goes deep into the nature of the sentence. Sentences are not different enough to hold the attention unless they are dramatic . . . All that can save them is the speaking tone of voice somehow entangled in the words and fastened to the page for the ear of the imagination."[12] In essence, this is Frost's theory of the sound of sense, or sentence sounds. His claims for speech and the dramatic organization of the sentence reiterate in an American context Yeats's enthusiasm for passionate syntax. Even the blank verse of an essentially meditative poem like "Directive" manifests dramatic energy through its sentence sounds:

> Back out of all this now too much for us,
> Back in a time made simple by the loss
> Of detail, burned, dissolved, and broken off
> Like graveyard marble sculpture in the weather,
> There is a house that is no more a house
> Upon a farm that is no more a farm
> And in a town that is no more a town.

Far from organizing itself according to some iambic drum machine, the first line is both syntactically and metrically disruptive. Though still within the contours of the vernacular, the line is speech that makes strange in a manner that, even more strangely, anticipates the contortions of Charles Olson's work. The second line intensifies the poem's energy through anaphora, the repetition of "back" placing the reader like the speaker in a kind of time warp. This is real retrospective movement and not nostalgia, a backward thrust and not merely a backward look. Were we to closely analyze Frost's metrical pyrotechnics here, we would find very few regular feet through the poem's first four lines, while the last three lines that comprise this opening sentence resolve into regular iambics—a sentence sound that shifts dramatically from a jarringly propulsive beginning to its soft landing, as it were, in the past. Though constructed word by word, the sound experienced in these lines is the entire sentence woven through the temporal grid of Frost's blank verse, and so to place the burden of Frost's music entirely on measure as though each note were greater than the symphony is to miss Frost's fundamental insight about the nature of working in traditional meter. The net is important, but the play is more important. As so often the case in Frost's greatest work, the sound of sense is both serious and ironic at the same time. There is no safety in the past, though there may be the illusion of safety, or a momentary stay against confusion, that the poet at once requires and keeps from hardening into finality. "Here are your waters and your watering place. / Drink and be whole again beyond confusion" epitomizes the paradox of closure with an opening, since the poem gives us no real faith that finding even a toy Holy Grail is at all within our power, though our better angels would believe that finding it must be possible.

One might say that for Frost the form of a poem emerges from the evolving shape of its sentence sounds, with the provision that Frost saw meter as the necessary skeletal frame that had already established itself in the greater body of the art. Something similar might be said of Yeats. Finding his paradigm in organic theories of form extending back at least as far as the Romantics, Robert Hass in "One Body: Some Notes on Form" locates the formal sense literally and not just metaphorically in a human biological necessity. "Maybe our first experience of form is the experience of our own formation," Hass remarks.[13] Not surprisingly, for Hass the intuition of the organic sources of form extend to poetry generally, and not just free verse: "We speak of the sonnet as a form when no two sonnets, however similar their structures, have the same form. . . . The form of a poem exists in the relation between its music and its seeing; form is not the number or kind of restrictions, many or few, with which a piece of writing begins. A sonnet imposes one set of restrictions and a poem by Robert Creeley with relatively short lines and three- or four-line stanzas another. There are always restrictions because, as Creeley says, quoting Pound, 'Verse consists of a constant and a variant.'"[14]

It is easy to misconstrue organicism in poetry as advocating a kind of free-flowing, intuitive profusion as if nature gave no restrictions to its apparently limitless productions. But variation is not formlessness. Coleridge, following Schelling, envisioned a poetry coincident with the *naturans*—the "organic form" shaping itself "as it develops from within"[15]—rather than the *naturata*, nature's particular manifestations. Yet Coleridge wrote in meter and form, and disputed Wordsworth's claim in his "Preface to the *Lyrical Ballads*" that poetry should be written in the common speech of ordinary people. On the contrary, like Yeats after him he believed it should be dramatized, heightened from life, but not antiquated or artificial. For Coleridge there was no inherent contradiction between organic form and the inherited conventions of poetry. In our own time, Hass's biological understanding of poetic form grows out of Coleridge's organic conception, and yet Hass himself remarks "now, I think, free verse has lost its edge, become neutral, the given instrument."[16] How extraordinary to find so eloquent an advocate of organic form in agreement with one of the basic tenets of the New Formalism, that the "official art of free verse" has become ineffectual, even decadent.[17] Conversely, when Timothy Steele laments the Victorian tendency to read "poems in a sing song way to bring out their metrical identity" as an unfortunate practice that obliterated "natural degrees of relative speech stress within lines,"[18] he essentially brings meter under the governance of speech. In this, he is in essential agreement with Hass's claim that "the pure iamb can't be rendered; it only exists as a felt principle of order, beneath all possible embodiments, in the mind of the listener. It exists in silence, is invisible, unspeakable. An imagination of order. A music of the spheres."[19] If scansion is not meter, then meter comes to life only in speech. The remote godhead of the *metron* cannot exist without the body of the living word.

The idea of meter as some outmoded deity relevant to only a few remnant disciples is an exaggeration, of course, but from the standpoint of some of the twentieth century's more radical declarations of poetic independence the likening of traditional meter and form to an antiquated and soon-to-be extinct faith is roundly inaccurate. In his essay "The Poem as a Field of Action," William Carlos Williams proposes "sweeping changes from top to bottom on the poetic structure. . . . I say we are through with the iambic pentameter as presently conceived, at least for dramatic verse; through with the measured quatrain, the staid concatenations of sound in the usual stanza, the sonnet."[20] If Pound for all his revolutionary fervor saw rhythm as a "form cut in time," then Williams in announcing poetry through with the measured quatrain and usual stanza shifts the locus of form from time to space. The poem is a field of action or energy, and if the temporal unfolding of passionate speech or sentence sounds exists, it is registered more in the spatial display of the page rather than in the temporal interplay of meter and line. The ramifications of this shift, so significant for some postmodern poetry, are even more emphatically articulated in Charles Olson's polemical treatise, "Projective Verse." In Olson's diatribe against traditional poetics, the tension within the "closed" and "open" attributes of poetry becomes a gulf between seemingly mutually exclusive approaches to the art.

The primary source of Olson's complaint against "closed" or "nonprojective" verse is that, he claims, poetry since Shakespeare has gradually lost its grounding in the voice and has become "print bred."[21] It therefore has ceased to be a "reproducer of the voice" since rhyme and measure have outlived their necessity as aids to memory.[22] In contrast, "projective" or "open" verse eschews the inherited line, stanza, and overall form in favor of "composition by field" in order to restore "a point-by-point vividness" to the speech of poetry. For Olson, the locus of vivid speech lies initially in the syllable and then in the line understood as a kind of inscription of the poet's breath. "The line comes . . . from the breath," Olson writes, "from the breath of the man who writes," though everything "starts from the syllable."[23] From this core idea Olson elaborates his program for revolutionizing modern poetry: "It is by their syllables that words juxtapose in beauty, by partaking of sound, the minimum source of speech. . . . It would do no harm, as a correction to both prose and verse as now written, if both rime and meter, and, in the quantity of words, both sense and sound, were less in the forefront of the mind than the syllable, if the syllable, that fine creature, were more allowed to lead the harmony on."[24]

The field of Olson's projective verse is essentially a field of the voice, but it is voice operating at a register of sound before sense—rather than the sentence sound, as in Frost's poetry. Here is an excerpt from "I, Maximus of Gloucester, to You":

in! in! the bow-sprit, bird, the beak
in, the bend is, in, goes in, the form
that which you make, what holds, which is

the law of object, strut after strut, what you are, what you must be, what
the force can throw up, can, right now hereinafter erect,
the mast, the mast, the tender
mast!

As should be clear from these lines, the speech of Olson's poem intends to
affect the listener in a manner that, initially at least, short-circuits any rush to
comprehension. The syntax of this speech likewise intends to be passionate,
but in a manner that elides the personal voice entirely, as we find it in Yeats's
poetry. What we hear instead is the voice-as-medium in which, to use Olson's
words, syntax is "kicked around" for the purpose of generating a different kind
of kinesis. The lines read either like the words of a person gradually losing
consciousness, or those of a person overtaken by an oracle whose meaning
cannot be fully expressed in completed thoughts. The emphasis finally is on
process rather than closure, since in Olson's understanding of poetry every
line break constitutes a new turn of breath that carries with it a possibility
for furthering the voice's projection, and therefore the poet's need to pursue
every worthy impulse. As they stand, the lines compress the action and thus
the metaphor of the boat's bow-sprit plunging into the waves like the beak of
a bird, and then pressing beyond that first sense to the matter of the poetic
process itself, the boat as seagoing craft transforming itself into the craft of
making: "the form / that which you make, what holds. . . ." Though the point
is that the craft of poetry should refuse holding, refuse closure for the sake
of what the force of breath itself "can throw up" in the process of discovery,
instead of being content to remain harbored (to push the metaphor perhaps
too far) within vessels of received form.

In addition to exemplifying his own practice, Olson's program of projective
verse is particularly significant because it both gathers into itself many of the
innovations advocated earlier in the century by Pound, Eliot, Williams, and
others, and sets the table for the more radical postmodernist poetries that
have followed us into the new century. For example, it is possible to foresee
Susan Howe's linguistic montages in Olson's claim that the new technology
of the typewriter can indicate "exactly the breath, the pauses, the suspensions
even of syllables, the juxtaposition of even parts of phrases" and so for the first
time "without the convention of rime and meter, record the listening [the

poet] has done" and so further "indicate how he would want any reader . . . to voice his work."[25] How much more would Olson see the computer developing this potential even further? Notice, however, that Olson's concern is with the breath, with speech, and that the page—the typewriter's field of action—suggests a spatial orientation exclusive of those oral traditions that have shaped traditional meter and form. Of course, stanzas by definition are "little rooms," but the spatial metaphor in the word's etymology does nothing to diminish the oral and therefore temporal dimension of poetry. People on the street do not speak in octava rima or blank verse, but Yeats's and Frost's uses of these conventions on the page have less of a visual appeal than the deconstruction of traditional form into atomized, "nontraditional" parts on the page, whether by pauses, syllables, or juxtapositions of phrase. The phrase "composition by field" clearly suggests as much, and concrete poems, *carmina figurata,* like George Herbert's "Easter Wings," and "The Altar," John Hollander's "Swan and Shadow," and James Merrill's "Christmas Tree," are exceptions that prove the rule. Today's "erasure" poems and "burn" poems where parts of an already established text are removed, while considered avant-garde, require the printed page for their effect. So, by a strange reversal of original intent, Olson's futurist program might be said to entrench the poet more deeply in the print-bred culture from which he sought to liberate it, as well as in the burgeoning digital culture, precisely because the freedom brought by scrapping traditional meter and form makes positioning on the page even more integral to indicating how the reader ought to listen to the moves the poem makes.

A second problem, suggested earlier, concerns the issue of what Charles Olson's friend Robert Creeley called restriction. Because projective verse (and potentially all free verse) calls for a radical adherence to openness, to a furtherance of the poet's impulse to discover, there is nothing to stop the poem from not stopping. The obvious result is shapelessness, which is one of the reasons why Hass fears that free verse has run its course. Pound's *Cantos,* Williams's *Paterson,* Olson's own *Maximus Poems*—all lose in formal integrity because, in the final analysis, they have no closure. In contrast, a long sequence like John Berryman's *Dream Songs,* though clearly open in its articulation of Henry's angst-ridden musings, nevertheless obtains an accrued sense of closure through Berryman's elongation and re-formalization of the sonnet. Likewise, though multifarious in the formal expression of its parts, Irish poet

John Montague's *The Rough Field* obtains closure through the leitmotif of the journey and the sequence's overall circular structure. It almost goes without saying that if the great pitfall of traditional verse is a staid satisfaction in filling out the form to the letter of its convention, the great pitfall of nontraditional verse is to make convention out of originality. The result is verse that reads like the proverbial chopped prose or, as seems more and more the case, verse that runs like words in spate across lines that confuse excess with passion. At the far side of the gulf between open and closed poetries lies mannerism: on the one hand the idolatry of tradition and form that mistakes security for achievement; on the other a pretentious radicalism mistakes faddishness for sophistication.

Whether Olson's is a program for a more sophisticated poetry or not, if literary historian David Perkins is right in observing that he "writes in a language that was never spoken anywhere,"[26] then the irony of "Projective Verse" is that it reminds us that poetry ought to have the strength and vigor of speech that the best poetry has never lost, and it does so with practical acknowledgment that speech is not merely a recording of what might be heard in conversation but is speech shaped by the ear of the poet. To redouble the irony, despite his desire to escape the metrical straitjacket, the last runover line from "Maximus" quoted above is pure iambic tetrameter ("the mast, the mast, the tender / mast"); which perhaps only suggests that measure does exist in the rhythms of speech, however "kicked around" that speech might become, and it is one of the poet's essential jobs to listen for it. Despite Olson's objection to traditional meter and form, some of the ancient salt gets into the American grain. Moreover, in instances where attentive listening shapes the process of composition, I would argue that the gulf between closed and open modes collapses, and does so regardless of the individual poet's particular aesthetic or polemical program.

A. R. Ammons's "Corson's Inlet" is undoubtedly a poem shaped by the poet's embrace of open poetics and his refusal to be limited by what he called in *Garbage* "the tidy boxes" of conventional stanzaic structure. I know of no other poem that locates itself and its poet more steadfastly within the tradition of organic verse. Indeed, the "field of action" envisioned in "Corson's Inlet" translates the biological metaphor underlying organicism into an overall poetic structure derived from contemporary physics. Like any shoreline, the size of Corson's Inlet depends on the scale of measurement. On the scale of maps, a given shoreline might be ten miles long, but even if one were to measure the inlet with a straightedge, the minute curves and juttings of the shoreline would be missed. To obtain the "actual" length of the shoreline you would need a still more subtle device, though the smaller and presumably more intimate the scale of measurement the more intricately formed the shoreline reveals itself to be. Corson's Inlet is a fractal shore, and as fractal geometry demonstrates, its ever-finer edges can be measured infinitely. Ammons's walk is an encounter with infinity, with the ultimate openness of form that finally composes all of nature, indeed all of physical reality, and the poem is not only shaped by the poet's recognition of that openness but becomes a self-reflexive model for it:

> I allow myself eddies of meaning:
> yield to a direction of significance
> running
> like a stream through the geography of my work:
> you can find
> in my sayings
>   swerves of action
>   like the inlet's cutting edge:
>   there are dunes of motion,
> organizations of grass, white sandy paths of remembrance
> in the overall wandering of mirroring mind. . . .

As these lines suggest, Ammons's poem intends to be an *ars poetica* mimetic of the inlet's own structure and organization, and not merely an objective meditation on the scene. As such, the ultimately open form of physical reality guides the poet's reflections. "I have reached no conclusions," he continues, "I have erected no boundaries / shutting out and shutting in, separating inside / from outside: I have drawn no lines. . . ." The poet's whole effort is to follow the motion forward, continually breaking beyond the boundaries of line and stanza into wider more rarified "fields of order." The poem is therefore a model of projective verse, its ideal "an order held / in constant change" without "finality of vision." In keeping with this open ideal, "Corson's Inlet" is a single sentence held together by permeable thresholds of colons. As such, the poem's self-reflexive liminality extends to grammar and syntax. What would Frost make of this sentence sound? Is Ammons just playing tennis without the net? And if, to borrow Yeats's phrase, any poem looks "out of shape' from toe to top it seems to be this one.

Yet, as in any successful poem whether open or closed, "Corson's Inlet" exhibits a perfect coincidence between content and form. At the same time, it could be easy to justify the arbitrary management of lines in a poem simply by appealing to the ephemeral nature of the world: "I make / no form / of form-lessness." In this scenario, a single line might read "as" as it does in Ammons's poem, a line arguably as far from any rhythmic vitality as from any metrical validity as one could possibly write. The success of Ammons's poem, however, even in the matter of this single-word line, springs from the poem's orchestra-tion of texture and structure in achieving its overall form. In her essay "The Flexible Lyric," Ellen Bryant Voigt describes the relationship between these three elements of a poem—texture, structure, and form—in the following way:

> To say a building has a sound structure means that the foundation and frame are adequate for the shape and weight. . . . By extension, structure in poems seems neither "paraphrasable" content . . . nor "achieved harmony." . . . but rather the support for both content and its embodiment in the words chosen and arranged in harmony or tension. That is, structure is the way all the po-em's materials are organized, whether they are abstract or concrete, precise or suggestive, denoted or connoted, sensory or referential, singular or recurring. Since almost all poems in English are linear—read left to right down the page—structure is also the purposeful order in which materials are released to the reader, whereas form creates pattern in these materials, to establish pleasing proportion, balance, unity—"a single effect"—in an otherwise overwhelmingly various texture.[27]

Given Voigt's incisive discrimination, the question to ask of a free verse poem like "Corson's Inlet" is whether and where "texture has been used in the service of structure" and where it has been used to achieve "a formal ar-rangement."[28] While one could trace how the poem successively and success-fully builds structure and formal integrity from the textural substructures of

Ammons's swerving lines, the poem's most achieved scale of measurement is precisely what Ammons says eludes him in the poem: the Overall. Though "Corson's Inlet" portrays a manifold and elusive order, the poem's formal achievement—the "shape of its understanding"—rests in its ability to attain a suitable and pleasing closure despite textures that easily could have dispersed into overwhelming variety: "not chaos." The overall pattern or form of the poem is circular: "I went for a walk over the dunes again this morning . . . tomorrow a new walk is a new walk." Across the span of its one sentence the circular movement of the poem is dynamic because it speaks to the deep reality of recurrence, and not just the poet's personal habit of taking walks. "Corson's Inlet," to borrow the subtitle of Ammons's book-length poem *Sphere*, has "the form of a motion." Recurrence is an open circle. It is the poem's overall formal organization, realized through its textures and structural "fields of action," that finally lends even a one-word line like "as" credibility, since the line finds its true measure on a different order of scale—not the syllable, not the *metron*, nor the line, but the overall. And "as" as a line also makes paraphrase-able sense, since the word embodies in microcosm the ambitious mimetic intentions of the poem, the coterminous spaces of the poet's mirroring mind and the equally mind-mirroring reality of the world.

Underlying Ammons's use of open poetics in "Corson's Inlet" is an idea of order that presumes a deep formal correspondence between the poem and reality. Unlike the seashore encountered by the singer of Wallace Stevens's "The Idea of Order at Key West," the inlet on which Ammons's walker meditates offers a version of the sublime that need not be "mastered" or "portioned out" because the poem and the world on which the poem reflects are finally all a part of one flow. The "blessed rage for order" has resolved into a blessed acceptance of organic and even subatomic form. The conflict between one poet's desire to impose order on reality by means of what Olson called "closed verse" and another poet's desire to discern in reality a more rarified and open conception of form originates in the apparent gap between two seemingly contrary ontologies. Do poems master or receive the world? But the opposition is false, since the world is rife with formal symmetries and mathematical structures, rhythms, recurrent measures, all manifesting themselves both within and as the natural expression of the flow. Perhaps, given the mainstream tradition of American poetry and the fragmented nature of our postmodern world, the traditional formal poem seems for many too tame, too tended, within the present historical and cultural context, while for those across the divide open verse appears a culpable indulgence in formlessness.

Steering her own craft beyond the contentious seas between these clashing rocks, Elizabeth Bishop offers a model art gratefully above polemics in which fixed ideas of order give way to the patient practice of the repertoire. Equally masterful at couplets, quatrains, ballads, sestinas, the villanelle ("The Prodigal" is formally a double sonnet), and free verse, Bishop's work has risen to such universally high regard precisely because her poems manifest an openness to the world's variety despite the poet's natural reserve, and do so without loss of control, intelligence, or descriptive energy. That is what gives Bishop's poems their unique brand of restrained but unmistakable passion. Written in free verse, "At the Fishhouses" exhibits Bishop's genius for showing us a world, for pacing us through that world with measured attention to the right detail given at just the right time until, by the poem's end, textures that might have seemed random have fallen together with explosive continuity:

Although it is a cold evening,
down by one of the fishhouses
an old man sits netting,
his net, in the gloaming almost invisible,
a dark purple brown,
and his shuttle worn and polished.

As the opening of her poem demonstrates, the acuity of Bishop's visual attention is fine almost beyond comparison, but what gives the scene its subtle intensity is the audible pacing of the lines. Each is a complete phrase that gradually releases and concentrates the poem's dramatic focus. Moreover, it contains the most delicate of alterations—the comma after netting and the subsequent line break—that place's the old man's net in clear juxtaposition to the gloaming which renders it nearly invisible. This blending of the human landscape with the surrounding non-human atmosphere will become crucial to the poem, and the net as a tool that permits access to the sea's otherworld resonates with the apparently frail but secure device of the poem itself as it lowers the reader ever more deeply into the liminal world of the fish-houses. Of course, the consonance and assonance of the lines does its work as well—"although," "cold," "old," "gloaming," "almost," "invisible," "purple," "shuttle," "polished." The poem's sonic textures, filled with plosives and liquids announce the sea's "heavy surface" as well as its unbearable depths before it even appears on the poem's thirteenth line, its opacity a muted contrast to the silver translucence of the dock area with its gangplanks, gables, wheel-barrows and fish tubs. But for the emerald moss of the shoreward houses and the rust on the old capstan like "dried blood" the world of the poem is nearly monochromatic.

Beyond Bishop's vivid description, the significance of these details derives from the pacing. After the opening five lines, Bishop departs from her focus on the old man and spends the next twenty-five describing the indigenous surroundings. In short, she slows the pace even further in order to widen the aperture of the poem's focus. The details and textures throughout these lines compose a living map and not merely a random survey of the scene. She is defining the space of the poem in a way that inevitably returns us to the old man who now ceases to be part of a painterly setting and is revealed as a friend of the poet's grandfather. How many lesser poets would have cut the preceding twenty-five lines, or condensed them and restructured the poem around this personal detail, thereby having marred the vivid surfaces—"the principal beauty"—that the poem regards so patiently, so lovingly? But neither is this personal detail superfluous, for it introduces the past and therefore time into the poem, a crucial move at this juncture, for it is between time and timelessness that the poem's spaces hover. This becomes apparent in the short strophe that follows with its interplay of verticals, "down" and "up" balanc-ing each other on the water's edge until the brief scene comes to rest on the horizontal tree trunks—again silver, and a threshold between the historical human world and the timeless world of the sea. Here, as it were, is the poem's spirit level, its balance point between alternate universes:

Cold dark deep and absolutely clear,
element bearable to no mortal,
to fish and to seals. . . .

Rhetorically these lines constitute a dramatic shift in tone in which the world's fleeting principal beauties, unlike the iridescent scales of fishes taken up from this otherworld, encounter an impenetrable limit. The arrival of the seal in the poem, to which the poet with marvelous good humor sings Baptist hymns, suggests the possibility of mediating between these worlds, the absolute world of the sea and the ephemeral human world. One might hear, even in a good workshop, someone suggest that this detail is distracting, an unnecessary re-direction in a poem that directs us all too often, before us and behind us, up and down. But the seal is a mediator, like the hymns to which it appears to listen and shrug off, a mediator between worlds. Likewise, the second re-direction to the tall firs, a million Christmas trees, underscores the restrained religious sense that has entered the poem. The poet, like the seal, is a believer in "total immersion," though so extreme a baptism in this context represents a loss of identity rather than a fulfillment of religious promise. Bishop, as always, moves by margins and reversals to the center, though none of those margins, reversals, or re-directions is extraneous to the shape of the poem's understanding. The icy freedom of the water above the stones and then "above the world" is a perceptual trick, an illusion that reveals the truth of the sea as a kind of radioactive sub-space, a metaphor not for the Ground of Being but for an ontological flow that finally permeates Bishop's shore as well, and that resists full translation into human terms:

If you should dip your hand in,
your wrist would ache immediately,
your bones would begin to ache and your hand would burn
as if the water were a transmutation of fire
that feeds on stones and burns with a dark gray flame.

The water *is* a transmutation of fire, like all things a metamorphosis from primal energy. At this point Bishop's lines lengthen to accommodate the increase in the poem's intellectual and emotional resonance. One would think the ontological nature of the world would be enough for one poem to tackle, and to do so in utterly concrete terms that allow for remnant old men as well as comical seals, but as its final move "At the Fishhouses" redirects us again, from ontology now to epistemology, and so to the historically conditioned nature of all knowledge, and therefore all talk about that Beyond the sea represents. As in "Corson's Inlet," Overall transcends the poem's widening scope, but whereas Ammons's poem confidently models the poet's work on a subliminal, primal, and recurrent flow Bishop's poem offers a more circumspect vantage. In "At the Fishhouses," to drink from the sea is not the same as drinking from Frost's imaginary grail to become "whole again beyond confusion," or to be lifted like Yeats's bird out of the sensual music. The world resists us, and knowledge of it is often bitter and briny, and certainly fleeting. With this final realization, Bishop's resolutely paced and tightly controlled free verse in "At the Fishhouses" offers a closure freer than the circular path of "Corson's Inlet," for at the poem's end she launches us expressly into the open. Tomorrow, a new walk might be a new walk by the fishhouses but, though flowing, eventually our knowledge of the world will be "flown." From the perspective of Bishop's poem, Ammons's faith in scientific knowledge as a model for poetic form is merely one more conditioned way of envisioning the world and the poems that seek to derive order from it. Despite his preference for open form, I doubt whether Ammons would deny Bishop's insight. In the final analysis the two poems offer overlapping rather than contrary visions of the world, and the formal approaches poems might employ to respond to the world.

"Everything only connected by 'and' and by 'and,'" so Elizabeth Bishop observes in "Over 2000 Illustrations and a Complete Concordance," a phrase that could have been incorporated by Charles Olson in "Projective Verse." And yet within her poems a world defined by contiguity and resistant to metaphor progressively gains in metaphorical intensity and revelatory power. In turn, the world of her poems resists neat closure while still embodying formal necessity, and retains its openness to new impulses while securing its textures within the larger order of the whole. Whether she is writing a villanelle or a free verse meditation her forms are always actively engaged with the world she encounters and imagines, never slack or intransigent or merely imposed on the elusive conditions of life, which finally is characteristic of all good poems whether packed in the ancient salt or orchestrated in the American grain. Regardless of school, program, or ideology, good poets are scavengers who somehow manage to find what they need, and good poems of any formal orientation embody the desire to clarify life out of the welter of experience.

In such poems the walker becomes a dancer whose mastery we know by the choreography of the dance, the world another dance we are called to join again and again in its passing, and in our passing to know with ever greater intimacy and integrity.

ONE ARC SYNOPTIC

Plot, Poetry, and the Span of Consciousness

O Choir, translating time
Into what multitudinous Verb the suns
And synergy of waters ever fuse . . .

—HART CRANE, *The Bridge*

DANCING ON THE BRIDGE

There is a scene near the beginning of *Saturday Night Fever* where Tony Maniero, after another late-night excursion with his friends through the discos of 1970s Brooklyn, parks his blue-collar, hand-me-down sedan in the middle of the Verrazzano Bridge. What follows is a ritual of testosterone-fueled whooping and strutting as Tony, hardware store clerk by day, aspiring dance sensation by night, climbs over the guardrail onto the span of girders, where he begins a sequence of pirouettes that requires him to balance precariously several hundred feet above the churning Narrows where the Hudson River opens into Gravesend Bay and the Atlantic beyond. This macho flirtation with death is a rite of passage, and Tony is the hero who must survive the film's "epic" trials, not least of which is overcoming his blue-collar upbringing to become an artist, battling a gang of Puerto Ricans from Sunset Park with his own tribe of Italian Americans from Bay Ridge, and finally winning the woman he loves—his ideal dance partner—by entering the big contest at the local disco, 2001. The movie is a late twentieth-century American male *Bildungsroman* (counterpointed by the falsetto voices of the Bee Gees) and its plot, true to the roots of Western narrative, composes a dramatic arc replete with temptations, reversals of fortune, and the birth of a new identity in the form of a more mature consciousness for our hero. Before he can leave the world of his youth he must, at the crucial turning point or *peripeteia*, refuse the dance prize he so desired and award it himself to the Puerto Rican couple whose dancing he judges to be better than his own and his partner's. He must also return to the girders of the bridge high above the flowing water of the Narrows between the human city and the vast inhuman ocean to witness the death of his sidekick, the pathetically sycophantic Bobby C, who plummets into the swell below while drunkenly trying to perform the same leaps his idol had mastered at the beginning of the film. It's as though Tony's transformation had to be sealed by the loss of his alter ego, his anti-self, the part of him that was mindlessly subservient to his origins. In the end he must even forgo an erotic for a purely Platonic relationship with his "beloved." In short, it's not until the "Bobby C" in him is dead that he can cross the other bridge—Hart Crane's bridge so it happens—into the promised land of Manhattan.

However we might interpret *Saturday Night Fever,* it may be said that the figure of the bridge presides over its plot from beginning to end and may be taken as an analogue of plot itself, in Greek *muthos,* the dynamic span of a story's essential action as it is structured through the succession of details and events. Plot is, in Robert Scholes's succinct definition, "the dynamic sequential element in narrative literature."[1] Working directly from Aristotle, Thomas Leitch defines plot as "a sequence of events or actions (*praxis*) which displays a particular end (*telos*)."[2] Given that Aristotle defined a poet as a maker of plots rather than verses, it seems plausible that this definition of plot should hold for narrative poetry as well as fiction and film. Surely the narrative poems of Robert Frost and Robinson Jeffers have plots. Yet, when I think of the situation of narrative poetry at the beginning of the twenty-first century the first name that comes to mind is neither E. A. Robinson, nor Frost, nor Jeffers, nor any of the significant contemporary poets working with narrative in our own time, nor even a poet in the stricter sense of versifier at all, but Virginia Woolf. "Examine for a moment an ordinary mind on an ordinary day," Woolf enjoins us in her essay "The Novel of Consciousness." "The mind," she continues, "receives a myriad of impressions—trivial, fantastic, evanescent, or engraved with the sharpness of steel. From all sides they come, an incessant shower of innumerable atoms; and as they fall, as they shape themselves into the life of Monday or Tuesday, the accent falls differently from of old; the moment of importance came not here but there; so that, if a writer were a free man and not a slave, if he could write what he chose, not what he must, there would be no plot, no comedy, no tragedy, no love interest or catastrophe in the accepted style. . . . Life is not a series of gig lamps symmetrically arranged; life is a luminous halo, a semi-transparent envelope surrounding us from the beginning of consciousness to the end."[3] Woolf's observations, revolutionary in their day, construe plot as anything but sequential. As a translation of time's endless flow into a narrative's beginning, middle, and end, plot becomes profoundly diminished, if not entirely marginal, in Woolf's formulation. Indeed, her remarks are observed for the purpose of undermining what she called "the tyranny of plot," and while clearly the genre she had in mind was fiction her implication that there is something contrived, artistically stultifying, and epistemologically deluded about plot begs the question of how poets both in her time and ours might effectively construct a narrative poem.

The legacy of modernism in both fiction and poetry asks writers and readers to rethink if not eschew traditional machinations of plot, or at least to make them secondary to character or other kinds of temporal organization. Through the experiments of Joyce, Faulkner, Lawrence, Woolf, and many others, the "realistic" novel of the nineteenth century becomes atomized and recast in the flow of modernist stream of consciousness. Often contemporary realistic novels minimize plot designs for character development, and the postmodern metanarrative tradition often manipulates plot in outrageous ways for the purposes of parody. In Woolf's case the realistic novel is anything but "real"; it is a warping of reality into false constructs, a lie of order that transgresses against time's inherent flow. What was for the mythic storyteller truth—the shaping *muthos* of some sacred or near-sacred idea of order—becomes an impediment to representing the world as it is in all its radiant complexity. What was for Aristotle the hallmark of art as well as life, plot, for Woolf seems almost an intrusion upon life and an impediment to art.

Aristotle's notion of plot as the mimesis, or representation of an action and not of character, emerges from that first world of ritualized narrative, of storytellers recreating strictly defined plots within the confines of oral tradition. Again according to Robert Scholes, traditional plot evolves from this mythic world on its way to what he calls "the secular narrative."[4] Moreover, for Scholes, though plot is dynamic in its construction of sequence, "the whole movement of the mind in Western culture . . . has been a movement away from dogma, certainty, fixity, and all absolutes in metaphysics, in ethics, and epistemology," and so by extension the very idea of plot as a plausible ordering of reality becomes ever more undermined even as it reaches its dominance in the "traditional story."[5] If Scholes is right—and it is hard to argue against this prevailing sense of things, regardless of one's philosophical, religious, ethical, or aesthetic persuasions—then the idea of plot is linked to fundamental issues of human self-understanding and desire for a world at once conceivable and representable in the truth of time's fugitive nature. In short, modern and contemporary questions of plot find their roots in primordial questions of time, consciousness, and the sacred. As always, one's idea of poetry, narrative or otherwise, emerges implicitly if not explicitly from one's idea of the order of things, even if one believes there is nothing but chaos at the ontological heart of experience.

Surely Woolf's misgivings about plot are made in support of her own narrative art, which is, paradoxically, intensely inward, character-driven, and lyrical. The lyric movements of her novels are, in a profound sense, a scandal to temporal structure. Her novels portray consciousness immersed in the fluid medium of time. How would Woolf represent the action of Tony Maniero's passage from dancing thug to the sadder and wiser aspirant we see at the movie's end? Perhaps the question isn't fair, since Woolf may well be the least obviously cinematic of twentieth-century novelists, and thought of any adaptation of plot in the traditional sense would be anathema to her. If one could imagine Virginia Woolf in 1970s Brooklyn, I doubt the bridge would loom so boldly in her exploration of Tony's consciousness. Still, plot as an orchestration and sequencing of "events" does not disappear entirely from Woolf's actual work, though it is minimized in favor of the envelope of accrued luminous details. Plot closure in Woolf is Lily Briscoe's final brushstroke through the center of her painting at the end of *To the Lighthouse,* almost an afterthought even as it satisfies the reader's sense of closure: "It was done . . . I have had my vision."

In addition to her disaffection with plot, Woolf's view of consciousness also reflects the diminishment of individual identity before the powers and dominions of modern life, and is not this reflection the inevitable consequence of Romantic claims to self-empowerment? At the same time, the rejection of the Romantic ethos by the modernist poets who were Woolf's contemporaries, most notably Pound and Eliot, ironically reveals a longing for the security of plot in the face of what appears a thoroughly atomized world, and this longing persists perhaps most visibly where plot seems most absent. Though as an epic it achieves far less closure than Woolf's *To the Lighthouse,* the structure of Pound's *The Cantos* is predicated on the submerged plot of Odysseus's journey home. Despite its seeming cacophony of allusions and voices, Eliot's "The Wasteland" achieves a kind of discordant symphonic coherence through its "subsumptive" myth. The action it represents is that of the dying and reviving god assumed like an archetypal code beneath its fragments, juxtapositions, and associations. To some it might seem ridiculous to mention "The Wasteland" in the same breath as narrative, but in addition to what one might call the poem's intertextual plot, "The Wasteland" has distinct narrative as well as dramatic elements. It is above all an orchestration of stories or fragments of stories that would fit together into one Ur-narrative. In a profound sense Eliot's assumption of his intertextual, archetypal plot brings him nearer to the *muthos* found in ritual where the action is sacred action, worthy of ritual repetition, to be later embellished by "the singer of tales," but not to be essentially departed from. Remarkably, in "The Wasteland," the potentially most secular of all plots—the fracture of civilization into incoherence and disorder, into the profane—is also the most sacred: a repetition of the infinite struggle between order and chaos leading, hopefully, to spiritual regeneration. Though one would be hard pressed to defend "The Wasteland" as a narrative poem in the strictest sense, plot understood as the essential action of *muthos* orchestrated through events and details is necessary for the poem's artistic success and integrity.

When Aristotle spoke of plot as a representation of action, or more specifically a sequence of actions leading to a justifiable end, he was speaking of Sophoclean drama as the highest form of *poesis.* What, however, is the nature of a poem's action, its *muthos?* For the lyric that action might ideally be described as an action of voice. Unbounded by story, the pure lyric gathers forward motion through an intensity of voice that gestures ultimately toward a suspension of time. Beginning, middle, and end exist as staging for the voice's aspiration to sing out of a state of pure being, or perhaps into that state through language, as in Rilke's "Sonnets to Orpheus"—"*Gasang ist Dasein.*" Song is existence. In contrast, the essential action of narrative poetry, like any narrative, must be accomplished with reference to time's forward motion; that is, in reference to becoming. Of course, it's debatable whether there is a pure lyric as described above, though, if there were, Rilke's poetry would come near to achieving that standard. Still, plot, as Thomas Leitch observes, is an essential part of the rhetorical structure of the English sonnet,[6] and Edward Arlington Robinson's Tilbury sonnets show him to be an essentially narrative poet within this lyric form. More broadly, in his essay "In Praise of the Impure: Narrative Consciousness in Poetry," Alan Shapiro demonstrates brilliantly how narrative informs such lyric poems as William Carlos Williams's "The Road to the Contagious Hospital" and Robert Hayden's "Those Winter Sundays." Conversely, to be successful the narrative poem must have a strong lyric dimension—it must combine story with song in the sonic and rhythmic textures of its lines—otherwise it might as well be written in prose. Yet, to complicate matters further, Paul Ricoeur in his magisterial work *Time and Narrative* reminds us that even in Aristotle's *Poetics* the representation (*mimesis*) of an action (*muthos*) manifests itself through "the medium of metrical language."[7] From this standpoint the adaptation of *muthos* into the belated world of prose is secondary to its fundamental presence in poetry. At the very least it suggests that the terms lyric and narrative are not strict generic markers but point toward something more fluid. At the root of the matter, song and story are not mutually exclusive but are rather mutually implicated in the reordering of time through which stories are told and meaning gets made in poems.

Questions over the nature of narrative's reordering of reality certainly fuel the discussions of narratologists, and it ought to be entertained by poets in their more extended musings about their art. "Plot alters . . . the world even as it provides an interpretation of it"; so Thomas Leitch describes what he sees as the fundamental paradox of narrative, its ability to at once comment on the world from a stance that transcends the world, a vantage of wisdom "outside the particular represented situation," while nevertheless operating through the narrative's sequence of events, its "process of development" or essential action.[8] This is exactly what Woolf finds so transgressive about plot, its presumption of having staked out the truth about life when it is merely a warping of life away from the truth of life's elusive nature. There is no outside for Woolf, no vantage except for being within the luminous envelope—hers is a narratology approaching pure immanence. Hers is a mimesis of consciousness rather than a mimesis of action or even character.[9] At the same time, without some dimension of plot neither a story nor a poem could obtain closure. Plot, therefore, may be understood as a fundamental trope of the poet's imagination, a shaping action or "organizing mimesis," to use Paul Ricoeur's phrase, that transforms a fluid temporal experience into self-conscious unity.[10] Plot for Ricoeur is "a synthesis of the heterogenous"[11] by which the fluid multiplicity of life obtains livable order on the human scale. To use Woolf's *To the Lighthouse* again as an example, it is in the middle section after Mrs. Ramsey dies and the nonhuman vibrancy of the house rises into narrative focus that life outside the human experience of time comes into focus as the wider truth of existence. The whirling line of light from the Lighthouse, like plot, can reach only so far across the flow surrounding it. It inevitably disappears. The human world is an island world and its plot concerns, even world wars, pale before the nonhuman flux that composes the greater elusive sum of reality. At its core, plot constitutes an ontological countermovement against the flow, even as it intends to articulate that flow. That is the core of its paradox. Plot therefore lives a double life, and finds in Frost's "West-Running Brook" an apt figure for its contrary nature:

> Speaking of contraries, see how the brook
> In that white wave runs counter to itself.
> It is from that in water we were from
> Long, long before we were from any creature.
> Here we, in our impatience of the steps,
> Get back to the beginning of beginnings,
> The stream of everything that runs away.
> Some say existence like a Pirouot
> And Pirouette, forever in one place,
> Stands still and dances, but it runs away,
> It seriously, sadly, runs away
> To fill the abyss' void with emptiness.

How tempting it would be to compare Frost's Pirouot and Pirouette with Tony Maniero's dance on the bridge above the Narrows, but such mindfulness about the ontological and epistemological roots of things really never enters the human neighborhood of *Saturday Night Fever*. In any case, plot as an arc of action assumes a vantage outside the flow of time, a contrary movement like Frost's white wave, since without that outside vantage, time itself would not exist as a succession of comparable moments: without plot time would not be time but "undifferentiated flow."[12] The paradox cuts in both directions at once, not unlike Frost's brook. Plot not only exists as a presumption that would impose order as if from outside time, it is an invention of time without which time would not exist. As poet Eleanor Wilner remarked once at a poetry reading, "We are hotwired for narrative." We are, it seems, hotwired more specifically for *muthos* at least in some measure, and the managing of plot in poems as well as stories is a dance of degrees that at once marks the human span, clarifies its longing, and admits its own countervalence in a flow that otherwise cannot be known.

It is interesting that poetic intelligences as alien to each other as Woolf's and Frost's would be drawn in their contrary ways to the same experience of time's flow and ultimately the question of how human experience seeks to determine meaning through the reordering of time. Both writers are ultimately concerned with consciousness, and in the human sphere that also means inherently living a double life, of being at once a part of the flow of life as Frost sees things: "It flows between us, over us, and with us," his spokesman, Fred, reflects in "West-Running Brook," and exists counter to the flow by our mind's awareness of its seeming separateness from nature. I think therefore I am: the Cartesian formula with its primacy of thinking over being speaks to the phenomenological truth of our inherent contrariness. Similarly, according to Colin McGinn in *The Mysterious Flame,* consciousness is a phenomenon that by its essential properties eludes our ability to describe it since, by his estimation, we cannot determine its true nature simply because we exist *as* humanly conscious beings. For humans to see consciousness for what it truly is would be for an eye to be able to see itself without the aid of a mirror. "Our ignorance here," he observes, "is an ignorance of a hidden architecture of the self. Something about the hidden structure of the self, determines its unity and identity, but we do not grasp this hidden structure, which is why we cannot answer questions about unity and identity with any reliability. It is not that we know the essential nature of the self but fail to understand under what physical conditions it exists; rather, we are ignorant of what the self intrinsically is."[13]

Speaking as a philosopher, McGinn writes persuasively and compellingly about the failure of both science and religion to answer this most fundamental question, but both Woolf and Frost in their own idioms brilliantly portray the essential action of consciousness reflecting on itself and, perhaps, reveal art's most basic mimetic aim—to represent the "hidden architecture" of our humanity. Though Woolf's art, by Paul Ricoeur's estimation, is "a masterpiece from the point of view of the perception of time" precisely through her ability to make "the incompleteness of personality, the diversity of levels of consciousness . . . and the evanescent character of feelings" the center of her portrayal of human beings,[14] her minimizing of plot in story does not eradicate what he calls "emplotment" as an indelible feature of narrative and, I would claim, a necessary feature of human self-reflection. From the first cave painting, art seeks to represent the essential action of the human consciousness seeking to see itself for what it is intrinsically and in relation to the world. If McGinn is right that is an impossible task, though what may be a failure for philosophy could well be a boon to art, and to poetry specifically, for with each failure the spur to represent, to create in an image the true nature of ourselves that forever eludes us, is renewed.

Does this scenario, however, lock us into a postmodernist hall of mirrors, the product of a tragic tautology or a fruitfully recursive journey inside the most formative of hermeneutical circles? The fundamental *aporia,* the seemingly "unbridgeable gap" as Ricoeur calls it,[15] falls between the representation of time in a reality independent of us and the representation of time as the condition for our experience in the world. Ricoeur's answer is to claim that "emplotment"—*muthos* as a creation of the structure of human consciousness—clarifies the gap but does not offer a solution to the problem. The bridge itself is a dance above that serious, sad running away of everything from everything else and from itself that is finally the emptiness that fills Frost's couple in "West-Running Brook" with "a panic fear." At the same time, the multifarious presence of plot in ways not normally construed in poetry permits us to extend our understanding of how poetry might be orchestrated outside the traditional "gig lamp" design and still maintain a dimension of narrative as well as coherence and viable closure. This is what Ricoeur means by "emplotment" as opposed to plot: it is the deep structure of the work that finally brings the intention of single action to the succession of events linked together by causality, and it is the product of that "rage for order" Stevens found concomitant of the poetic impulse. In my view such causality in poetry need not be apparent in the traditional sense, but may exist through narrative elements and nonnarrative elements in a poem's orchestration. Hence my example above of "The Wasteland." Ricoeur's sense of emplotment might also allow us to see more traditional narrative designs in the manner of Robert Frost's dramatic narratives as being far less the series of "gig lamps" they may at first appear to be, particularly when the poet effectively confronts themes that resist the human order of things, which is something Frost does all the time in his best work. Finally, it may help us begin to rethink some of the assumptions that have led to a balkanization of American poetry into mutually exclusive camps whose artistic assumptions are underwritten by profoundly antipathetic views of reality and how reality, self, and time, ought to be represented.

MACROCOSM: POLYPHONY AND CONFIGURATION

Beginning. Middle. End. I am riding in the back seat of my family's new Rambler station wagon on a Friday afternoon in Brooklyn, my father having left work early to beat the traffic. We have driven the ten blocks to 95th Street along Fourth Avenue, made the left turn just before the Harbor Theater, resumed the trip after the red light on the corner of Fifth by the White Castle—a light we always seem to catch whatever time of day—and now with the next right after Vesuvio Italian Restaurant and Joe's Garden World we're merging along the on-ramp of the Verrazzano. It's 1968 and the Vietnam War is still raging just before the catastrophic events—King's assassination, Kennedy's assassination—that would transform history. We glide along the rise over the Narrows between the two towers I watched ascending through some of my earliest memories and down the gradual arc to the toll plaza cut into rock beside Fort Wadsworth and above the emptying Hudson, one brief leg of the trip west finished, an ending to be followed by other markers—The Outerbridge, Perth Amboy Refineries, The Wishing Well Tavern on Route 206, signs for Lake Hopatcong, Andover, Newton, Don Bosco College—that had become my way of pacing the journey that ended, at least until Sunday night when we started back, at Cherry Wood Trail in Crandon Lakes, New Jersey. This paced organization, the way of finding significant milestones as a means to mark time is, I think, a way of not only enduring *chronos*—what Frank Kermode calls "waiting time" or "passing time" in *The Sense of an Ending*—but of shaping it into "significant time," what he in contrast identifies as "*kairos*."[16] Though Joe's Garden World and The Wishing Well Tavern hardly stand as significant markers outside my own memory, and only then in retrospect, it is this reconfiguring of time from mere chronology to meaningful order that most distinguishes the Western conception of history, particularly in the Judeo-Christian tradition. We find the significance of our place in time by seeing our lives somehow in concert with the *kairoi,* those events that stand out as emblematic of an encompassing story that lifts us above the passing flow, that configures the plots of our lives within the purview of some larger and deeper emplotment.

Assurance of the validity of such an overarching conception of temporal order has, of course, been greatly undermined as much for most poets as for theologians and philosophers. If the grand arc of a world-defining story could be believed any longer it would have to be believed with the provision that its truth claims provide only a glimpse at best of the reality toward which the grand scheme points, itself having become one story in a potentially infinite number of stories all pointing in their limited ways to some still grander and ever-elusive universal emplotment. At the same time, the urgency of so eminent a design exists like a ghost in the machine of poetry. Stephen Dobyns, a poet notable both for his narrative gifts as well as his skepticism in matters of ontology and epistemology, underwrites as much when he reflects "the way a poem is created is a metaphor for the ordering of chaos, not only through the use of pattern, but also through structure, which is the presence of a beginning, middle, and an end."[17] Dobyns's insight is profound for it makes the poet's task akin to the mythmaker's. The poet's ultimate success is an image of order wrested from a disordered world—the representation of a single essential action that is the poem realized through the formal patterns established through the poet's various choices. Beginning, middle, and end—that deep structural integrity—achieve their meaningful unity of time in a victory of concordance over discordance.[18] This is, as Dobyns observes, a structural victory, but one that nevertheless is accomplished through the poet's ability to bring all the patterns and textures of the poem into concert with each other—Frost's momentary stay against confusion.

The most astounding example of a poem that organizes itself at every level according to the scheme of some grand emplotment is Dante's *The Divine Comedy*. The beginning of the poem is the middle of the poet's journey—"*Nel mezzo del cammin di nostra vita*"—though his life is also "our" life, the one life, the one archetypal plot line. The poem's terza rima, its thirty-three cantos in each book but for the *Inferno* which has thirty-four and brings the poem's number to a perfect hundred, the tripartite structure of the whole—all reveal an orchestration of scale reflective of the Trinitarian unity of Dante's spiritual and physical universe. The fiction of Dante's journey of descent and ascent, the epic romance of the soul, is a passage through scales of one divinely ordered *muthos* for human beings, history, and the entire universe. Dante's encounters along the way, both the damned and the saved, are personal *kairoi* that further and deepen his spiritual knowledge and finally enable him to represent that which paradoxically cannot be represented: the Divine Life itself which is ultimately the beginning, middle, and end of human life. Whether one still believes in Dante's universe is beside the point. In *The Divine Comedy* time has become fully humanized. What the narratologist would call the prevailing "discursivity" of life, its absence of plot, has been reconfigured to achieve a teleology, an end, one that is conducive to meaning and therefore human habitation in time. Narrative becoming has arrived at the lyric apotheosis of being, only to find that it has been being all along!

Like Stephen Dobyns, Alan Shapiro envisions poetry, and in particular narrative poetry, as intimately bound to human self-definition and reflective of human consciousness as well as our innate desire to create order in a world that sorely resists our efforts in these matters. Shapiro's sense of narrative, though far removed from Dante's cosmic unity of scale, nonetheless retains the idea of unity of action, emplotment, as a dynamic structural organization that necessarily involves all aspects of the poem. "I regard narrative," Shapiro declares, "as having more to do with a particular activity of consciousness than with technical matters, or with anecdote, or with the mere sequential nature of external happenings." And he continues:

Narrative involves what W. S. DiPiero calls "states of becoming," the enactment as well as imitation of action (mental, physical, emotional, or intellectual) in the unfolding of the verse. The complete rendering of an action implies an arc connecting origins and ends—how have I come to this (past) is implicit in what I am doing (present), and what I am doing is unintelligible from what I am doing it for (future). Anything in the poem which clarifies or contributes to the rendering of this action has narrative meaning. Thus, it is possible to talk about meter and syntax as narrative elements, and about how the evolving shape of the sentence, for instance, or the developing contour of a particular rhythm, forms a segment of the arc which the poem as a whole describes.[19]

Shapiro's observation here is important because it essentially shifts our attention from the contrivances of plot that so troubled Woolf to the very matter of consciousness that Woolf sought to better represent by removing plot in any conventional sense from her fiction. In turn, it adapts DiPiero's concept of "states of becoming" in a manner that amends the Aristotelian notion of *muthos* as an imitation of action. For Shapiro, plot is an "enactment," an idea that in one sleight of word restores the fundamentally dramatic emphasis of Aristotle's *Poetics* and makes it central to narrative poetry. Finally, it reiterates the likewise fundamental connection between narrative and lyric poetry, correctly seeing the difference between the two as a difference of inclination and degree, and reaffirming implicitly if not explicitly that a successful narrative poem must have something lyric about it in its employment of rhythm, sonic texture, syntax, and form.

The linking of narrative to states of becoming in Shapiro's thought underscores what Robert Scholes affirms is the now long-standing shift in narrative literature "from myth seen in the context of a cyclical concept of time, to myth seen against a linear concept."[20] For Scholes, moreover, "this change in the human conception of time is an aspect of that universal movement toward a rational understanding of the cosmos which tends to make itself felt in most cultures but is virtually the identifying characteristic of our Western culture."[21] The birth of narrative literature in the West that by and large coincides with the epic vision we identify with the name Homer may itself be understood as a secularization of myth into progressive narrative. Dante's sacred journey combines his soul's linear "state of becoming" with an encompassing cyclical revelation at the visionary summit of the *Paradiso*—the whirling, kaleidoscopic Rose that is the poet's admittedly feeble figure for the communion of divinity and humanity, transcendence and immanence, that is being in its essence. Dante's poem unites being with becoming, linear time with cyclical time, by joining microcosm with macrocosm in a final commanding figure that seeks to represent that which cannot be represented. In contrast, Odysseus's journey home after Troy, fraught as it is with delay, binds action to character. He is *polytropos,* the multifaceted man, and by inscribing the arc of his journey the plot of *The Odyssey* manifests the same polytropic character. What Thomas Leitch calls "the polytropic principle"[22] is essentially a conception of plot that would reconcile its discursive dimension—the potentially endless narration of events in the manner of Scheherazade—with its equally necessary teleological impulse, the requirement for closure.

In modern poetry the mythic impulse at the root of narrative finds its expression in the modernist "epic" sequence. Of course, there is no modernist (or postmodernist) epic in the pure sense of the word since we no longer have the luxury of a shared, all-encompassing paradigmatic story. Homer, Virgil, Dante, Milton assumed a unifying *muthos* for their cultures. Blake invented his own mythology. In Wordsworth's *The Prelude* we see the displacement of the epic impulse into the poet's own "becoming"—a psychological epic, the inward journey. In the twentieth century, Pound's *The Cantos* expresses an epic impulse, but the sequence's failure rests in its unbridled discursiveness. Despite their roots in Homer (and their multifaceted cultural allusions from Confucian China to Troubadour France) *The Cantos* finally has no *telos.* The modernist and postmodernist epic plot from Williams to Olson displays itself as a quest for the very organizing principle that would provide it with closure—they are discursive searches for the end that never comes. Dana Gioia's remark in "The Dilemma of the Long Poem" that the modern long poem is "doomed to failure" reflects his stance, and the New Formalist stance in general, that only the narrative structures of epic can satisfy narrative teleology. The narrative poet should adopt traditional narrative structures to avoid the pitfalls of endless discursivity, according to this analysis, since by Gioia's estimation the need to create "the form" of one's own poetic discourse assumes an outright rejection of received methodologies.[23] However, Gioia's assumption that the modern long poem refuses to adopt traditional narrative structures simply does not hold, unless one is limiting the phrase "traditional narrative structure" largely to blank verse. Though Pound does not write in blank verse, *The Cantos* attempts to incorporate the essential narrative structure of the journey as a way of organizing the poem's discursivity. Pound fails mightily to infuse his poem with a formal *telos,* but his failure is not born of rejecting all traditional narrative structure. Rather, he fails to adapt the Homeric motif sufficiently into the poem, becoming ever more distracted by his own centrifugal wanderings in the vast storehouse of human cultures. Both *Patterson* and *The Maximus Poems,* as brilliant as individual parts might be, at times, likewise lack teleological focus, though in both cases it is not due to the utter rejection of traditional narrative structures but, I would argue, the failure of Williams and Pound to adapt tradition in a way conducive to reconciling the long poem's need for discursiveness with a reliance on teleology to achieve satisfactory closure. They fail, in short, at being polytropic, at reconciling these two fundamental elements of plot.

One modernist long poem that does not fail to achieve adequate closure despite its incorporation of multivalent perspectives that amplify the discursive aspect of its structure is Hart Crane's *The Bridge.* Most believe Crane's poem to be, in Dick Allen's words, "a noble failure,"[24] and there are indeed individual parts of the sequence that do not contribute much to the overall design, or excel merely as individual moments within the whole. These are "Indiana," the last poem in section II entitled "Powhattan's Daughter," and section V, the loosely juxtaposed "Three Songs." There are also moments of vatic bombast, excesses of Crane's ambitious and operatic conception of the poem. Nevertheless, the governing action of *The Bridge,* its plot, is the eternal metamorphosis of Divinity into time through history, and the human effort of creation in material form by which new incarnations are made. Every section of the book intends to be revelatory of that end. The Brooklyn Bridge is the representative figure or trope for this action, and it is anything but static. Dick Allen's observation, then, that the noble failure of the modern long poem results from attempts by poets to extend the "imagistic lyric" into epic form without regard for "narrative and dramatic elements"[25] does not quite hold for Crane's ambitious work. Indeed, the opposite is true: the sections identified above fail because they are imagistic relative to the scope of the whole, and the sections that do further the poet's vision are at once more lyrically vital and more vitally formed within the structure of the narrative. From its multiple perspectives, and really its multiple voices, *The Bridge* is Hart Crane's attempt to realize a modern myth.

From a narrowly traditional vantage, it is an affirming myth, shaped by a shared belief in progress, surely the one popular overarching, largely untested value of our culture despite the high modernists' demurrals to the contrary. From another vantage, a vantage chastened by a knowledge of American history appropriately skeptical of America's presumptive myth of fully achieved democracy, Crane's "epic" can be read as an offensive celebration of supremacist distortions of history resulting in the brutal oppression of native peoples. From this perspective, Crane's *The Bridge* is really a poem supportive of empire, akin in its way to Virgil's *Aeneid*—a poem of mythically self-justifying origins, which is its *muthos.* Such a view, while mindful of our needed reconsideration of American history, misses and ultimately distorts the aesthetic intent of the poet, which is to give voice to Crane's optimist's vision of America coming slowly and painfully into the full promise of his democratic vista. By virtue of Crane's orchestration of that *muthos,* through a variety of voices and temporal incarnations, *The Bridge* does achieve a satisfactory reconciliation between discursivity and teleology within the work's polyphony, the many songs of its various embodiments resounding into "One Song." *E pluribus unum.* It is not my intention here to advocate for Crane's vision of America, only to underscore the point that as a poem of epic ambition *The Bridge* does indeed go a long way toward achieving the scope of its intended design. How the elaboration of that design distorts or suppresses certain necessary and incontestable voices remains a crucial consideration.

Yet many voices are indeed heard in *The Bridge.* There is the poet's voice, sometimes animated by Orphic rapture as in the opening "Proem: To Brooklyn Bridge" and particularly in the sequence's final section, "Atlantis," sometimes more quietly meditative as in "Cutty Sark" and "The Tunnel," and sometimes punctuated by slang. The variety of tones is so great, and the shifts sometimes so sudden, that this "authorial" voice actually becomes multivalent in the poem. The poet's voice shifts abruptly from slang to biblical rapture at times within the span of a line, as though the poet had suddenly become an oracle. It is, in fact, the integrity of the plot that gives the presiding voice a core intention that runs through its variety of tones. In addition to this dominant voice, there is the voice of Columbus in "Ave Maria," and the voices of women throughout the individual poems of "Powhattan's Daughter," each of whom is a historical permutation of the female archetype or anima that is also the continent itself. There is the sailor in "Cutty Sark" whom the poet meets on one of his night wanderings. Then there is the voice-over prose narrative running alongside the verse that provides yet another more omniscient perspective on events. The polyphonic orchestration of voices in Hart Crane's poem achieves its unity of action primarily through the poet's recursive figuration. The looming figure of the poem is, of course, the Brooklyn Bridge itself, which is as much the embodiment of the poem's nameless Deity as it is the material structure:

> And Thee, across the harbor, silver-paced,
> As though the sun took step of thee, yet left
> Some motion ever unspent in thy stride,—
> Implicitly thy freedom staying thee!

One of the Bridge's prevailing attributes is its status as a figure that unites opposites, a *coincidentia oppositorum,* a figure whose ambition Dante certainly would have admired. From the start, Crane depicts the Bridge as theophany, a revelation of the divine that combines both motion and stillness, at once spiritual manifestation and product of the creative libido of the world: "O harp and altar of the fury fused, (How could mere toil align their choiring strings!)," the poet exults. Yet, the Bridge is matter shaped by human design to manifest its destiny as spirit incarnated. Thus it "condenses eternity."[26]

The figure of the Bridge recurs throughout the poem in literal form when, for example, the poet encounters the sailor on South Street in "Cutty Sark," whom he eventually leaves to walk home back across the Bridge. In "Cape Hatteras," Crane's great evocation of Walt Whitman—the true presiding spirit of the poem—he identifies the bridge not merely as a physical entity but as the fulfillment of Whitman's imaginative vista:

> Our Meistersinger, thou set breath in steel;
> And it was thou who on the boldest heel

Stood up and flung the span on even wing
Of that great Bridge, our Myth, whereof I sing.

This is Crane at his bardic and operatic best, in which the figure of the Bridge permits him to mythologize his imagination's hero and thereby channel that hero's vision into his own. The Bridge is the myth of America, carried forward from Columbus's "spanning" the ocean—*Te Deum laudamus* for thy teeming span," Columbus exclaims in "Ave Maria." Or is it the poet, or a fusion of the poet and the historical figure? The metaphorical span of the Bridge, its ability to incorporate and designate the "amplitude of time," is made manifest through the plot of the poem and it is precisely this figural trope that allows Crane's voices to metamorphose in their archetypal fusions across the span of the poem. Though the poem constitutes a myth of America, its true subject and aim, its action as confessed to Walt Whitman, is "to course that span of consciousness thou'st named / The Open Road. . . ." Like Columbus and Whitman, the other principal human figures in the poem manifest the Bridge's attribute of "spanning" space and time by configuring it anew through the power of their imaginations. Edgar Allan Poe is yet another figure who appears in "The Tunnel" as the shadow side of the poet's imagination, the destructive anti-self who must be expiated, something, tragically, the suicidal Crane was unable to do in his life. The feminine principle of "Powhattan's Daughter," in turn, seeks to infuse Native America into the poem, though the contemporary reader might well (and probably should) cringe at her appearance as at an earnest but lavishly insensitive stage production. Nevertheless, she and her various manifestations introduce a conception of cyclical time, which moves in contrary motion to the apparent linear organization of the sequence from Columbus in "Ave Maria" to the utopian future of "Atlantis."

The reconciliation of these time frames, cyclical and linear, is yet another fusion of opposites the poem seeks to accomplish through its plot. At the same time, one might argue that the cyclical conception of time, allied as it is in the poem with Native America, actually contributes to the poem's unreflective stereotyping of native peoples, effectively de-historicizing them into the caricature of an archetype. Though many voices are heard in Crane's polyphonic poem, the archetypically feminine voice of "Powhattan's Daughter" renders Crane's conflation of archetypal significance into stereotype doubly offensive. At the same time, to his credit, there are moments when Crane does not shy from portraying the violence of America toward those who have been marginalized and silenced inside the "One Song," as when the poet identifies murdered African Americans floating in the Mississippi:

> The River, spreading, flows—and spends your dream.
> What are you, lost within this tideless spell?
> You are your father's father, and the stream
> A liquid theme that floating niggers swell.

One might object, given our current moment in American history, to Crane's use of the "N" word. Then again, would one really want to soften the racism that, in essence, pulls mightily against the current of Crane's own progressive vision? Note that Crane's self-address suggests a loss of American identity that permits the poet to himself become the exemplar of generations of Americans, a paternity that in the line following reveals tides of hate. When the section ends, the River lifts on a dream, the American dream one must presume, "a mustard glow / Tortured with history. "

Perhaps it is too much to ask, considering when Crane was writing his poem, that there should have been more such moments, and a deeper and more pervasive exploration of manifest elisions, and inconsistencies, within the poem's configuring design. In any case, ambitious as the design may be, its realization at times pitches the poet too vigorously forward and away from ugly realities—historical and social realities rather than mythic ones—from which he should not be distracted. Rather, the poet needed more vigorously and comprehensively to allow the span of the poem's design to take the combustible stress of those realities, rather than suspending the completeness of his gaze. We do find something of a more fulsome take on these thorny subjects in a letter Crane send to his friend Jean Toomer: "*Cane* has come and I am grateful—and happy for your words. My mood is naïve and somewhat awed today. The strange tempest has left off. . . . It has left one conscious thing (at least this and perhaps more) that evil accumulates, if not *in* us, at least in pockets and domains of the world without. And the mark + gauge of our progress is quite obviously to be told in the successively more intense attacks of the dark force upon us—as we continue to defy it in ways more persistently."[27]

The evil Crane refers to, the "dark force upon us," comes into view with the arrival in print of Toomer's *Cane,* one of the great books of his time, and one that deals expressly with racism. Crane also appeals to "the mark + gauge of our progress," which likewise places his reading of *Cane* within the frame of the poet's progressive vision for America, to be published some seven years later. As a gay man who himself knew trauma and prejudice because of his sexual orientation, and given his friendship with Toomer, it appears unlikely Crane would use what we now call the "N" word glibly or merely decoratively in his poem. The poem's context proves this, moreover. At the same time, one might have hoped for a greater purchase in the poem on the cumulative evil to which he alludes in his letter, the cumulative national evil of racism. There is nothing in Crane's would-be American epic to equal in such crucial matters Hayden's "Night, Death, Mississippi" or Brooks's "A Bronzeville Mother Loiters in Mississippi, Meanwhile, a Mississippi Mother Burns Bacon," or lucille clifton's "Jasper, Texas 1998," or even in his own time Claude McKay's "The Lynching" or "If We Must Die." Of course, we have the advantage of nearly a century of reconsideration, now, however belatedly, to be more acutely and justly forthright in such matters. The historical frame has moved and has been reconfigured, to a degree, from Crane's time.

Movement, motion—and so reconfiguration—is in fact a central theme in *The Bridge.* The Proem begins cinematically with the pivot of a seagull's wings above New York harbor, and the poem places the reader inside that motion, as if there were a camera fastened to the seagull's breast. Then in a series of movements "elevators drop us from our day," then we are with the "multitudes" in the "panoramic sleights" of cinemas to which they hasten. A "bedlamite speeds" to the parapets of the Bridge to jump into the East River, noon accelerates down Wall Street, derricks turn, traffic lights "skim" along the Bridge's own "unfractioned idiom." In the midst of all this movement the Bridge stands, an embodiment of movement and stillness. The Bridge "vaults" both the sea and "the prairies' dreaming sod" as the poet prays for it to descend to us, the lowliest. All of this motion at the outset of the poem puts me in mind of Philip Glass's film *Koyaanisqatsi,* where the composer's rapidly modulating score accentuates the scenes of urban energy. Glass's film is meant to portray "life out of balance," but Crane's poem intends the opposite. All the movements in the poem coordinate and ultimately dovetail with its singular action, its *muthos:* the ever-more-encompassing revelation of the Bridge as figure of Divine energy incarnating itself in matter.

To arrive at its final crescendo in Atlantis, the sequence moves us from Columbus's journey west to the New World. The poem then accelerates time through its motion in space so that, in "The Harbor Dawn," we arrive at the present with its bedded lovers. As the reader moves through this section, the poems at once shift us spatially, so that we follow the way west with the Twentieth Century Limited as well as the Mississippi River's flow, and temporally—first back into mythic time in "The Dance," and forward to the present-day Indiana woman who is meant to be the latest incarnation of the feminine archetype. In "The River" the poet declares "I knew her body there / Time like a serpent down her shoulder, dark, / And space, an eaglet's wing, laid on her hair," and what he knows is more than conjugal pleasure but an eternal principle that manifests itself, paradoxically, in the river of time. The linear movement of time in this section of *The Bridge* is actually enveloped by the circular movement from present to past to present. The structure of "Powhattan's Daughter" establishes time as cyclical. The same is true for the poem in its entirety. For example, in "Cape Hatteras" as the poet reflects on the "imponderable" reaches of time bedded into the space of the continent ("the dinosaur / sinks slow, / the mammoth saurian / ghoul, the Eastern Cape. . . ."), and before he invokes Walt Whitman who himself is "in speed with vast eternity," the poet glimpses fleetingly "that star-glistered salver of infinity, / the circle, blind crucible of endless space, / Is sluiced by motion—subjugated never." The circle is indeed the geometric figure that recurs throughout the poem, and demonstrates that throughout *The Bridge* Crane uses figuration as a plot device to orchestrate the poem's development through the discursive movements of its individual poems and to maintain continuity with the sequence's teleological imperative, its guiding myth.

Crane likewise accomplishes unity of action through other figures, such as Columbus himself, who returns in "Cape Hatteras" as "the Great Navigator," like Whitman a great imaginer and purveyor of the Open Road of consciousness. He returns again allusively as the poet crosses Columbus Circle in "The Tunnel." The motion of the subway in this section is likewise at once a linear progression that furthers the heroic consciousness on its journey into the underworld and its encounter with the shadow self, and a return to the poem's beginning—Brooklyn, and the Bridge. The overall motion of Crane's poem might best be described as neither linear nor cyclical but recursive, an evolving movement forward that likewise continually doubles back on itself through the efficacy of its figuration. Both motions are necessary for the essential action of the poem to find representation of its structure. Recursive as it is, that structure brings us back to the Bridge, but at a still more encompassing level of consciousness than at the beginning of the poem:

> O Choir, translating time
> Into what multitudinous Verb the suns
> And synergy of waters ever fuse, recast
> In myriad syllables,—Psalm of Cathay!
> O Love, thy white pervasive Paradigm . . . !

As the visionary onslaught of "Atlantis" shows, the final coincidence of opposites in the poem is multiplicity and unity—*E pluribus unum*—a truly democratic metaphysical vision that makes *The Bridge* at once a myth of America and much more. The poem's last crescendo (there are many crescendos in Crane's tour de force) further invokes the Bridge as "Everpresence," which is something yet more encompassing than mere eternity, since Everpresence is not the antithesis of time but a synthesis of time and eternity: a vision akin to Dante's cosmic Rose at the end of the *Paradiso,* though without recourse to his Thomism. Crane's is a hierophany fueled by modern dynamos. In the penultimate line of the poem, the serpent of time and the eagle of space return again before "whispers antiphonal in azure swing." All along we've been following in leitmotifs of figures an encompassing Jazz symphony whose highly orchestrated plot, despite lapses, excesses, and deficiencies, nevertheless forms in Crane's phrase "one arc synoptic" through its multiple voices and visions.

This short exegesis of *The Bridge* in light of plot does scant justice to the brilliance of Hart Crane's orchestration at every level of scale, every aspect of narrative and lyric texture in the poem, despite its rhetorical excesses, the insufficiencies of some individual poems in the sequence, and of course the culpable limitations and distortions of his mythic conception. Though not a narrative poem in the strictest sense, Crane's long poem demonstrates that a too narrowly held conception of narrative poetry perhaps hides more than it discloses. In so doing, it may limit the possibilities of narrative structure in contemporary poetry, as well as how we understand narrative's role in poets like Crane who modulate from tradition without abandoning its teleological imperative. Some contemporary narrative poets see narrative as antithetical to modernist and certainly to postmodernist experimentation. Crane is certainly from the second generation of modernists, and his eclectic use of various poetic methods places him outside the tradition of Frost and even Jeffers, both of whom loomed large as models for New Narrative poets. However, by looking even briefly at a major long narrative poem like Andrew Hudgins's *After the Lost War,* it becomes clear that Crane's modernist methods and this narrative poet's stricter adherence to traditional narrative structure are not wholly incompatible.

The major difference in plot structure between *The Bridge* and *After the Lost War* is that while Crane's poem develops recursively to achieve closure Hudgins's poem adopts a linear chronology. Discursiveness in Crane's poem is given teleological form through a *muthos* that incorporates an earlier cyclical conception of time. To use Paul Ricoeur's term again, in *The Bridge* plot operates through a highly ritualized brand of configuration, something close to myth. Plot as configuration in Hudgins's poem operates according to a principle of linear selectivity rather than ritual circularity, though obviously Crane had to be selective in shaping the multiple voices and vantages of his poem. In *After the Lost War,* Hudgins renders the life of Sidney Lanier univocally rather than polyphonically and most often in blank verse. He also places us in Lanier's life *in medias res,* after the war, and allows Lanier's speech to render the character's consciousness as overheard by the reader, and as re-imagined by Hudgins himself. By Hudgins own estimate Lanier as portrayed is a hybrid character, part nineteenth-century American poet and part Hudgins. "I'd like to thank Lanier for allowing me to use the facts of his life—more or less—" Hudgins remarks in the Preface, "to see how I might have lived it had it been mine."

The univocal nature of the poem, it seems, is perhaps not as stable as it first may appear. More significant to the notion of plot, however, is that Hudgins's long poem, like Crane's, is a sequence of poems and that, like Crane, Hudgins uses recurrent figures to create continuity. The figures of the child, Lanier's flute, bees and insects continually resurface in Lanier's meditations that turn as often to metaphysics as to history. The two poems share thematic concerns as well. Most importantly, while obviously the tone of Hudgins's poem shows he aims to de-mythologize a life more than mythologize a paradigm as in Dante or Crane, the principle of selection the poet uses to choose the facts and experiences of Lanier's life on which to focus is essentially a principle of gleaning *kairoi*—representative "spots of time"—from the available chronological record of Lanier's life, and often inventing them. These *kairoi*, as in the stories told by Dante's shades, reveal the life; and, as in Wordsworth's "spots of time," they offer vantages on the hope of transcendence, or at least moments of clarity within the life that constellate into a pattern of coherence. The plot structure of *After the Lost War* is the sequence of these *kairoi* that, while arranged in chronological order, nonetheless *configure* into an order of time that is not merely discursive but teleological, as these lines from "The Hereafter" demonstrate:

> For so long I have thought of us as nails
> God drives into the oak floor of this world,
> It's hard to comprehend the hammer turned
> To claw me out.

Chronologically, death is the end of life, where the beginning and the middle find their completion and, hopefully, fulfillment. "Only through time, time is conquered," Eliot wrote in *Four Quartets* with somewhat greater faith. These lines taken from the last poem of Hudgins's long sequence reveal, however, that Lanier's life has been shaped all along by the plot or *muthos* of the Christ story. Though Lanier expects death to be death, unlike Crane who expects transfigurations on an operatic scale, that does not prevent his fictive life here or Hudgins's poem as a whole from being organized by a more subtle orchestration of the paradigm in the very process of de-mythologizing Lanier's life. Indeed, because it requires attributing equal value to time as well as eternity, since the figure of Christ is both human and divine, the Christ story as a shaping paradigm allows ample room for discursiveness, digression into time and along the flow of time; for time is the necessary medium by which the eternal is made known. Regardless of Hudgins's assent to belief, this paradigm provides the narrative of the poem with its figural organization. Though *After the Lost War* does not seek to "condense eternity" in the manner of *The Bridge*, both poems in their different idioms use plot as a principle of configuration to shape narratives that ultimately engage supreme questions of human destiny. In doing so, even within their limits, both poems force us to confront enduring and intractable questions of American history, democracy, and justice, as well as poetic construction.

MICROCOSM: PLOT AS SENTENCE SOUND

Both Crane's *The Bridge* and Hudgins's *After the Lost War* are book-length works that depend on large-scale figural strategies of emplotment to orchestrate their parts into a whole greater than the sum of those parts. Such orchestration necessarily depends on what chaos theorists call recursive symmetries between scales. Such symmetries become operative through each poet's use of figures, despite the obvious differences in the kinds of figures each poet employs. In both cases, successful closure is achieved, paradoxically, through the extravagance of the individual poems and sections, their individual narrative and lyric satisfactions. Still, in the current postmodern milieu, the idea of closure accruing out of individual parts has become seriously undermined. Over a century ago Edgar Allan Poe proclaimed the long poem impossible. In a paradigmatic conceptual problem, the Greek philosopher Zeno proposed that in reality an arrow fired toward a target never reached its mark since the space traveled always could be divided by half, and half again, into a minimalist infinity. The like problem is encountered today when we consider a fractal shoreline whose size reaches infinity as one conceives of its surfaces measured in ever finer dimensions of space. Measurement depends on scale. To build a bridge across that fictional shoreline to the other side would be to span infinity, according to this paradox of scale. That is what plot does in narrative, the nominalist's refusal of universal claims surmounted by the realist's impossible dream. In his essay "Nature" Ralph Waldo Emerson makes this paradox constitutive of human life and consciousness when he affirms: "We live in a system of approximations. Every end is prospective of some other end, which is also temporary; a round and final success nowhere."[28] Such a vision of reality is near to Virginia Woolf's idea of life as a transparent envelope, and implicitly foreshadows both what Alan Shapiro calls "the subjectivist esthetic"[29] of modernism, and the acceptance of some postmodern writers of a world devoid not only of approximations but of linguistic reference. It also presages the historical and cultural milieu of recent times, characterized by Tony Hoagland in his essay "Fear of Narrative and the Skittery Poem of our Moment," as evincing "a widespread mistrust of narrative forms, and, in fact, a pervasive sense of the inadequacy or exhaustion of all modes other than the associative."[30] Behind this recent and current fashion, among undoubtedly other converging influences—historical, cultural, and academic—is a pervasive skepticism about language itself.

Based on Ferdinand de Saussure's notion that linguistic signs comprise the foundation of discourse, and that such signs become knowable through difference among each other rather than through any intrinsic quality of self-identity, one of the core ideas of postmodernism as it is usually advanced is that language constitutes a field of play in which meaning endlessly slips and defers so that neither the world nor the play-space of language itself is anything more than a shifting approximation of a reality that, to echo Fred in "West-Running Brook," "seriously, sadly runs away." Where Fred articulates the fact of reality's "slippage" from our powers of identification, many contemporary poems intend to perform that slippage. By contrast, Paul Ricoeur in discussing this fundamental problem of language refers to Émile Benveniste's alternative conception that sees the sentence and not the sign as the basic unit of discourse.[31] "If," Ricoeur proposes, "we take the sentence as the unit of discourse, then the intended of discourse ceases to be confused with the signi-fied correlative to each signifier in the immanence of a system of signs."[32] The difference between these two conceptions is a difference in the perception of scale within the space of language proper. Like those who might see a shore-line as infinitely devisable by virtue of a fractal reality, making that prospect the ground of their understanding of the world, those who hold with Saussure that signification is founded on difference see the world of language as a world of difference in the most profound sense. There is no bridge outward from language to the world, or even across signs within the field of language itself. The idea founds the most extreme nominalism. In such a world narrative, as anything more than a parody of its endlessly faltering intentions, cannot exist. Ricoeur, after Benveniste, essentially affirms that the sign as a vehicle of discourse is the wrong order of scale to describe how language operates in the reality we inhabit. A bridge can be built from language to reality, for "with the sentence reality is oriented beyond itself."[33] Likewise, Alan Shapiro sees narrative as a "going toward" the other.[34] Paul Ricoeur again summarizes the issue neatly when he states that "narrative time is like a bridge set over the breach speculation constantly opens between phenomenological time and cosmological time," that is, between time as it is humanly experienced and time as it exists physically on the still larger scale of universal motion. The breach must be bridged. To deny this is to deny that reality has a ground in objectivity, though objectivity may only be a series of approximations that, as Emerson would have it, we must plumb again and again with no final success. To refuse the validity of this higher order of scale in language is self-defeating, for to do so is to subvert one's own claims to meaning (the meaning in this case that there is no meaning, only difference) as a categorical *a priori*—the figure of a snake eating its own tail and wholly swallowing itself.

Of the many modern and contemporary poets who have thought about their craft in relation to such definitive questions, no one made the sentence so central a principle as Robert Frost. "I alone of English writers have consciously set myself to make music out of what I may call the sound of sense," Frost wrote famously to his friend John T. Bartlett.[35] For Frost the music of poetry was fundamentally "the sound of sense" transposed by the poet from the living voice of actual speech, a capturing of cadences that the poet skillfully breaks "with all their irregularity of accent across the regular beat of the metre."[36] In short, the music of poetry is embodied in the sentence, which Frost defines as "a sound in itself on which other sounds called words are strung."[37] By regarding the sentence as a sound in itself Frost, like Ricoeur and Benveniste, lodges expression and the integrity of expression in a higher order of scale than the sign. Of course, Frost is a practicing poet not a theoretician, but that does not subvert the sophistication of his thought on the matter. It also does not prevent him from building ambiguity into his best poems in a manner that is as dramatically vital and disturbing as any appeal to what Charles Bernstein called "the wordness of language."[38] Indeed, as Richard Poirier observes, "saying things that almost but do not quite formulate is a central achievement of Frost's poetry from the first volume onward."[39] Frost, in fact, turns Saussure's paradigm on its head: the sentence rather than the sign is the vehicle of ambiguity, of meanings shading always into difference. At times this can happen with such subtlety the reader easily misses the sleight, as in

"The Road Less Traveled By," where the divergent roads are "worn about the same" though Frost's perhaps deluded speaker persists in his affirmation that his choice "has made all the difference." What has made all of the difference is Frost's play with ambiguity in the poem, achieved artfully through his orchestration of the sentence, though that hasn't prevented naïve schoolteachers and automobile advertisers from so reiterating the speaker's delusion as to make it a commonplace.

Frost's guiding principle in making sentence sounds is musical, but the other guiding principle is the poet's action of "stringing" words together to make the sentence sound. On the scale of the sentence this action of stringing words together is both musical and, I would argue, plot driven. If plot is the representation of an action, then the action a sentence sound represents is the action of the speaker's voice. This constitutes the lyric dimension of Frost's poetry since the orchestration of this action is primarily musical; at the same time, the representation of this action has a narrative dimension since the sentence likewise functions as a kind of drama of the voice. Here is a particularly wrenching moment from "Home Burial":

> "There you go sneering now!"
>   "I'm not, I'm not!
> You make me angry. I'll come down to you.
> God, what a woman! And it's come to this,
> A man can't speak of his own child that's dead."
>
> "You can't because you don't know how to speak.
> If you had any feelings, you that dug
> With your own hand—how could you?—his little grave;
> I saw you from that very window there,
> Making the gravel leap and leap in air,
> Leap up, like that, like that, and land so lightly
> And roll back down the mound beside the hole.
> I thought, Who is that man? . . ."

In his interview with the *Paris Review,* Frost said poetry was "all performance and feats of association" and a way of "thinking forward."[40] If we look briefly at the husband's words to his wife, we find that they are clipped. Medial caesuras define the first three lines, a way of "sounding" his frustration, a frustration that is minimally released in the unstopped line that follows. This is a musical orchestration of the sentence, but it is also dramatic. Frost plots the action of the husband's distress and anger into the curtailed sequence of sentences that move jarringly down the page, associatively, but nevertheless representative of the husband's hurt and tragic inability to read his wife's own despair and anger. Perhaps even more impressive is the wife's sentence sound that begins "If you had any feelings. . . ." The sentence runs on, unlike her husband's jarring staccato registry of grievances. At the same time, the way the sentence's delays and interruptions are strung together "plot" the action of her grievance against him leading to the scene of the child's burial. Simply to transpose the crucially moving interruption "How could you" from right before mention of the grave to, say, the head of the sentence would be to ruin both the sentence sound and the sentence's dramatic portrayal: the sonic action of her speech through the sentence's syntax cuts across the loose iambic lines and enacts the representative action of the woman's consciousness in turmoil. What Frost, amazingly, achieves here is a representation of two consciousnesses at odds with each other and not even fully aware of their own buried motivations, the depths of their denials, the depths of their hurt, and their inability to transcend their grievances against each other because of their emotional blindness. Frost's sentence sounds together perform this infinitely complex action.

To move up from the scale of the sentence to the scale of the whole poem, it is likewise possible to discern still more apparently the workings of plot in Frost's conception of a poem's dynamic structure as it moves, sentence sound by sentence sound, to its denouement: "The figure a poem makes. It begins in delight and ends in wisdom. The figure is the same as for love. No one can really hold that the ecstasy should be static and stand still in one place. It begins in delight, it inclines to the impulse, it assumes direction with the first line laid down, it runs a course of lucky events, and ends in a clarification of life—not necessarily a great clarification, such as sects and cults are founded on, but a momentary stay against confusion."[41]

Frost's affirmation about "the figure a poem makes" binds that essential figural impulse to plot—and specifically the archetypal plot of love—as an orchestration of events with a beginning, middle, and end the movements of which, while discursive in the course of lucky events, nonetheless reveal the teleology of life clarified into meaning. This definition of a poem's dynamic representation of life finds its origin, however unspoken by the poet, in the conception of *muthos,* an order of representative action that on the still larger scale of culture and history founds religious paradigms. "Drink and be whole again beyond confusion"—Frost's imagined grail excavated from the ruined house of childhood at the end of "Directive" points, for all of Frost's ambiguity and skepticism, to the same endangered but stubborn wish as Eliot's grail housed in the ruins of culture: the wish for an appeasing but supple order underlying a seeming chaos—a *muthos,* a plot. These issues, finally, do not only bear on poetry but on our understanding of consciousness itself, as limited as that is at the present time. For a thinker like John R. Searle, consciousness is an emergent property that ultimately is more than the sum of the physical parts in the brain. In contrast, for Daniel Dennett, consciousness is reducible to the brain's remarkably complex network of causal relations and therefore carries no meaning except as a vehicle for Darwinian survival. There is something analogous in Dennett's conception of consciousness to Saussure's atomistic conception language; likewise, in contrast, there is something emergent about the sentence in Ricoeur's understanding of how syntax raises the level of scale with regard to the production of meaning. That emergent property of language and consciousness is further driven home by Frost's "figural" understanding of the poem, for all his skepticism and confrontation with the slippery nature of reality. For poetry, like consciousness, the surrender to the mere associations of physical or linguistic cause and effect is not enough— even the most "skittery" set of affairs requires the emergent property and greater sum of a plot.

BETWEEN SCHEMA AND SCHEHERAZADE

Nevertheless, as soon as one mentions plot, one conjures its shadow side: the scheme and not the design, the contrivance and not the storyline—in short, Woolf's gig-lamps. This is particularly problematic in our contemporary milieu in which Woolf's universe of impressions resists the ordering vehicle of a shared frame of reference. As we've already considered, without this shared cultural context it becomes exceedingly difficult if not impossible and more often than not debilitating for poets to aspire to the epic ambition if not its satisfaction. "Overall is beyond me," A. R. Ammons wrote in "Corson's Inlet," who sought to create a shared culture in the context of a science with cosmic significance. Though he eschews traditional narrative, for Ammons the plot is motion in his long poems, a transfiguring into the poem of nature's endlessly creative action. In other hands plot as such becomes transposed into an errancy endlessly rehearsed, like one of John Ashbery's dazzling ruminations, or Woolf's transparent envelope devoid of its letter. In a situation absent of anything resembling common poetic consensus the reliance on traditional narrative strategies can gain appeal, at least for those poets for whom an ethos of radical skepticism proves unsatisfactory and ultimately a brand of decadence. Still, the question remains: How can individual contexts resonate beyond the confines of their own self-referentiality, if not in epic terms, then in terms that appeal to a deep human circumstance, not simply for popular, ideological, political, or personal appeal?

In contrast to some postmodern views on the subject of narrative, John Barth in his "4 1/2 Lectures: Chaos Theory" affirms the traditional Aristotelian conception of plot as a representative action in light of contemporary physics. For Barth, plot is "the incremental perturbation of a homeostatic system and its catastrophic restoration to a complexified equilibrium."[42] Barth's definition is only superficially tongue-in-cheek since he goes on to translate his admittedly amateurish adaptation of science to narrative into explicit Aristotelian terms. The point he intends to make is that chaos theory does, indeed, constitute a shared cultural context in the way that Thomism infused Dante's *Commedia* through what he calls "the principle of metaphoric means," that is, "the writer's investiture in as many aspects of the text as possible with emblematic significance."[43] Barth's principle clearly resonates with Leitch's "polytropic principle." In both, *muthos* is an essential aspect, even to Barth as an avowedly postmodern writer. Moreover, as he elaborates his discussion of chaos theory in the essay, and in a manner that recalls the figuralism of Crane and Hudgins, Barth likens the kind of nonlinear models of narrative production to "recursive symmetries between scales—swirls within swirls within swirls, replicated over numerous scale levels."[44] Though, as we've seen, Crane's myth organizes itself recursively to orchestrate closure, for Barth the narrative exemplar for such organization is Scheherazade, whose stories within stories within stories are told to fend off death by her captor, King Shahryar. Such storytelling is the model for the ateleological narrative, the narrative that potentially digresses endlessly without closure. Reified in this manner, Scheherazade's narrative is all flow, but if Barth is right that doesn't mean it is without *muthos,* without order, without plot. At the same time, Barth's claim that stories formally deploying the principle of metaphoric means "will be stronger and richer than those that do not"[45] suggests that works exhibiting contrary structural principles to those seemingly untested by contemporary ontological claims (the "linear" novel uninformed by experimental design, the "straight" narrative or lyric poem as I heard one avant-garde poet quip derisively) are at best lower order achievements, at worst nostalgic holdovers from an outmoded aesthetic.

The one-time exponents of the New Narrative and the New Formalism contest such claims vigorously. In appealing to Yvor Winters's "the fallacy of imitative form," Christian Wiman urges us to be skeptical of the simplistic notion that because the world is disordered, chaotic, and resistant to meaningful representation poetry likewise should reflect formally that distressing condition. The critic Marjorie Perloff is guilty of this fallacy when she claims that only poets who write in "indeterminate forms" avoid the nostalgia for some determined order.[46] Wiman places against this fallacy the proper claim that good poems, narrative or otherwise, allow their ideas of order to be "contested" by the disorder of the world.[47] Such poems effectively assume disorder like an antibody into the poem. The assumption need not be a formal one, or at least not in the most obvious sense. Frost's work is highly formal, but few have assumed disorder so effectively into the work by means of such formal control. His "momentary stay against confusion" is achieved not by denying the disorder of the world but by plotting it, in every sense, into the poem. Certainly, the sheer disruptiveness of sense at times in Crane's operatic myth of modernity assumes the very disorder out of which he would construct his "Paradigm." Like Frost, Wiman also maintains, "it's sometimes precisely in those works which exhibit the greatest degree of formal coherence . . . that a reader may experience, and thereby more likely endure, the most intense anxiety and uncertainty."[48] To claim otherwise, it seems to me, is to delude oneself into believing that one's particular sensibility is somehow reflective of some ultimate reality and therefore no less an uncontested idea of order as any strenuously held religious or ideological belief. The same is true for those who hold that only a return to traditional forms can save contemporary poetry from its own cultural and artistic irrelevance. Between plot manifested as schema—an abstract structural organization used to shape a poem's action as it assembles toward closure—and plot as Scheherazade—discursivity for discursivity's sake, for which closure is an afterthought or mere cessation of speech—narrative poems find a range of efficacious, compelling, and emblematic formal investitures of at once intensive and broad human significance.

If there is any poet who inhabits the dynamic space between plot as an abstract structural organization and the kind of discursivity that eschews closure as an afterthought it is Elizabeth Bishop. She is equally adept at writing highly formal verse as free verse, and in particular a free verse that "plots" the poet's perceptions in a resolutely discursive way. There is a seemingly random recounting of the speaker's travels in "Over 2,000 Illustrations and a Complete Concordance," though her strategy of letting her precise and brilliant eye linger on each detail of the unfolding scenes makes for the poem's gradual but no less powerful revelation of the "missed" nativity that would have permitted us "to look and look our infant sight away." Bishop's poem is about the fall away from a guiding revelation, the divinely inspired *muthos* of Christ's birth as the central moment of God's plan for the world's salvation, into travels that indeed appear plotless:

> Entering the Narrows at St. John's
> The touching bleat of goats reached to the ship.
> We glimpsed them, reddish, leaping up the cliffs
> Among the fog-soaked weeds and butter-and-eggs.
> And at St. Peter's the wind blew and the sun shown madly.

Between the speaker's recollection of the Narrows and her recollection of being at St. Peter's, time becomes telescoped by a simple "And at . . ." What follows is a catalogue of places—in Mexico, in Dingle Harbor, in Marrakesh. Her travels in the poem, vivid as they are, trace the errancy of life lived without *muthos,* of life in which everything is "only connected by 'and' and 'and.'" From its opening lines, "Thus should have been our travels: / serious, engravable," the poem announces that it will lead us through a discursive would, a world without any true *telos*, however vivid its digressions may be. At the same time, Bishop's arrangement of these brilliantly observed details reveals a plotted shapeliness resolving into closure. The poem's first stanza leads the reader through a series of illustrations that depict time and space from the vantage of sacred history: the Tomb, the Pit, the Sepulcher, the decorative arrangement of emblematic signs as though infused by Barth's "principle of metaphoric means." All proceed to the image of "God's spreading fingerprint" in the storm images made by the burin that, in turn, ignite "in watery prismatic white and blue." In short, the stanza comprises an arrangement that moves the reader from the emblems of truth to the nearest truth of God's identity—His fingerprint. The stanza also progresses in a manner that is self-reflexive of the poet's method in that the arrangement of illustrations mirrors Bishop's own strategy of focused detail accruing larger and larger significance as the reader lingers over the poem. The "page alone" and the "page made up / of several scenes" "when dwelt upon, they all resolve themselves." That is, the seemingly chaotic scales of association begin to reveal order, emplotment, reconfiguration at higher levels.

If the first stanza of Bishop's poem constitutes the speaker's record of a bygone sacred *muthos* puzzled together through cross-cuts of emblematic scenes, then the second stanza represents its antithesis: the travels that are mere digressions in a world devoid of sacred history. Cunningly, Bishop segues from the first stanza to the second by carrying over the water imagery associated with God's signature into the water journey into the Narrows. The arrangement of travels in the second stanza in turn brings us to paynims; that is, back to the beginning of the poem with its tongue-in-cheek, ironic Arabs "plotting against our Christian empire." As a plot, then, the poem begins with a thesis that is elaborated in the first stanza. The second stanza constitutes the antithesis. The poem's final stanza, not unexpectedly now, constitutes Bishop's synthesis of the contraries in an optative revelation that never actually occurs—the fulfillment of the "should have" at the poem's outset into the implied "would have" of the Nativity. The poem likewise therefore organizes itself from Sepulcher to manger, from death to birth, or from end to beginning. That beginning, the Nativity scene, is also a most vivid and satisfactory end, the perfect closure to a poem that shrewdly contests both the idea of *muthos* as teleological ground and the reliance on discursivity or digression as an associative method of organization and resolves them in a way that includes both brilliant divergences—Barth's "incremental perturbations"—and strong closure that, as in all great poems, resonates beyond "the system" of the poem itself and into our being in the world.

Bishop's "Over 2,000 Illustrations and a Complete Concordance" is exemplary for its achievement in dynamically joining contrary organizational imperatives, though her greatness stems from her larger achievement of succeeding over and over again in this regard. In poems like "At the Fishhouses," "In the Waiting Room," and "The Moose," to name only a few, her strategy of employing digression as a way of realizing closure makes for astonishing resolutions and at times revelations in a world that is supposed to be devoid of such measures. Her poems typically move by peripheral vision to an unforeseen center, as in "The Filling Station" where filth and grease, an arrangement of oil cans (Esso-so-so), and a briefly but crucially sustained anaphora on the word "somebody" lead to the explosive and completely convincing insight within the context of the poem that "somebody loves us all." At the end of "At the Fishhouses," Bishop declares that "our knowledge is historical, flowing and flown," though that revelation is likewise prepared through the painstaking arrangement of details, a configuration through peripheries of an essential action revelatory of our fragile place in the universe. Bishop's genius is her ability to shape that flow to include closure without transgressing against the world's luminous details or our consciousness of its fleeting nature. As such, she manages by a sleight of perception worthy of Escher to include Scheherazade in the defined schema of beginning, middle, and end.

Entering the Narrows at St. John's with the poet in "Over 2,000 Illustrations and a Complete Concordance" is to place oneself *in the middest,* apart from the sure path, with no hope of recovering the security of a Dante ascending, however uncertainly, toward paradise. Tony Maniero's cinematic dance above another Narrows likewise places him and the viewer *in medias res* on his path to maturity, though, like my own journey with my family over the same bridge above the same Narrows in real life and now only in memory, such travels inevitably point to possibilities outside the frame of immediate reference. At the same time, it is the poet's job not merely to mimic the ongoing in a dispersal of recursive associations but to shape the time of the poem to human ends. Even a poet like Robinson Jeffers, wary on an ontological if not metaphysical scale of humanity, places the human story in the context of ends that transcend human time as its stands in relief of a natural sublime. After Frost, Jeffers's work constitutes the purest narrative impulse in modern poetry—perhaps more so than Frost since Jeffers's narratives are less dramatic and more plot-driven. Not surprisingly, along with Frost he constitutes an important model for new narrative poets like Mark Jarman who would, as in the book-length poem *Iris* for example, use Jeffers's model to tell a story in verse. By contrast, Robert Hayden's "Middle Passage" uses pastiche, collage, and association—shards of narrative lyrically arranged—to tell the story of the slave trade and in particular of the *Amistad:* "passage through death to life upon these shores." Though less ambitious in scope than *The Bridge,* "Middle Passage" is nonetheless a poem of epic travel that in essence demythologizes Crane's grandly sublime vision of the modern world and its indulgence in a skewed vision of history untainted by brutality. Given the span of possibilities for narrative in our time, is one mode really more vital or viable than the other? Imaginative vitality as always rests in the poet's employment of poetic craft in a manner that surpasses the mere execution of craft into poems, regardless of one's aesthetic temperament.

Emerging from the crowd of poets born during the time modernism had reached its height and coming to prominence after modernism had "morphed" into that various cultural and creative state of affairs known as postmodernism, John Ashbery wrote a lifetime of poems that from the first seemed to breathe the same air as Scheherazade. This is certainly true of Ashbery's longer productions—"Flow Chart" for example, or "Litany," or "A Wave"—that unreel in an associative flow that would forestall closure indefinitely. Ashbery's productions, however, both large and small, whether strictly formal in the traditional sense or more open and experimental in their formal appropriations, resist "plot" and closure first and foremost on the scale of sentence organization. One could say, strangely enough, that like Frost, Ashbery is primarily concerned with "sentence sounds," though unlike Frost, living speech in an Ashbery poem becomes "warped" through an intellectual prism that has dislodged itself from the requirements of objective representation. There is not much world in an Ashbery poem, except as an occasion for manifesting a linguistic sublime. Though one moves through an Ashbery poem when reading it, the poem has no movement in the traditional sense. Instead, as in

"Self-Portrait in a Convex Mirror," what one typically encounters is a sequence of beginnings without end. Time itself in such an art, and hence plot, never advances:

> The time of day or the density of light
> Adhering to the face keeps it
> Lively and intact in a recurring wave
> Of arrival. The soul establishes itself.
> But how far can it swim out through the eyes
> And still return safely to its nest?

The answer to Ashbery's question is that the soul cannot travel past each new beginning, and so "Self-Portrait in a Convex Mirror" articulates an aesthetic of continual emergence, poems that are journeys composed of departures alone, no middles or ends, for there is only the moment-by-moment: "The soul has to stay where it is, / Even though restless . . . Longing to be free, outside, but it must stay / Posing in this place." There is no "going towards" in such a poem, only gestures that finally round to self-enclosure—consciousness wrapped in its own rapt subjectivity.

Ashbery's poetry puts into ideal practice the ethos that *muthos* is impossible. For Ashbery this is a matter beyond contention, beyond testing in any dramatic way, as even in Frost's more ambiguously constructed forays. It simply is the world his poems inhabit, or more rightly, construct. Since plot requires movement, the poems may be read as brilliantly textured rehearsals for journeys that never take place beyond the moment, or perhaps only just beyond. The moments are vivid and lush, but they must be savored for themselves like the swirls of recurrence in Barth's "homeostatic system," though without resolution, catastrophic or otherwise:

> Other dreams came and left while the bank
> Of colored verbs and adjectives was shrinking from the light
> To nurse in shade their want of method
> But most of all she loved the particles
> That transform objects of the same category
> Into particular ones, each distinct

Within and apart from its own class.
In all this springing up was no hint
Of a tide, only a pleasant wavering of the air
In which all things seemed present, whether
Just past or soon to come. . . .

These lines from "Scheherazade" are indubitably gorgeous, an ontological meditation that envisions, among other possible readings, the making of poetry as Scheherazade's potentially endless process of generation, though there is no tide, no passage, and hence no time. The lines also unmistakably echo Wallace Stevens's "The Idea of Order at Key West"—"She sang beyond the genius of the sea"—though in Ashbery's poem the "blessed rage for order," "the maker's rage to order words of the sea," has become a pleasant receptivity to the patterns or orders momentarily revealed by the chaotic system of the sea itself. The stories that the poem rehearses as it shifts tones slightly and continues on give evidence of an obstinacy that borders on delusion, the notion that "none knew the warp / Which presented this major movement as a firm / Digression." That major movement, ironically, is merely "a new fact of day," which is no different from the old fact of the day before, composed as it is merely of moments juxtaposed. It is as if the poem's stream of sentences unfolds from discrete present to discrete present, luminous as photons beamed from Woolf's proverbial lighthouse, and blotting out any afterglow of gig lamps. As the poem later states, the echo of stories becomes merely "Anticipation that was only memory after all, / For the possibilities are limited." Where Bishop admits a world in which everything is connected by "and" and "and," her poems are organized in such a way as to position a counterforce against mere discursivity unshaped by human ends. In contrast, Ashbery in a superficially dazzlingly way divests teleology of any force whatsoever except as it is realized in the luscious surfaces of language encountered in the moment.

The argument to be made against such a poetry has nothing to do with its lush articulateness, its dazzling spikes of grandeur and tonal amplitude, its surface elegance and flow, but with an aesthetic that refuses, like Blake's Thel, to enter the fraught world of Experience, and so to make the journey beyond its own protected self-defined and self-enclosed boundaries—its own self-enwound luminous envelope of what Sven Birkerts calls "semantic slippages" and nonsequiturs.[49] It is this refusal that distinguishes Ashbery's poetry from Frank O'Hara's work and the work of A. R. Ammons, two poets of his generation with whom he is often compared. Where O'Hara captures the moment with the context of ordinary human time, Ammons shapes his poems in such a way as to inhabit in language the larger motions of order discovered in nature. There is much of Scheherazade in both these poets, though there is also engagement with the world that makes the idea of endless digression something to be contested, though not an endorsement of strict closure. In contrast, those poets of the same generation, like Anthony Hecht and Richard Wilbur, who have become models for formalist and narrative poets of recent decades clearly embraced a contrary aesthetic in which the "scheme" of form and plot shapes the utterance of the poem. These two broad orientations in the art define a gap that needs to be bridged for American poetry to advance beyond the mere reiteration of disputing traditions.

Given the legitimate doubts in our time about language, culture, knowledge, and consciousness itself, what, we might ask again could be more intransigently rooted in the nostalgia for plot and so the determination of identity than narrative? Tony Hoagland likens the recent shift away from narrative to "crop-rotation,"[50] though the shift itself suggests that the more serious impact on the culture portends a loss of confidence in the authenticity of meaning-making in our poems as well as our institutions.[51] The characteristic mistrusts of such poetries—"a fear of submersion or enclosure by narrative,"[52] the limitations and presumptions of the confessional poem including serious epistemological and metaphysical doubts about the veracity of something we might call the self—have generated "elliptical" work attractive in Hoagland's view for its "speed, wit, and absurdity."[53] At the same time, he identifies the potentially trivial nature of such poetry when it becomes a mere homage to dissociation. Indeed, if the danger of narrative is that it might enable us to relax into "the pretense of order"[54] then the danger of dissociative modes is that they may perform and perpetuate the vacuity of sense that so pervades the culture at large. Such untested "disorderliness" is potentially as culpably self-indulgent as narrative's rage for order. This is not to confuse poetry with propaganda or to prize the message over the medium of the art, but merely to affirm with Hoagland that "one of poetry's most fundamental reasons for existing" is "the individual power to locate and assert value"[55] and that to abscond from that purpose may be in the long run to render one's work irrelevant.

Nostalgia for permanently stable orders has its own culpabilities, of course, that surely breed irrelevance at best and, at worst, far graver legacies. If, however, a guiding *muthos* of our time is that there is no *muthos,* and that any shaping plot for our identities as well as our art must be held provisionally (if at all) to have any hope of authenticity, then perhaps as a matter of course poetry need not be as atomized and ephemeral as the world it inhabits. "There is something in disorder that calls to me," Louis Simpson writes in "Searching for the Ox." Rather than passively and "performatively" reiterating the scattered atoms of his world through an artifice utterly mimetic of that world, Simpson's speaker dramatizes the crisis of consciousness. At the same time, Paul Ricoeur's claim that "we tell stories because in the last analysis human lives need and merit being narrated"[56] stands as a cautionary observation for any poet who would turn away wholly from the world. For, as he continues, "this remark takes on its full force when we refer to the necessity to save the history of the defeated and the lost. The whole history of suffering cries out for vengeance and calls for narrative."[57]

American poets employing narrative in various ways are mindful, in practice at least, of Ricoeur's affirmation. For example, Eleanor Wilner's re/visions of myths and biblical narratives use narrative itself as mode of inquiry into the sources of culture with an aim toward re-envisioning those sources and redressing cultural injustice at the level. She aims, among other things, to awaken us to a counter feminine tradition—her version of the Shekinah—hidden inside the prevailing Western religious and mythic narratives. In contrast, Rita Dove's *Thomas and Beulah,* though it claims to tell a personal story, convinces primarily as a lyric sequence, though it is a sequence shadowed by the history of civil rights. The plot of the two sides of her grandparents' lives together gives chronological and circumstantial scaffolding for the lyric epiphanies. Though book length, *Thomas and Beulah* finally affirms an aesthetic of compression rather than expansion, and that is its particular success. Like Wilner's work, it is also a testimony to the under-represented who have been largely absent from the historical narrative. Dove's *Sonata Mulattica,* on the life of Beethoven's friend George Bridgetower, also builds on that trajectory.

Another work that has achieved similar status is Natasha Trethewey's *Native Guard,* and in particular her titular sonnet crown, voiced as the reflections of a recently freed slave and member of the historically neglected regiment. In their own spheres, Wilner, Dove, and Trethewey seek to give amplitude to their poetry by engaging cultural and historical contexts, the storylines that shape our lives as a matter of irreducible course and not merely of personal circumstance.

This, it seems to me, is a condition for truly expansive poetry—not length alone but breadth and depth of vision, the desire to portray as fully as possible the complexity of the human journey from any number of historical perspectives, artistically achieved. The admirable desire to link the individual consciousness to the collective life may likewise be found in Ellen Bryant Voigt's *Kyrie,* her justly praised sonnet sequence that takes as its subject the flu pandemic of 1918—prescient, given more recent history. Here, in a manner that takes inspiration from Frost though with a strong infusion of montage, Voigt blurs dramatic, lyric, and narrative genres. Her shorter narrative work, particularly in *The Lotus Flowers,* as well as powerful lyric narratives written by a diverse retinue of other poets show that a strong narrative cast still is present in American poetry regardless of any affiliation with the new expansive poetry, or claims of nostalgia from the imaginative heirs of Scheherazade. Among the expansive poets, Mark Jarman and B. H. Fairchild stand out, with Andrew Hudgins, as significant practitioners of narrative in contemporary American poetry, as does Alan Shapiro, whose many narrative and lyric-narrative poems enact his incisive reflections on plot with delicacy and power. Poems like Fairchild's "Beauty," "Body and Soul," and "The Blue Buick," and Jarman's book-length *Iris,* as well as an array of shorter narratives, have achieved critical recognition beyond the confines of the New Formalist canon. Over the last decade or more other narrative poets, unaffiliated expressly with "expansive poetry" or New Formalism, have gained prominence. William Wenthe's *The Gentle Art* and Ryan Wilson's *The Stranger World* come to mind, as do the associative poems of Bruce Beasley's *Prayershreds,* which point to sacred emplotments within and around the surfaces of language. One book-length narrative work is Adrian Matejka's *The Big Smoke,* on the life of boxer Jack Johnson. Matejka's long poem, a polyphonic orchestration similar to Crane's

The Bridge, underscores the important influence of that earlier poem, for all of its excesses and limitations.

Regardless of affiliation, it should go without saying that in the case of every successful poem, especially narrative poems, the line and the storyline are intimately related. It should go without saying that, like memory itself, narrative works by selection, though like life it must leave ample room for the intractable, the unexpected, the disorderly, which is to say that the linear impetus of plot of course requires digression and diversion into the textures. This is so much more the case in the narrative poem that by necessity must embody plot, the arc of the whole, in image and metaphor, line, syntax, and poetic structure. Perhaps, then, it also goes without saying that any poem, large or small, lyric, narrative, or dramatic, is nothing without intensity. That being said, poetry is consciousness released from its dream of accidence into a new dream of achieved form that, like any good plot, surprises and satisfies, and in the end may illuminate us with a clarity and recognition never entirely foreseen.

FORMS AFTER FORMS

On Metamorphosis and Improvisation

DIGRESSION

"My mind leads me to speak now of forms changed / into new bodies," so begins Ovid's *Metamorphoses* in Charles Martin's contemporary translation. The sweep of Ovid's culturally formative epic encompasses all of history, as Ovid saw it, from the creation of the world to the deification of Julius Caesar. Suffice to say, without providing a summary of the exhaustive myths and stories that comprise this classic of global literatures, Ovid orchestrates his epic around the prevailing theme of the poem's title: metamorphoses, or "transformations." One should underscore at the outset that the arc of the poem's entire narrative is shaped, as I have quietly implied, by its own uniquely defining cultural perspective relative to the natural world, that is, physical reality; the mercurial and often perverse actions of the gods, that is, metaphysical reality; and finally the unfolding of human history leading to the apotheosis of one human being, Julius Caesar, transformed into a god—a god whose deification redounds to the imperious rule of the state. One might pause briefly here to acknowledge that while politics inevitably informs art, it perhaps need not inevitably circumscribe aesthetic achievement, that is, a particular work's greatness. How else could a work outlive the conditions of the artist's life, its own time and place, the historical and cultural conditions of the poet's inherited identity, or even its own language?

This brings me by slippage of phrase, if not sleight of form, to life, albeit in somewhat broader consideration. "Metamorphosis" in nature, the witness of which must have spurred Ovid's imagination is the process by which an animal after birth undergoes rapid physical transformation. Larvae become flies; the caterpillar crawling on my metal storm fence one spring morning slowly wraps itself inside the cowl of its own making only to later wrestle free, to be reborn, having become the swallowtail alighting on my wife's fennel, potted, incidentally, for the purpose of attracting this form changed into its new body. Whether accomplished singly and rapidly, as with flies, or in stages as with our swallowtail, metamorphosis in its etymological root combines "morphe," meaning "shape, form," with the Greek "meta," which has a still more various etymology. "Meta" could mean "after," "behind," "among," "between," or "changed, altered," or "higher, beyond," or even "in the midst or middle of," or "together." The range of "meta" suggests much more in life, and therefore in art, than what we habitually mean when we use "metamorphosis," a change of form, or "metaphysics," where the term typically signifies a realm "higher" or 'beyond" the physical. And come to think of it, in a moment of meta-discourse, my mind thinking of "metamorphoses" leads me to think of "metaphor," from the aforesaid "meta" combined now with the Greek "pherien," which means "to carry, bear," which in turn derives from the PIE root "bher," "to carry"; also, "to bear children." In contemporary Athens, one can take a metaphor to work—a bus or train—since the word also conveys the meaning "transport," to carry across or beyond.

Words, it appears, too, when we venture to see into them deeply enough, with enough depth of field, are bodies giving form to new bodies having themselves been born of the "meta" matter of the world. They are, like the stuff of nature, improvisational, turning eventually, if not immediately, toward the "unforeseen," which is what the root "improvisation" means. In music, jazz most obviously, though actually in any kind of musical endeavor, improvisation happens with an appearance of spontaneity, an extemporaneous development—process and discovery favored over the lineaments of any received composition. The same would be true of acting, and comedy, where the players forego scripts, or depart from them, for the inspiration of the moment. The risk in such instances is discord, chaos rather than creation. Regarding poetry, what interests me is how some vital relationship between metamorphosis and improvisation spurs creation. Improvisation points to an emergence of "the unforeseen," seemingly without any previous preparation; metamorphosis recognizes that "new bodies," to again use Ovid's phrase, emerge from previous forms, even if it is only the apparent formlessness of chaos. To risk another etymological play on words, metamorphosis provides for the improvisational, the genuinely innovative. It enables the unforeseen "to be seen ahead," and therefore to carry something into "the new." Ovid suggests this paradox in his depiction of creation:

> Before the seas and lands had been created,
> before the sky that covers everything,
> Nature displayed a single aspect only
> throughout the cosmos, Chaos was its name,
> a shapeless, unwrought mass of inert bulk
> and nothing more, with the discordant seeds
> of disconnected elements all heaped
> in anarchic disarray.

In the case of Ovid's *Metamorphoses*, Chaos is the unformed "form" of Nature, its shapeless and discordant aspect out of which the Cosmos becomes wrought in the original metamorphosis, the original improvisation that modulates the "single aspect" of the cosmos" into plurality. It is, in short, not nothing. "Some god (or kinder nature)" does the transformative work of creating the new body of the cosmic ordering, which is an ordered variousness. In our own mythically resistant time, chaos theory provides for the emergence of order through concepts like strange attraction, in which ordered patterns emerge spontaneously out of disorderly systems—like life from non-life through the crystalline, emergent structure of DNA. The implication, for Ovid's poem and for us in our own belated and apparently skeptical time, is that all metamorphoses must be improvised out of previous forms, "forms changed / to new bodies," the unforeseen out of the foreseen, and as such the "meta" fulfilling itself in its apparently contradictory vectors of meaning: the "after" from the "behind," the "beyond" in the "midst," and each to each with equal recognition and regard.

It seems appropriate to take this elemental interplay between metamorphosis and improvisation and, ultimately, innovation, as a metaphor—or is it a meta-metaphor?—for the evolution of poetic forms in English. Through its complex and undeniably fraught historical evolution, the English language has found means and inspiration to adopt and adapt poetic forms from other languages. Likewise, its poets have tuned their powers of innovation, as with the blues and other forms, to new and vibrant expressive means. The cultural convergence of Anglo-Saxon and French with the Norman invasion of England altered the English language irrevocably. One might say that this seismic metamorphosis enforced a culture-wide demand for linguistic improvisation within the gradual burgeoning of what would become Britain's own empire. In any case, the initial colonizing of the eventual colonizer resulted in a diversification that inevitably impacted and utterly transformed English verse. Consequently, one might argue that, in turn, the French language influence on Chaucer's poetry, the development of blank verse from classical models, the modification of Greek meters, the incorporation of the sonnet, ballade, villanelle, and other continental forms into the repertory of poetry in English, as well as more recent vital importations like the ghazal, all broadly witness the adaptive capacities of poets writing in the language, regardless of place.

I make this general point with full awareness of the complexities and bitter contentions involved in contemporary considerations of canon, questions of canonicity, de-colonization, the politics of identity, and identity-directed poetics, and do so with the utmost assent to what for me is Agha Shahid Ali's incontestable point that "every literary culture has a canon"[1] and, therefore, that when it is not merely serving ideology, canon inculcates "levels of artistic accomplishment, of achievement" and, as such, of "standards" that ultimately transcend the ephemeral impositions of taste,[2] even when those tastes, and trends, are influenced by valid political and cultural concerns. Ali affirms this crucial point with full awareness that English literature was introduced into England's colonies "for reasons other than aesthetics"; rather "it was put to political uses in service of class and empire."[3] Moreover he maintains, paradoxically, that as a result of the political use of canon he himself is "assured of a privileged position" in that as a poet he "has three major world cultures available to him without effort, cultures that [he] can appropriate, mix, and exploit."[4] It is precisely his uniquely capacious vantage of writing at the intersection of multiple cultures that enables Ali to hold the likes of Chaucer, Shakespeare, Marlowe, and Milton, with Faiz Ahmad Faiz and Ghalib, as exemplars of the utmost in artistic achievement, while simultaneously recognizing the displacements and disruptions of his own colonial history. Ali's own formal powers of improvisation are positively fueled by historical metamorphoses at once multifarious, nearly intolerable, and irreversible.

This does not mean artistic achievement outweighs irreparable loss; it

does mean even the more chaotic burdens of history can breed transformative rages for order, of re-ordering. What we find in Ali's complex perspective
is the interfusion of canonicity and diversification, the measuring "cane" of
canonical achievement, which is, etymologically, a strict rule or bar derived
from "kanna," "reed" that implies at the root an organic metaphor. At the root,
it is wedded to the spirit of inclusion. Or, to carry ahead my previously evoked
metaphor of transport to Ali's vision, the standard-bearing requirements of
canon are bound to an "omnibus," from the Latin, meaning "to, for, by, with,
or from all." Whatever formal improvisations come to periodic prominence
in the metamorphoses of poetry in English, the double imperative of artistic
measure and inclusion ought to remain a guide for an individual poet's particular transformations.

ON THE BUS

With these admittedly broader considerations in mind, I want to narrow my
focus to a few examples of recent formal improvisation that may well be re-
garded as unforeseen, but whose innovative transformations of received forms
embodies all the nuances of metamorphosis I have sought just now to evoke.
The first of these, the bop, was invented by Baltimore-born poet Afaa Michael
Weaver in 1997 while he was teaching at a summer retreat for Cave Canem.
He has since become an elder in that organization, and a model for African
American poets in the generation following Robert Hayden and Gwendolyn
Brooks. Weaver's poetry draws from his experience as a Black American male,
a member of the working class, as well as from his long immersion in Chinese
language and culture, especially Taoist philosophy. The term "bop" riffs the
musical slang term "bebop," of course, and implies the kind of tune that would
make a person want to dance. Structurally, a bop is composed in three stanzas:
an opening sestet followed by an octave, which in turn is followed by a second
sestet. Within its structural progression, the first stanza is intended to present,
or dramatically embody, a problem or crisis. The second stanza explores that
crisis, considers the problem, and expands on it, or seeks to pursue an alternative that might resolve whatever is haunting the speaker in the first. The final
stanza presents or articulates whatever resolution might have been achieved,
though if there is no viable resolution the final stanza explores or dramatizes

that impasse. In addition to its stanzaic structure, the bop incorporates a re-frain following each stanza. While the bop refrain like all refrains provides no uncertain musical allure, the repeating lines of the refrain are intended to resonate somewhat differently after each stanza and at the end of the poem, thereby underscoring the bop's complex thematic progression even as it creates a powerful sonic unity. Here, by way of example, is Weaver's "Rambling":

RAMBLING

in Lewisburg Federal penitentiary

In general population, census
is consensus—ain't nowhere to run
to in these walls, walls like a mind—
We visitors stand in a yellow circle
so the tower can frisk us with light,
finger the barrels on thirsty rifles.

I got rambling, rambling on my mind

In general population, madness runs
swift through the river changing, changing
in hearts, men tacked in their chairs,
resigned to hope we weave into air,
talking this and talking that and one brutha
asks *Tell us how to get these things*
They got, these houses, these cars.
We want the real revolution. Things . . .

I got rambling, got rambling on my mind

In the yellow circle the night stops
like a boy shot running from a Ruger 9mm
carrying .44 magnum shells, a sista
crying in the glass booth to love's law,
to violence of backs bent over to the raw
libido of men, cracking, cracking, crack . . .

I got rambling, rambling on my mind

In this paradigmatic bop, the first stanza places the reader with the speaker, a visitor, in the confined space of a specific prison with all its institutionally controlled violence—a prison that itself becomes a reflexive metaphor for the mind. The refrain that follows resounds with the speaker's desire for escape from a place that he has chosen to enter, since he is merely a visitor. At the same time, the refrain implies the mental state of the men incarcerated there, and that is what is precisely evoked in the octave that follows—an elaboration at once of the scene and the internal world of prison life, as well as of a constricted hope that gestures, ironically, outward from the prison walls to the economic and social conditions that, the poem implies, likely contribute to the dehumanizing conditions of imprisonment. After the octave, the refrain explicitly underscores the plight of the incarcerated, with all their frustrations and fraught hopes. The final sestet dramatizes the apparently insoluble nature of the scene with a scene of violence that breeds further violence, sexual violence, the violence of the hopeless in the pervasively violent culture of America, with the racial divisions of the society likewise encoded in speech—brutha, sista—as well as in the wider and deeper implications of what is said about economic and social opportunity, that still wider prison, in which, the poem infers, we are all incarcerated. By the end of the poem, in a mere twenty lines plus three lines of refrain, the reader has advanced from the perspective of a single visitor to a vision far more immersive, and then panoramic, in its rendering of the world.

In an interview, Weaver observed, the aesthetic influence that led him to invent the form was "the golden mean," and he goes on to suggest his early interest in 35 mm photography likewise influenced him to become interested in depth of field.[5] Depth of field, in fact, he confesses, is what he seeks in his poetry. One can see in "Rambling" how the bop intends to develop depth of field as the poem unfolds through the opening sestet, through the octave, and then through the final sestet, with the refrain employed musically but also as a kind of prism through which the widening scope of the poem becomes clarified. One can also see and hear how Weaver's evocation of the golden mean resonates with the proportions of the sonnet, albeit elaborated to 6-8-6 from 8-6, with the three iterations of the refrain working within the overall symmetry to create a sonically resonant space inside the symmetrical structure, a kind of musical dynamic that keeps the form from becoming rigidified in its conceptual architecture. One can also discern in the bop, within its tripartite structure, something of John Berryman's dream songs. Berryman's nonce form likewise derives from the golden mean inflection of the sonnet and functions as a kind of elaboration of that preeminent English form, derived of course from the Italian. Across its three sestets, Berryman's dream song form improvises hairpin tonal shifts, dialogic bends and swerves, almost ecstatic ascents, emotional plummets, and everything from precision logic to scatology. What the dream song does not incorporate to the same emphatic degree is the bop's explicitly dialectical structure.

Berryman's formal invention, one might say, permits greater frenetic movement and vocal improvisation, though the improvisational impulse behind the bop, while more structurally controlled, also interfuses the formal attributes of the blues within Weaver's adaptation of the sonnet's "golden mean." The refrain in "Rambling" is very much a blues refrain. The classic blues stanza is a tercet with the first two lines repeating and the third declaring the cause of the emotional malady. Taken at another glance, the whole tripartite, dialectical structure of the bop does not appear entirely inconsistent with the tercet structure of the blues. Rather, it can be viewed as itself a dramatic, narrative, and meditative elaboration of the blues, a form Ralph Ellison defined as "an autobiographical chronicle of personal catastrophe expressed lyrically" (189). From this standpoint, one can see in the bop a kind of superposition of formal means in which the poet's improvisational impulse draws from multiple traditional sources. The result is a formal metamorphosis in which innovation brings a "new body" into the world of poetry in English, and does so, paradoxically, without loss to the original formal imprint. The DNA of the forms that spurred Weaver's invention remain at work, crystalized in the new body of the bop.

Jericho Brown's still more recent invention, the "duplex," goes further in what I am calling the metamorphosis of inherited forms, but which might also be understood as a hybridization of formal means through strategic improvisation. Invented for his Pulitzer Prize-winning book, *The Tradition,* Brown's duplex combines formal aspects of the sonnet, the blues, and the ghazal, though unlike Weaver's bop and its inspiration in the golden mean, Brown's improvisation with and from inherited forms arises from a deeply founded skepticism. When he was asked in an interview with *The Rumpus* about his new form's origin and inspiration, he makes his skepticism abundantly clear:

> I sort of had been thinking about gutting a sonnet. We go fourteen lines to get to what will be in that fourteenth line, a repeated line. I kept thinking, "Why can't I just skip all the lines in between? What would that make?" In my head I kept thinking that it would make a ghazal. A ghazal is couplets that seem disparate because there's something in between them that is not said. Do you see what I mean? So first, it started with me asking, "How do I gut the sonnet crown?" But I guess the question before that is, "Why do I wanna gut the sonnet crown?" I feel completely in love with and oppressed by the sonnet. You know, because I'm a poet. I can conjecture about my obsession with the sonnet. I mean, I'm educated in the sonnet. It's been pushed down my throat the entirety of my life. There is something in me that doesn't like that, and doesn't trust that because I'm a rebellious human being. I need to be a rebellious human being because I'm black and gay in this nation and in this world which has not been good to me or anybody like me. I have this responsibility to be skeptical, even of what I love.[6]

One might say, speculatively, that where Weaver's invention of the bop responds to tradition or, rather, traditions, within a hermeneutic of trust despite the poet's obvious repudiation of systems of injustice, Brown's invention of the duplex does so within a hermeneutic of dis-trust, even within the wider frame of what he calls "love," which clearly has much to do with the art of poetry and with nothing but repulsion for the long experience of racism and social injustice.

Regardless of its contrarian origins in the poet's impulse to gut the sonnet, and Brown's sense of being to some degree imprisoned by it, the duplex retains an incontestably generative relationship to the form. The duplex, like the bop, or the dream song, would not exist without the sonnet, and, indeed, the sonnet crown, since the five duplexes seeded throughout *The Tradition* form, in fact, a kind of divagated crown, ending with a cento duplex in which lines from the previous four are woven together by the poet to form the book's coda poem. The first duplex in Brown's broadcasted sequence exemplifies the form at once self-reflexively and arrestingly:

A poem is a gesture toward home.
It makes dark demands I call my own.

> Memory makes demands darker than my own:
> My last love drove a burgundy car.

My first love drove a burgundy car.
He was fast and awful, tall as my father.

> Steadfast and awful, my tall father
> Hit hard as a hailstorm. He'd leave marks.

Light rain hits easy but leaves its own mark
Like the sound of a mother weeping again.

> Like the sound of my mother weeping again,
> No sound beating ends where it began.

None of the beaten end up how we began.
A poem is a gesture toward home.

At fourteen lines, the duplex is sonnet-length, though it moves structurally along with couplets that are nine to eleven syllables in length, both akin to the ghazal. Ghazals, however, resist narrative, as Brown himself acknowledges. They permit the poet and reader, to use again Ali's phrase, "to be teased into disunity."[7] Ali, of course, must be credited with bringing true ghazals into the world of contemporary poetry in English, and the form moves in his description with "a stringently formal disunity."[8] Though Brown has, as it were, grafted the sonnet and the ghazal together, unlike a true ghazal the duplex uses the formal components of the ghazal differently. The *matla,* or opening couplet, does not repeat, though it does set up the repetition of recurrent rhyme through repeating words, the *radif* in a ghazal, and the refrain, or *quafia,* has more the sonic effect of a variable blues line, particularly when the line repeats across couplets, though the blues form itself has been lifted out of the classic tercet.

In this initial duplex in Brown's sequence of duplexes, the first couplet reflexively considers the nature of the poem itself as a gesture that simultaneously and metaphorically implies a demanding journey toward home, the place of origin, though "toward" strongly suggests that a final arrival is not something one ought to expect. The contemplative frame of the poem elaborates in the third line to include memory, though with the second line of the second couplet both the poem's frame and its tonal shift: "My last love drove a burgundy car." The poem has modulated from meditation to narrative, and the narrative proceeds through the ghazal-like "disunity" of a leap from the speaker's "last love" to his "first." Yet, the seemingly discontinuous leap across the couplet embodies, nonetheless, a continuity of memory in the speaker's recognition of a physical fact: the burgundy car.

As it progresses from this juncture of memory back into the deeper, indelibly fraught family history of the speaker, the "gesture toward home" that is the poem lands on the father's contrarily violent gesture—the beating of his son. We have moved eight lines into the poem, and with the ninth line the reader arrives, as in an un-gutted sonnet, at a volta: "Light rain hits easy but leaves its own mark." The turn is tonal, it is also softer in its imagery than the brutal scene that precedes it, though the matter of the line itself suggests an ongoing trauma. That trauma is underscored in the line that follows where, contrary to the father's violence, we encounter a mother weeping. The penultimate couplet binds the archetypal mother of the previous line to the speaker's own mother, and the second line of this couplet expressly reiterates the profound effect of violence on the traumatized mind. The first line of the final couplet, in turn, announces the poem's irrefutable conclusion—the brutalized can never end where they began, they are altered forever; and the final line—an exact repetition of the first line of the poem—transforms utterly what might have been construed as a hopeful departure. On the contrary, in this instance the duplex embodies and enacts the closed system of physical and especially psychic trauma in the almost claustrophobic recurrences inside this hybridized form, ending with the final envelope closure the form requires.

"The blues is an impulse to keep the painful details and episodes . . . alive in one's aching consciousness," Ralph Ellison wrote, "to finger its jagged grain, and to transcend it, not by the consolation of philosophy but by squeezing from it, a near-tragic, near comic lyricism."[9] While there seems little comedy in Jericho Brown's "Duplex," there is certainly the urgent impulse to transcend pain through formal lyricism. That lyricism draws from at least three formative sources—the sonnet, the blues, and the ghazal. Though I would add that the envelope structure of the duplex inevitably enjoins the exact formal requirement of the pantoum as well, and not only the sonnet crown. Here, again, with this newly invented form, we can and should discern the effect of one poet's needful improvisational impulse creatively enjoining earlier forms in a spirit—however uneasily and indeed traumatically inherited—of innovation both rooted and routed in metamorphosis.

This same improvisational impetus informs Tyehimba Jess's "syncopated sonnets," notably those found in his Pulitzer prize-winning *Olio*. Where Weaver's bop elaborates the structural dimensions of the sonnet, and Brown's duplex deconstructs and hybridizes the sonnet through the influence of the ghazal and blues, Jess's syncopated sonnet form maintains the lineaments of the sonnet exactly even while it reconfigures the sonnet's rhetorical structure with the introduction of vocal counterpoint. In short, he interfuses the sonnet with the contrapuntal, a form derived expressly from music. Contrapuntal poems have become more and more present on the contemporary poetry scene, especially among poets of color, but what is unique to Jess's syncopated sonnet is the combination, the interfusion, of both forms inside the sonnet's traditional "little song." Here is Jess's "Millie and Christine McKoy":

We've mended two songs into one dark skin   We ride the wake of each other's rhythm
bleeding soprano into contralto   beating our hearts' syncopated tempo
—we're fused in blood and body from one thrummed stem
budding twin blooms of song. We're a doubled rose
descended from raw carnage of the South   with a music all our own. With our mouths
bursting open our freedom. We sing past rage   seeped in the glow of hand-me-down courage
grown from hard labor that made our mother shout,
spent with awe. We hymn to pay soft homage
to the worksong's aria. It leaves us   drenched in spiritual a cappellas,
soaked in history like our father's sweat   flowing soul from bone through skin. We pay debts
born of beyond the flesh: we are just

                              two women signing truths we can't forget
          from plantation to grave. Lord, here we are,   from broken chattel to circus stars,
    freed twin sisters who've hauled our voices far . . .   we sing from this nation's barbwired heart . . .

    To read down the left side of Jess's poem is to listen to Millie McKoy's song; to read down the right side is to hear the song of her twin sister, Christine. The lines in the middle sound both their voices in unison when their individual voices join in harmony. As such, as in a true contrapuntal, the reader encounters three poems in one. In the case of "Millie and Christine McKoy," however, Jess also incorporates the exact dimensions and rhyme scheme of the Shakespearean sonnet, both internally to Millie's voice on the left and to Christine's voice at the line end on the right, as well as in the shared vocal lines. The execution of this syncopated sonnet's formal means is a tour de force of compositional ingenuity, and it is only one of numerous such orchestrations in *Olio*.

    Tyehimba Jess's "Millie and Christine McKoy" is also formally reflexive, in that the poem's opening phrase, "We've mended two songs into one dark skin," is exactly what the contrapuntal intends to do, but doubly so since Jess has likewise mended the sonnet and the contrapuntal into a single song whose very doubleness orchestrates a more comprehensive unity-in-difference: *e pluribus unum* achieved in and through the body of the poem as bespoken in the shared bodies of the twins. This embodied unity of mended songs, and its resonant melisma, are therefore further mirrored in the bodies of Millie and Christine, which are conjoined into one: they are pygopagus twins. Born in Whiteville, North Carolina, in 1851, Millie and Christine were born into slavery and forced to perform at fairs and freak shows. As Jess's internally doubled, syncopated sonnet recounts, the contrapuntal song of Millie and Christine analogically embodies the tragically counterpointed and conflicting history of the nation as well. The other poems of *Olio* do likewise, through the thematic prism of Jess's restorative panoply of Black musicians and performers who lived in the nineteenth and early twentieth centuries. In an interview discussing *Olio*, Jess reflects that he had two intentions in mind with the syncopated sonnet. First, he says he wanted "to provide a voice for those who have been left out of the dialog of history. In some cases, a quote is provided from a public figure or outlet, and I have written an adjoining or complimentary voice that adds the subject's point of view. In these cases, the objective is generally to create a syllabically symmetrical counterpoint to the quote, to inform the historical record in a way that is matched breath for breath with the original quote."[10] His second intention was to "imagine a conversation between two historical figures that are otherwise silent. In this case, the two figures may be in accordance with each other . . . or in opposition with each other. . . . In these cases, the dialog opens up a host of issues that are germane both to the individuals and ourselves—issues of freedom, choice, morality, love, courage and cowardice."[11] What is important to underscore in the immediate context is that Jess's project in the syncopated sonnet stands as an astute and compellingly intricate improvisation on the traditional sonnet form even while the "little song" retains all of its formal requirements without alteration or elision. The two contrapuntal songs expand the sonnet from within to make a combinatory third. Jess's is, in fact, an improvisation that through his use of the contrapuntal initiates a metamorphosis, a transformation, within this perhaps most canonically resonant of inherited forms in English.

The sonnet is an import that has become almost synonymous with verse in England and in America. Terrance Hayes's *American Sonnets for My Past and Future Assassin,* as well as Brown's "gutting" of the form with his invention of the duplex, and Jess's contrapuntal orchestration, extend the tonal and expressive range of the form. To expand the range of improvisation further, beyond the Italian origins of the sonnet, one might add to Weaver, Brown, and Jess's innovations, Terrance Hayes's invention of "the golden shovel." His form, conceived in homage to Gwendolyn Brooks, finds a formal template in the French poetic game of *bouts-rimés,* where a poet takes the rhyme scheme of another poet's poem and fashions a new poem by means of the end rhymes. Though not as widely practiced as yet as the golden shovel, bop, or duplex, Allison Joseph's new form she calls the "sweetelle" also appears inspired by French repeating forms—a kind of expanded, bulked-out triolet. Where the triolet is an eight-line poem in which the first, fourth, and seventh lines repeat, the sweetelle is a ten-line poem or dizain of fourteen syllables per line in which lines one, five, and ten repeat. Not unlike the bop relative to the sonnet, the sweetelle allows for greater discursivity or lyric development beyond the tight frame of the triolet, the form from which the sweetelle improvises its own form. In a similar vein, yet another newly invented form, the "gigan," might be said to dilate the sonnet to sixteen lines, allowing for extension where a curtal sonnet compresses, intensifies. Ruth Ellen Kocher, with a nod to postmodern hierarchy-busting, named the gigan after the cinematic cyborg who battles Godzilla in the famous Japanese film series. The gigan is a *keiju*, a "strange beast," and indeed the form assumes assorted structures into its singular form. A gigan begins with a couplet followed by a tercet, which in turn is followed by four more couplets, then another tercet, and ends on a final couplet. The stanzas need not rhyme, though the first line of the poem is repeated in line eleven, and the sixth line of the poem is repeated in line twelve, with some variation permitted in the repetition. As such, in its dilation of the sonnet, the gigan introduces something of the sonic repetition found in certain French forms, like the rondeau or ballade. Unlike those forms, the gigan concentrates the repetition in about the same proportional location where the volta might occur in a traditional sonnet. The final couplet, in turn, offers an amplification or twist on the poem's subject, achieved after the doubling up of the repeated lines in lieu, one might say, of a volta. In sum, the improvisational spirit at work in all of these new forms could not exist except in conversation, in dialogue, with tradition and a living canon that affirms its inherent vitality in transformation, in metamorphosis.

EN ROUTE

I began this discussion, somewhat elusively, with a digression on the metaphor of metamorphosis (illustrated through Ovid's great work), in which ruminations on the etymological origins of the word offered a kind of prism, I hope, through which I might briefly explore the improvisations of form, the formal innovations, produced recently by prominent American poets. In making my way toward a consideration of the bop, duplex, and the syncopated sonnet, along with passing reference to other new forms, I situated all of them within the historical context of English language poetry, principally of the sonnet. The ghazal and the pantoum, likewise, have been taken into the language from nonwestern traditions—the ghazal from the Persian, Arabic, and Urdu, the pantoum from the Malaysian. The blues, arguably, constitutes a tradition inside the broader tradition of poetry in English and America—in Raymond R. Patterson's words it is "a uniquely American poetic form with roots in oral performance and musical improvisation."[12] To complete my digression, I cited Agha Shahid Ali on matters of tradition, and canonical standards. All of the aforementioned new forms find their relevance in view of Ali's incisive handling of urgent and often conflictive aesthetic and cultural issues. I see Ali steering a middle path between the need for standards—he invokes them unapologetically across cultures—and the cancellation of standards for political reasons which he discounts as a version of philistinism: between tradition narrowly defined and tradition pluralized in the very evolution of its self-conception.[13] The pluralizing of tradition is inevitable, given the history of poetic forms in English, as well as what T. S. Eliot called "the historical sense," without which neither tradition nor the individual talent remains aesthetically viable for long.[14]

It may appear surprising at first to see the notoriously staid Eliot and the vivaciously open Shahid Ali as aesthetic and theoretical bedfellows in their thinking about poetry. It is important to note at this point that of the many etymological roots and routes of "tradition" one prominent meaning is "to hand over," as in offering a gift. As Eliot observed, tradition as a form of "handing *down*," meaning timidly, blindly following the ways of the immediate generation before, "should be positively discouraged."[15] Such would be a wholly conformist approach to tradition. Rather, for Eliot, a poet should write with a feeling for "the whole of the literature of Europe in his bones." There of course is the rub—just Europe and only "the mind of Europe," one asks? Only *his*? And what of the injustices of European colonial history, as well as the artistic triumphs? Given the vitality of his embrace of his nonwestern as well as his European literary forebears, and his acute consciousness of colonial history, Ali poses such unavoidable questions pointedly when he calls out Pound for his fascism, Eliot for his antisemitism, and the entire apparatus of the British Empire for aiming guns at his ancestor's hearts.[16] And yet, when Eliot says, "No poet, no artist of any art, has his complete meaning alone. His significance, his appreciation is the appreciation of his relation to the dead poets and artists,"[17] Ali implicitly gives his assent, though from a globalized vantage. In so doing, he anticipates by more than a quarter-century our often-volatile contemporary discussion about decolonizing the canon. Ali's is a brilliantly instructive negotiation between a defense of canon and the recognition that the canon of poetry in English (as well as literature globally) cannot be narrowly construed within the framework of "the mind of Europe." On the other hand, to those who would oppose the very idea of canonicity he demands, again, "What are your standards?"[18] In short, to those who would specify canonicity based on anything other than artistic accomplishment Ali gives the lie. In such a view, even in relief of Ali's forthright condemnation of the imperial intentions of canon vis-a-vis education in Britain's colonies, "decolonizing" the canon as an interpretive or educational position, if it is to have validity, should not become an exercise in retroactive cancellation; any recognition of canon or tradition understood as a living compendium of historical and artistic achievement must be considered an additive and prudentially reconfiguring enterprise. It must never, as Ali's conception would have it, intentionally or unconsciously prize ideology over aesthetics.

Ali amplifies his comprehensive perspective on the subject of canonicity with reference, like Eliot before him, to the individual talent when he cautions "in many cases we find a writer distracted from his real work into a facilely executed sense of social justice, rather than letting . . . passion for justice emerge organically from the courage to implicate the writer formally and thus truly take a stand."[19] In matters of making poems, in matters of art more generally, "ideology simply doesn't function as it supposed to when, indeed, it isn't directly threatening the work of art by trivializing it and trivializing as well the importance of the ideas it seeks to dramatize."[20] It is important to underscore at this juncture that Ali has no intention of repudiating an artist's commitment to social justice in favor of a belated conception of "art for art's sake." Rather, as he reminds us, "subject matter is interesting only when through form it has become content. The more rigorous the form, realized formally, openly, or brokenly, the greater the chance for content. I am not endorsing any mechanical fidelity to any rules."[21] From this vantage there is no trivializing of art or idea in Afaa Michael Weavers's "Rambling" or Jericho Brown's "Duplex," or Tyehimba Jess's "Millie and Christine McKoy," for in all these poems "subject matter" has been transformed into "content," to follow Ali's important distinction. Moreover, what positively distinguishes Weaver's bop, Brown's duplex, and Jess's syncopated sonnet, in Eliot's terms, is their incontestably acute historical sense, not only in terms of subject matter but in terms of form. Theirs is a historical sense that is in crucial ways more probing than Eliot's in matters of social justice, ethnic, racial, and cultural inclusion. Weaver, Brown, and Jess, as well as Hayes, Joseph, and Kocher, attune their work both to the transformation of tradition, its ongoing metamorphosis, as well as to vitalizing standards of excellence. This last point resides in complete agreement with Eliot's most powerfully resilient observation about tradition: that tradition has less to do with reified monuments—tradition as inert bulk—and more to do with tradition's inevitable transformations, its own evolving metamorphosis. "The whole existing order of tradition" Eliot observed, is altered with the incorporation of the genuinely and, by inference, the excellently new. Rather than conformist, or wholly nonconformist, such a vision is inherently transformational.

What we misperceive as static monuments are, in short, exemplary embodiments of the poet's work that have become standard bearers of tradition's own ongoing metamorphosis, standard bearers whose light alters and broadens in view of the genuinely new. Blindly following tradition is no way to make it. Eliot is right about this, but he is also monocular from today's vantage by the limitations of his own historical sense—a narrowness in this case in what we might call his depth of field, to borrow a phrase from Afaa Weaver. Ali himself confesses that he thought Eliot "horrible" when he discovered Eliot's antisemitism, though he also owns that he had to reassess that position when someone pointed out that he kept quoting Eliot's poems all the time. Ali had to change his mind about Eliot in recognition of Eliot's own transformational artistic achievement. In accordance with his aesthetic principles, he had to parse his leftward leaning politics from the incontestable urgency of his artistic judgment. Then again, as Eliot also observed, the mind of tradition changes, though ultimately "this change is a development which abandons nothing *en route.*" One need only read the opening of Derek Walcott's "The Schooner Flight" alongside the opening of William Langland's "Piers Ploughman" to witness, and to bear witness to, the vitally generative and improvisational capacities of tradition, and poets, across the distances of time and place. Will the bop, duplex, and syncopated sonnet as new forms, "new bodies" in the ongoing metamorphosis of tradition—like the golden shovel, the sweetelle, and the gigan—emerge into tradition's ever-evolving fullness? It is certain that those aspects of traditional forms incorporated into these new forms are now incontestably part of the "new body" of each. To borrow a phrase from poet Marilyn Nelson, these poets have sought to add vibrantly to the general body of poetry in English by "owning the masters," by improvising forms after forms in concourse with tradition's, and canon's, ongoing metamorphoses.

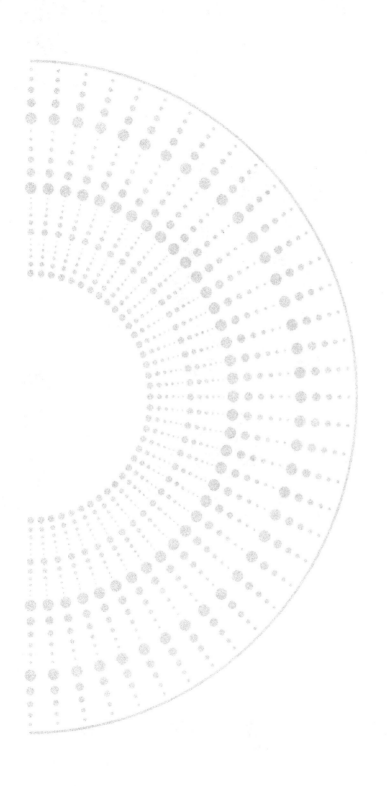

"HELLO, I MUST BE GOING"

The Poetry of Farewell

At the risk of trivializing a rich and varied body of poems that set before themselves the task of holding up a mirror to the moving and universally human experience of saying goodbye, I want to begin by quoting in its brief entirety the duet that Groucho Marx sang for the first time opposite Margaret Dumont, aka the whimsically redoubtable Mrs. Rittenhouse, in the Marx Brothers' second film, *Animal Crackers.* In the scene, Groucho as Captain Spaulding, with his trademark swallowtail coat incongruously paired with a white pith helmet, dances gleefully in front of the partygoers gathered in his honor. When his legs and arms aren't akimbo, he looks very much the skater gliding along a shelf of rapidly melting ice. This is what they sing:

SPAULDING: Hello, I must be going.
I cannot stay
I came to say
"I must be going."
I'm glad I came
But just the same
I must be going.

MRS RITTENHOUSE: For my sake you must stay,
For if you should go away
You'll spoil this party
I am throwing.

SPAULDING: I'll stay a week or two,
I'll stay the summer through,
But I am telling you,
I must be going.

Written by lyricists Bert Kalmar and Harry Ruby expressly for Groucho, "Hello, I Must Be Going" quickly became a lifelong theme song for comedy's answer to Tristan Tzara. Groucho's lightning wordplay and absurdist "schtick" saw him through a somewhat brief but legendary film career with his progressively disappearing troupe of brothers—Gummo, Zeppo, Chico, and Harpo—followed by a wildly off-color stint as host of the fifties game show *You Bet Your Life* and then a gradually diminishing role as a regular on variety hours, specials, and late-night talk shows though the sixties and seventies, until he died in 1977 at the age of eighty-six. For one who was always going, it took him a long time to leave. And he certainly appeared to enjoy the party he never came to, or was it the party he never left, or the one he kept leaving whenever he showed up on his way out?

For all the Dadaist foolery in "Hello, I Must Be Going," there is I think a rather subtly realized interfusion, to borrow a word from Wordsworth, between the experience of arrival and the experience of departure. Like a deeply enwound double knot or a Janus face the two become very nearly the same thing; or as T. S. Eliot muses in his *Four Quartets* "in my beginning is my end" and, again, "in my end is my beginning." Or, as he still more memorably announces at the end of "Little Gidding":

We shall not cease from exploration
And the end of all our exploring
Will be to arrive where we started.
And know the place for the first time.

Admittedly, it is hard to reconcile two artists as widely divergent in tone and medium as Julius "Groucho" Marx and Thomas Stearns "Tse Tse" Eliot capturing the same paradoxical convergence of departure and arrival, as though, taken together, whether flung away or whirled back, saying hello and saying farewell constituted a single parabolic motion; or perhaps, more strangely, assumed the form of what physicists call a Calabi-Yau shape—a multidimensional space, a manifold, that can be curled or folded into a single point[1] Stranger also that Groucho Marx, New York son of Jewish immigrants, and T. S. Eliot, Anglican expatriate to London from St. Louis, some of whose poems occasionally exhibit strongly antisemitic portraits, exchanged several agreeable letters when the two men grew older, each acknowledging their admiration for the other: Eliot even invited Groucho and Eden Hartford Marx to dinner when they visited London. "After such knowledge, what forgiveness," to quote "Gerontion." Or from Groucho's perspective: "Goodbye, I must be staying."

It is, in fact, the imperative "must"—whether to stay or to go, but especially "to go"—that bespeaks the urgency behind poems of farewell, and I would argue that animates a poet's search for formal and expressive means to embody the emotional urgency one encounters in that little tightly enwound knot that subjectively at least will one day constitute all of time for each of us. In the announcement "I *must* be going," not "I *choose* to go," the extension of departure collapses into the starkest insight of existential brevity expressive of a condition as much as of an occasion. *Tick,* as Frank Kermode observed in *The Sense of an Ending,* inevitably leads to *tock,* such that *tick-tock* really constitutes a single phenomenon.[2] Or, more philosophically, *tock* is embedded in the teleology of *tick,* for the end as Eliot said is in the beginning. We can hear that pervasive clock resoundingly in Wallace Stevens's "Waving Adieu, Adieu, Adieu" where, in addition to engaging the theme of farewell, the poem must find efficient artistic means to encode the poet's response to this head-on look at mortality, encountered without the traditional assuaging answers: Here are the first two stanzas:

> That would be waving and that would be crying,
> Crying and shouting and meaning farewell,
> Farewell in the eyes and farewell in the center,
> Just to stand still without moving a hand.
>
> In a world without heaven to follow, the stops
> Would be endings, more poignant than partings, profounder,
> And that would be saying farewell, repeating farewell,
> Just to be there and just to behold.

In Stevens's poem the moment of farewell is the centrally emblematic crux of our being on which, you can be sure, you can bet your life. It is the still point that, for a split second, hushes all becoming, neither apostrophe nor elegy; whereas Stevens further observes "in a world without heaven" there is only this mutual beholding, a "being there together" that would be "enough" as he affirms in "Final Soliloquy to the Interior Paramour," but for the fact that this moment cannot hold, and by not holding the moment of farewell becomes central to our experience. Despite the inherent drama of its title, "Waving Adieu, Adieu, Adieu" is a poem that emphatically eschews the dramatic, or seems to. Indeed, the action of the poem is conditional: "that would be waving, and that would be crying." The poem posits no heaven, but nonetheless places the reader in the vantage of looking down with the speaker from the heights of his rhetorical empyrean. How, then, does Stevens's poem, lacking nearly all dramatic content, offer a counter strategy for convincing embodiment?

To begin with, the poem's first sentence is a tour de force. The verb "to be" expresses the existence and the condition of a subject, which in this case is the action of the title. Remarkably, the poem's first sentence renders existence itself conditional as a performance of the title's action, the more so since the right-branching clauses that follow create a slippage in the condition of the sentence's immediate objects, especially "crying," such that they become subjects before the sentence evolves across these first four lines only to stop, abruptly, in a stillness that is ontological as much as it is physical—a stillness of being achieved, paradoxically, though movement. Consider again that Calabi-Yau shape, or walking along the border of a courtyard in a Maurits Escher print only to find yourself on the ramparts above, or think of those mirror hands that miraculously draw each other into existence.

As the poem develops, its verbal repetition as well as its elaboration and modulation of right-branching syntax becomes further self-enwound with the poem's prevailing dactylic rhythm. In the first stanza the word "farewell" repeats three times within two lines, with the particularly halting combination in the turn between lines two and three. "Farewell" repeats twice more in stanza two and finally again in stanza four. We also find "behold" and "beheld," "still" "ever-jubilant" through stanzas three and four, and the nicely framing repetition of "heaven" near the beginning and at the end of the poem. More emphatic still is the piling on of clauses, both in the first two stanzas and most especially in the long sentence running again across stanza three and four, followed by the two short sentences that come successively at the outset of the poem's final stanza. The poem's cumulative progression is achieved through a strategy of syntactical delay that moves in counterpoint to its insistent meter.

This is progression as regression. In Stevens's poem, syntax has become a kind of leash that pulls against the lines' dactylic urgency to run ahead. "Waving Adieu, Adieu, Adieu" thus feels a bit like the experience of dragging a prescient and thereby seriously recalcitrant dog to the vet for neutering. Wait—there are also instances, as in the poem's sixth line, where the dactyls suddenly transform into anapests, caught as they are in the currents of the poem's syntax. Am I mixing metaphors to explain the dynamic knot of Stevens's poem? I am, and the poem itself would accept that protean rhetorical gesture. Beyond such richly shifting dynamics, one could also highlight the poem's interplay of liquids and plosives orchestrating its sonic textures, and especially the alliterative effect of "poignant," "partings," and "profounder" repeating, expressively, with "repeating" and "stops" in the poem's second stanza. Stevens's use of a variety of modes of repetition in the poem accomplishes a motion forward that, paradoxically, contains its own counter-motion. The total effect resonates with the idea of a consciousness, the poem's "single self," seeking to halt time, to fend off the end, and that is the medium of the poem's drama in spite of its rather abstract vantage.

Similarly, in her poem that begins "My life closed twice before its close," Emily Dickinson grasps the centrality of the moment of farewell for the human condition, but does so in a way that captures the emotional gravity of the experience with greater self-evident drama than Stevens's more musing treatment:

My life closed twice before its close –
It yet remains to see
If Immortality unveil
A third event to me

So huge, so hopeless to conceive
As these that twice befell.
Parting is all we know of Heaven
And all we need of Hell.

Unlike Juliet who found parting a "sweet sorrow" before the tragedy unfolded, Emily Dickinson sees right into the heart of parting—it is, ultimately, inconceivable, the promise of death realized in life that knots together even the supreme contraries, Heaven and Hell. At the same time there is something epigrammatic about the end of this Dickinson poem that appears at first to steer slightly away from her typical modus operandi to "tell it slant." Looking more closely, however, one can see how Dickinson quietly unsettles the poem. The most evident disruption comes in the penultimate line when Dickinson's emphatic iambs reverse with the trochaic substitution, "Parting." The iambs resume immediately but slip again with the final hypercatalexis, or feminine ending, "Heaven" at the end of the line, before we are eased again into the perfect iambic line that ends the poem. That last line, to my ear, feels almost too neat, but deceptively so. The more disruptive nuances of Dickinson's poem are registered earlier, within the rhyme scheme. While lines two and four of each stanza rhyme perfectly, "see/me," and "hell/befell," lines one and three of each stanza carry their sonic DNA through a single letter: the "l" in "close/unveil" and the "v" in "conceive/Heaven." "Close" and "unveil" are opposites, as are "conceive" and "Heaven." To close something is to shut it out or shut it off; to unveil something is to open it to view. Conception is a beginning; Heaven an end in every sense, one hopes, teleologically as well as theologically speaking. Poetically, both pairs frame the beginning and end of things within the world of Dickinson's two quatrains. Together these pairs of opposites embody the crux of the poem's fundamental hermeneutic, its circuit of understanding that ultimately subverts any neatness of meaning. Beyond any pretense to epigram, Dickinson's poem bespeaks the reality of an insurmountable transcendence, an unknowing so profound as to fuse Heaven and Hell together and therefore to render any definitive conception of them purely fictive.

Dickinson's immense unknowing resides physically at the heart of the poem, specifically in the enjambment between its two stanzas, that which exists formally between the speaker's self-articulation, "me," and the descriptive phrase "So huge," a spondee that constitutes the primary metrical break from the poem's strong iambic rhythm. Here is another proverbial "white sustenance" for Dickinson, beyond even despair: the blank of the page that is the richest signifier for what ultimately lies beyond conception and yet resides at the core of all parting, whether in the beginning, or the end, or successively experienced in time. Is Dickinson's "me" so huge, or so infinitesimal in relation to the vastness that "me" intuits as to be little more than nothing? Beyond these questions, or at the core of them, one might ask how immortality can unveil an event, since immortality by definition lies outside time, unless the poet insinuates here the perspective from time's fullness and not merely one of its points. Dickinson, in the genius of one of her seemingly "less-than-slanted" poems, places us squarely at the tipping point of an understanding that cuts both ways at once, a paradoxically blank unveiling that contains both immortality and time.

The sidelong glance by which we come to see the central emptiness at the heart of Dickinson's poem unveils what is so central in saying goodbye. At the heart of every farewell there is an apophatic shock, a recognition and prefiguration of that final parting, even of ourselves from ourselves. In contemplative thought, the apophatic tradition emphasizes our inability to think what is ultimate and therefore lies beyond representation—the radically dark. Facing this, Stevens turns away at the end of "Waving Adieu, Adieu, Adieu," where he affirms "what spirit / Have I except it comes from the sun?" The sun also blinds. Dickinson looks still more deeply into the eclipse. It is a hard thing to do, which is perhaps why Groucho's absurd little song "Hello, I Must be Going," has something in common with Joycean wakes, or a Becket play.

What appears as a semi-slantwise inference in Emily Dickinson's "My life closed twice before its close" moves into the forefront in Stanley Kunitz's "The Image-Maker." The title of Kunitz's poem announces from the outset its primary subject—the maker, the poet, who seeks to represent reality, that is, to re-present it anew within the analogical frame of the poem. Embedded in the title as well, however, is the ancient religious taboo against "graven images" that resides in the cultural makeup of Judaism and Islam. Christianity's embrace of representation, its reliance on the figural, as Eric Auerbach demonstrated so completely in his classic work, *Mimesis,* is an outgrowth of its fundamentally Incarnational theology, though contemplative traditions within it likewise stress the apophatic moment of unknowing. The entirety of this complex Western cultural inheritance stands behind Kunitz's poem and underscores its first line, which parallels the opening lines of Genesis in the context of an individual life: "A wind passed over my mind. . . ." With this initial declaration Kunitz makes his life—and most especially his life as a poet, "a maker"—a microcosm of all created life, as though he were enacting Coleridge's classic definition of the imagination: "a repetition in the finite mind of the eternal act of creation in the infinite I Am." Needless to say, Coleridge's definition reiterates and re-frames for poetry the biblical name for God: YHWH, "I AM THAT I AM," which technically, in true apophatic fashion, should never be uttered. From the richness of its opening, the poem moves into progressively less reassuring territory—into a reality where words themselves evanesce into shadows and the poet's senses confuse in synesthesia—the poem's "black rustle of wings." The conflicting perceptions mount: a summons gives way to blessing, belief to punishment. From here on "The Image-Maker" unfolds with all the associative power of consciousness following the cross-cutting knife edge of itself as it approaches its very limit:

> Perhaps it is time to go,
> to slip alone, as at birth,
> out of this glowing house
> where all my children danced.
> Seductive Night! I have stood
> at my casement the longest hour,
> watching the acid wafer
> of the moon slowly dissolving
> in a scud of cloud, and heard
> the farthest hidden stars
> calling my name.
> I listen, but avert my ears
> from Meister Eckhart's warning:
> *All things must be forsaken.*
> *God scorns*
> *To show Himself among images.*

There is something Keatsian about Kunitz's casement window, but this seductive Night, notably capitalized, is more a dark night of the soul than a lush encounter. "Oh, for a life of sensations rather than of thoughts," Keats reflected, or as Kunitz exclaimed in "The Long Boat," "Oh to be rocked in the Infinite!" In this poem, Kunitz has reached the point where thought and sense meet like anti-particles that cancel each other out of existence, a mutual effacement captured ironically enough in the brilliant image of the moon as an acid wafer dissolving. That black rustle we heard earlier is not a nightin-gale's—does Kunitz wake or sleep? Yet by entering that apparent negation in which image consumes itself, in which the poet's whole *raison d'être* evapo-rates, Kunitz's poem performs a miraculous trope: it pulls the proverbial rabbit of presence, and therefore image-making—the artist's directive to re-present—out of the underlying emptiness of things. By listening and simultaneously averting his ears, and thereby by speaking the very words of the mystic he says he averts, Kunitz at once unties the knot at the core of making, the built-in conflation that exists "as at birth" in the essence of farewell, then ties it all back together again.

Stanley Kunitz's "The Image-Maker" incorporates in the fullest sense of that verb the apophatic condition at the heart of poems of farewell, or any-thing for that matter. As its Greek root indicates, "apophasis" means "speaking off," which makes "apophasis" an essentially rhetorical move, a way of speaking about something by moving away from the mark, telling the truth by telling it, proverbially, slant. In Dickinson's and Kunitz's engagement with the term's metaphysical applications, apophasis may be read as a denial, and it appears that the poetry of farewell finds ways to orchestrate that denial, to create the poem out of a denial of death itself, as a way of transfiguring the unthinkable so life can move forward, so out of the brokenness of "farewell" a deeper sense of wholeness might emerge. That would make human love emblematic of the image-maker's effort to rescue life from loss, and therefore akin to a kind of heaven. That is exactly what John Donne presumes in "A Valediction: Forbid-ding Mourning." Like many of Donne's poems, "Valediction" proceeds through contraries, in this case love founded on the greater refinement of a spiritual eroticism, cast by contrast against love of the purely sensuous kind, which Donne deems "dull" by comparison—and merely "sublunary." Because he and his beloved are "inter-assured of the mind," the physical nature of love itself obtains an alchemical refinement by which the carnal transmogrifies into the soulful without evaporating into contentless spiritualism. In the poem's final conceit mind and body, soul and flesh, conjoin in a trope that is as sexually provocative as it is famously ingenious:

Our two souls, therefore, which are one,
    Though I must go, endure not yet

A breach, but an expansion,
　　Like gold to airy thinness beat.

If they be two, they are two so
　　As stiff twin compasses are two;
Thy soul, the fixed foot, makes no show
　　To move, but doth, if th' other do.

And though it in the center sit,
　　Yet when the other far doth roam,
It leans and harkens after it,
　　And grows erect, as that comes home.

Such wilt thou be to me, who must
　　Like th' other foot, obliquely run;
Thy firmness makes my circle just,
　　And makes me end where I begun.

If Donne's conceit succeeds in denying death by engineering a ritual return in which flesh and spirit exist in the ever-expansive knot of love, then he does so by using an infinite extension of space as the metaphor that trumps mutable time, and likewise does so by keeping the bonds of love, encompassing and potent. This is the image-maker at his most consummate and consummating. Donne's witty double-entendre in the poem's penultimate stanza, "and grows erect," is unmissable. The male lover's return, his coming, proceeds inevitably and in every sense from his going. Through that dialectical expansion, "like gold to airy thinness beat," Donne would obliterate the eclipse of death by making flesh simultaneously the literal and alchemical tool of embodied spirit.

The movement of Donne's encircling conceit, ending in the poem's expansively hopeful outcome, mirrors a structural process inherent in what some see as the nature of understanding itself—or rather the never-ending process of coming to understanding. Hermeneutics, the process of coming to understanding, is best figured as a circle, or more specifically a circular movement that really constitutes a cycle "constantly expanding" in which the whole "always affects" the individual part, and part the whole. Such is philosopher Hans-Georg Gadamer's view.[3] For Gadamer, this cycle is endless, moving into new horizons that fuse and enlarge through an ever-widening compass of tradition and history: Hello I must be going, coming back, and going again, and again, and again. What interests me here, relative to poetry more than any philosophical consideration, is what Gadamer calls "the structure of movement" that characterizes any kind of play of understanding, including the play of the work of art.

The sense of an ending, whether bound for return or not, defines the conceptual structure of the poems we've looked at thus far as well as their "structure of movement." The *form* of the poem that proceeds from that conceptual frame, however, is what the poet must discover, and each discovery means certain presiding strategies come to carry forward a poem's individual unfolding—the form of its movement so to speak, rather than its incipient structure or idea. In "Waving Adieu, Adieu, Adieu," the form of the poem's movement is carried along principally by its halting interplay of syntax and rhythm, one step forward two steps back, to the end. In Dickinson's "My life closed twice before its close," it is a steadily iambic and essentially epigrammatic neatness cast in dire counterpoint to the calyx of the Inexpressible hidden in the poem's center. In Kunitz's "The Image-Maker," it is the tracking of consciousness moving from biblical allusion, though abruptly shifting association, into the conundrum of bespeaking on the page what one averts one's ears from hearing. In Donne's "A Valediction: Forbidding Mourning," it is the metaphysical conceit that denies or delays in its circular eternity the prospect of the lovers' permanent departure from each other, at least in purely bodily terms. However orchestrated, the formal movement of each of these poems presumes a commonplace too often forgotten: that the aesthetic object, in this case the poem, doesn't have a form, it is a form.[4] Yet, underneath the formal elaborations of these poems composing their individually movements or arcs from beginning to end is the fundamentally dramatic condition of announcing the end of something, and not merely observing it.

Though it pivots toward abstraction, Donne's metaphysical conceit embodies a very physical gesture; the intellectual ingenuity of the poet's trope ultimately serves a dramatic purpose. However much embedded the drama may be in Stevens's, Dickinson's and Kunitz's poems the same essentially dramatic circumstance impresses itself on the poet's artistry. By contrast, John Keats in his devastatingly moving valediction, "This Living Hand," refuses the saving ingenuity of the metaphysical conceit entirely in favor of a wholly gestural solution:

> This living hand, now warm and capable
> Of earnest grasping, would, if it were cold
> And in the icy silence of the tomb,
> So haunt thy days and chill thy dreaming nights
> That thou would wish thy own heart dry of blood,
> So in my veins red life might stream again,
> And thou be conscience-calm'd—see, here it is—
> I hold it towards you.

Where Donne's "Valediction" turns on a metaphor of extension and return to the self-transcending center of an idealized relationship, Keats's poem, written almost literally in the face of death, turns on a decisive threat that would transpose the condition of the dead and the living. Keats's poem was written in a blank space beside "The Cap and Bells" and may address his lover Fanny Brawne, or his critics, or even more evocatively his readers. It doesn't matter. In Donne's poem, the relationship between the lovers, perfected despite distance, here collapses into another kind of perfection, one entirely mortal. Death itself has become the center from which the poet's living hand paradoxically reaches. There is something profoundly cinematic in the way the hand seems literally to reach out at the poem's end and gesture to the reader as to the beloved, as if the reader were eternally placed in the position of the beloved—the reader is. Appearing strategically and suddenly out of the long complex sentence that precedes it, Keats's blunt declaration enacts the same kind of fictive movement as the images that blazon across his Grecian urn, at once forever in motion and forever still in that motion. It reminds one of the way Dante's entire *Divine Comedy* turns on a fiction of actual descent and then ascent from the lowest depths to the highest heavens. Here, the eternal gesture, however, is utterly mortal rather than the perpetual motion-in-stillness of a divine revelation achieved through epic passage. This motion-in-stillness is the same condition embodied in Stevens's "Waving Adieu, Adieu, Adieu." By establishing death as an imminent condition that has become vividly present, "This Living Hand" becomes very nearly a postmortem farewell in which the lover virtually takes hold of the beloved, and the reader. Hello, I must be going, and you must be going, too.

Gesture, whether elaborated into conceit or captured with dramatic immediacy lies, then, at the heart of the poetry of farewell. But gesture can also be effectively withheld as a way of communicating the loss of parting, parting that ultimately and inevitably prefigures the final loss of death. Martha Rhodes's poem, "Mother, Quiet" powerfully *withholds* gesture to communicate the emotional trauma of farewell to the departed in a life-before-death made actual through the devastating self-erosion of Alzheimer's disease:

I, too, felt chased, hunted—
So when I passed your room
I didn't stop for you,
Didn't lift and carry you
Out of that "pit"
I heard you call it,
That square, that bed.

Up into my arms I did not bring you,
There, there, I did not say, Mother,
Quiet, I've got you now.

Unlike Keats's "This Living Hand," or any of the other poems we've looked at, Rhodes's poem accomplishes its formal and emotional satisfaction through actions that do not take place, and therein resides the drama. In "Mother, Quiet" there is no hand to be held out either from the brink of death or as a final gesture to the dying, for it is as if there is nothing left of the other's self to "get" since that self appears already to be gone. The poem's movement, its verbal cinema, thus takes on the vivid outline of a negative—non-action or the refusal of action portrayed paradoxically as the poem's relentless gesture, its unyielding and indelible dramatic act. What "Mother, Quiet" does is orchestrate a sequence of negations—things not done, not said, not ventured on behalf of the beloved—as a means to deny the denial of death or, in this scene, to deny the reality of a death-in-life.

There is a similar relentlessness of scene and tone governing the drama of

Louise Glück's "Here Are My Black Clothes." Not surprisingly both Rhodes's poem and Glück's resonate as strongly in their approach to farewell as Keats's "This Living Hand." All step back from any luxuriance to confront the circumstance of ending with unsparing accuracy:

> I think now it is better to love no one
> than to love you. Here are my black clothes,
> the tired nightgowns and robes fraying
> in many places. Why should they hang useless
> as though I were going naked?

Though the speaker of this poem may not be going naked, the language certainly is, with its unremitting gesture of a gift emblematic of the death of intimacy. Certainly, there is much to be said in tracing the brilliance of Glück's free verse lines, the underscoring line ends of "fraying" and "useless," "thin" and "I," just for example, as though in her orchestration of the free verse line she had accomplished what the still traditionally formal Yeats sought in "walking naked" after he dropped his coat of "old mythologies." Glück drops the formalities. One of the principal ways she imbues directness with dramatic amplitude, thereby saving the poem from devolving into mere reportage, is her use of the metonym "black clothes." Like the proverbial emperor's crown, the female lover's black clothes, a gift that will keep on giving of a love forever gone, embodies the death of love with brutal honesty. And, of course, black clothes are the garments of mourning as much as they are the raiment of sexual allure. Significantly, like apophasis, metonymy, from the Greek *metonymia* meaning "a change of name," is a trope derived from rhetoric that addresses the truth of a thing through re-direction. In Glück's "Here Are My Black Clothes," the name has been changed from the betrayal of love, or its slow dissolution to an array of eponymous black clothes, to indict the guilty. She will not, as the poem tells us at its close, "need them in her new life."

All of the poems I've touched upon thus far exemplify perhaps only a small range of "the poetry of departures," as Philip Larkin calls it. Given the nature of the subject, lesser poems in the genre could easily be prone to the maudlin and sentimental. Stevens, Dickinson, Kunitz, Donne, Keats, Rhodes, and Glück all avoid these pitfalls through their idiosyncratic (though equally uncompromising) engagement with the signature human experience of having to depart. It is the formal success of each of these poems that saves them from bombast or from simply missing the genuine pathos inherent in the moment. In his poem "The Poetry of Departures," Larkin offers a wry critique of the genre, and especially the tendency to romanticize the regret attendant upon the experience of farewell:

> Sometimes you hear, fifth-hand,
> As epitaph:
> *He chucked up everything*
> *And just cleared off.*
> And always the voice will sound
> Certain you approve
> This audacious, purifying
> Elemental move.

If any poem were the antithesis of "A Valediction: Forbidding Mourning" it is Larkin's skeptical meditation that would do nothing if not expose Donne's deliberate conceit-making as an effort to wrench both legs of the metaphysical compass from their center; though in fact nothing misses Larkin's skeptical eye—neither the audacious act of departing forever, nor the staying home. For Larkin, whether one stays or goes, nothing is perfect; though it may seem to be, it is only "reprehensibly" so, as the poem tells us at the end. On the other hand, "that vase" that remains after all the people have gone at the end of "Home is So Sad," another of Larkin's poems of departure, may offer a somewhat ameliorating alternative, though that alternative really is no more comforting.

What makes Larkin's poem "The Poetry of Departures" so perfectly achieved in the singular Larkin idiom is the brilliant marriage of lineation and rhyme. It is hard to say whether Larkin's characteristic tone of deeply engaged skepticism accomplishes the poem's brilliance, or whether the formal brilliance accomplishes the tonal flare, the two are so mutually sustaining. This is a poem that not only is a form but has a form—structurally it is constructed out of eight-line stanzas rhyming *abcbadcd*. Elsewhere in the poem, Larkin playfully modulates the tight form by broadly varying his line lengths and therefore the stresses in the lines from two ("As epitaph") to five ("Yes, and stagger the nut-strewn roads"). The rhyme scheme, in fact, is mostly off-rhymes, "hand / sound" in the first stanza, "think / junk," "crowd / did," "fo'c'sle / artificial," "life / if" in those that follow. Such moves intensify the poem's tone of plainspoken directness, its edgy, blunt, more-than-a-little cranky dissatisfaction with all of it. At the same time, while the *abc* rhymes generally torque and bend away from perfection, the *d* rhymes rhyme perfectly at the end of each of the poem's four stanzas. As a structure, the poem is sturdy, though the enjambments, at times strong between lines, and strong also between stanzas two and three, and three and four, create a feeling of acceleration through the middle that, were one to track them closely, underscores and inscribes Larkin's unique brand of staid petulance. Choosing to depart is for Larkin, as for all of us, an "elemental move" however evocatively "nut-strewn" the roads may be, but this poem is nothing if not wary of the artificiality of how that elemental fact of existence gets treated. Or perhaps it is mistreated, in the creation of an aesthetic object with—as Larkin's brilliantly vicious oxymoron declares—its reprehensible perfection.

Of course, at the very moment Larkin calls art into question for its artificiality before such an elemental *fait accompli* as the simple fact that everything is going even in the best circumstances, relatively soon after its arrival—or as Frost called it in "West-Running Brook" "the stream of everything that runs away" that 'seriously, sadly runs away"—he knows that it is only through the "art" in "artificiality" that that anything *can* come to move "against the stream," to borrow from Frost's poem again. And Larkin, like Frost, would probably say that it is this counter-motion against entropy, or more floridly "the universal cataract of death," as Frost's spokesman Fred effuses, that is most of what it means to be human: "most us," what we most "see ourselves in."

Agha Shahid Ali's intricately orchestrated poem, "Lenox Hill," exemplifies most movingly the human refusal of the universal flow of things toward inevitable ends, and the poet makes it so by choosing one of the most artificial and difficult of structural choices—it is a canzone. "Canzone" comes from the Latin *cantio,* meaning "song," and in fact the term comprises a variety of verse forms, mostly from the Italian. That said, the most frequent canzone assumes a complex stanza structure that involves iterations of five repeating words according to the following pattern: stanza 1—*abaacaaddaee*; stanza 2—*eaee-*

beeccedd; stanza 3—*deddaddbbdcc*; stanza 4—*cdcceccaacbb*; stanza 5—*bcbbdb-beebaa*—with an envoi of five lines running *abcde*. In this way it resembles a manifold form, self-enwound, folding inward even as it evolves forward like a kind of origami. In short, if one thought sestinas were formally involved, canzones are still more complicated and difficult to achieve with artistry consummate enough to trump the artificiality of the form. Canzones, one might say, are sestinas on steroids, and it takes formal mastery to write a convincing one. Here is the opening of "Lenox Hill":

The Hun so loved the cry, one falling elephant's,
he wished to hear it again. At dawn, my mother
heard, in her hospital-dream of elephants,
sirens wail through Manhattan like elephants
forced off Pir Panjal's rock cliffs in Kashmir:
the soldiers, so ruled, had rushed the elephant,
The greatest of all footprints is the elephant's,
said the Buddha. But not lifted from the universe,
those prints vanished forever into the universe,
though nomads still break news of those elephants
as if it were just yesterday the air spread the dye
("War's annals will fade into night / Ere their story die"),

the punishing khaki whereby the world sees us die
out, mourning you, O massacred elephants!
Months later, in Amherst, she dreamt . . .

"Lenox Hill" begins with parallel recollections, the first a wantonly brutal historical act of monumental proportions, a murderous transgression against nature if ever there was one; the second a dream in which the cries of the murdered elephants driven off the cliff in Mirahgula turn to sirens in Manhattan heard in delirium by the poet's dying mother. This initial move, the juxtaposition of historical reality and personal dream that shifts immediately into something closer to an interfusion of the two, is what comes to be elaborated through the canzone form, its structure of reiterative association as the repeating words are shuffled and re-shuffled through the five stanzas and the envoi. Each of the words, "elephant," "mother" "Kashmir," "universe," and "die," feature most prominently in the stanza in which the canzone structure determines that a given word take the fore. Fore-grounded in the first stanza, the elephants with their unjust deaths, presage the mother's unjust death— not out of human callousness, but out of the callousness of the universe itself that drives all things toward death, from mothers to nations—Kashmir, the geographical and cultural link that binds together all of the poem's losses including, eventually, the son who is the poet lamenting all, but especially the loss of his mother:

> If only I could gather you in my arms, Mother,
> I'd save you—now my daughter—from God. The universe
> opens its ledger. I write: How helpless was God's mother!
> Each page is turned to enter grief's accounts. Mother,
> I see a hand. *Tell me it's not God's.* Let it die.
> I see it. It's filling with diamonds. Please let it die.
> *Are you somewhere alive, somewhere alive, Mother?*
> Do you hear what I once held back: in one elephant's
> cry, by his mother's bones, the cries of those elephants
>
> that stunned the abyss? Ivory blots out the elephants.
> I enter this: *The Belovéd leaves one behind to die.*
> For compared to my grief for you, what are those of Kashmir,
> and what (I close the ledger) are griefs of the universe
> when I remember you—beyond all accounting—O my mother?

Though the canzone is structured to sing, in Agha Shahid Ali's hands it also roams, and roams vastly through its structure from dream to dream, from time to time, from space to space—from historical Kashmiri legend, to New York City, to Amherst, to a festival from childhood memory where the poet is crowned Krishna, to the bed of disease, to Paradise, back to Amherst, back to Kashmir, to a jungle far from Kashmir where an elephant (surrogate for the poet himself) touches with his trunk the bones of his mother, across religious traditions, to the outer reaches of the universe and beyond, venturing the compassionate (or is it the terrible) presence of God's own hand—and refusing it, the son preferring "beyond all accounting" his mother's impossible presence and the purity of his grief. If the poem of farewell tends to bind into a knot by some trope or strategy—syntax, association, conceit, metonymy, drama—the dialectic of arrival and departure, "Lenox Hill" unwinds that knot in the very knottiness of its formal accomplishment orchestrated fearlessly, brilliantly, and devastatingly.

"To conclude," Walt Whitman muses in *his* poem of farewell, "So Long," "I announce what comes after me," and onward un-spools the catalogue that would triumph over death. Poems of farewell, though, are not always so optimistic, and even when they are, as in Donne's "Valediction," it takes great ingenuity to arrive at some redressing vision of renewal. "Hello, I must be going." And so must you. The stream of everything, seriously, sadly, runs away. So long, but life isn't really so very long, is it—nor is it so long before we see each other again (or will we?) since forever is so long, too. All poems of farewell presuppose that everything to which we say goodbye is a part of the same precariously shared reality, the same passing world. In this sense they are, perhaps, meta-poems, emblematic of an aesthetic as well as a physical and metaphysical condition. Inevitably, as Keats brilliantly envisioned in what is surely an emblematic poem of farewell, "Ode to a Nightingale," we are like the poet "thrown back" to our "sole selves," having to bid adieu, adieu, adieu to "the immortal bird" whose song fades beyond the nearest distant valley. Though because the bird is immortal, it never actually leaves, or leaves only in relation to the one being departed from. It is as though the listener, not the bird, were in accelerated motion away from that which transcends death, since time with space is motion and the listener is still in space and time. The nightingale, as the poem witnesses, embodies the unconditional. And so, Keats's great ode reverses the polarities of parting, for now it is the one who must stay who must say goodbye, and thereby must remain for now bereft and mortal. For the listener, the nightingale's fading song constitutes an intimately distancing double departure, but it is not so far as that farther distance where all things must be going, even the one who stays, and where in true apophatic fashion we will neither wake nor sleep. Or to say this in a way that "speaks to" rather than "speaks off" is to call on the words of the great spiritual: *we'll* have flown away.

WRITING FOR THE DEAD

TWITTERING WORLD

Whether to the advantage or disadvantage of the present, it was an insight of great prescience when at the onset of the world's second brutal upheaval in two decades T. S. Eliot composed the phrase "this twittering world" for "Burnt Norton," the first of his *Four Quartets*. Grave as his own present was, one has to presume that for Eliot a world characterized by empty chatter (though prompted by the needful exchanges of birdcalls) defined a condition much more encompassing than his own historical moment. For a poet of such considered metaphysical and artistic awareness, a world characterized by twitters expressed one sadly ubiquitous condition of an existential and ultimately spiritual mise-en-scène. The twittering world was not ultimately reality at all, but rather an ever-pervading source of distraction from the really Real. The goal, even in the midst of its bewilderingly inescapable static, was to sufficiently quiet the interference and to begin to listen for something coming out of the silence, which for Eliot was ideally "the silence of God." That silence filled the emptiness with genuine presence and pregnancy—as if all the noise of the world might designate a kind of sonic contour. Coming to its edge, one desires to hear something essential and transformative rather than contributing to the cacophony.

Of course, in this twenty-first-century technological nexus of global interfusion lifted by consuming swells of social media, one can only imagine the ex-patriate Eliot "gobsmacked" by just how pervasively this twittering world has become more virtually, literally, and (one might say) allegorically circumscribed by the tenor and vehicle of his original metaphor. Virtual because our world has become shaped and reformed by virtual reality. Literal because in a world of infinitely iterative and interactive "Zoom rooms," the virtual appears to have collapsed entirely into the literal. Allegorical because the cultural topography only so briefly sketched codifies an existential investment in the superficiality and expendability of discourse. Perhaps it is not overstating to say we have become a world defined by the screen rather than the window, which lends Eliot's "twittering world" a visual as well as auditory aspect.

In any case, in such a literally and virtually twittering world we run the risk continually of losing the necessarily distancing perspective of the allegorical. The twittering world enwraps and enraptures, nets us in every respect. The potential danger for poets especially is a loss of depth perception that can deform sensibility and derisively impact one's apprehension and practice of the art. It is hard to get the news from poetry, Eliot's staunchest detractor William Carlos Williams wrote, and harder still for the poet to get the real news to begin with when so much in the twittering world militates against discernment. Or to take a further cue from Gary Snyder, to reserve space in one's often distracting life for the "real work" of poetry the poet needs to find ways of securing purchase on what is "really real" within and beyond the ever-passing and often engulfing stream of our collective and barely reflective consciousness.

One should never presume one has a universal grasp of a condition or circumstance, however one might hope to "penetrate the mirror," to borrow Michael Donaghy's phrase.[1] Though such considerations about the attitudes of poets toward their work put me in mind of an encounter at the front desk of the writing department where I work. I had come off the elevator after class and saw a klatch of graduate students talking, one of whom said—I couldn't help but overhear—that all of the poets she most admired had Twitter accounts. The work of this student was among the strongest in recent years, and while my own work's placement in her personal hierarchy apparently had been cast aside (I did not, alas, maintain a Twitter account), I found myself less piqued than struck by what so confident a declaration meant for this promising poet's frame of aesthetic regard. I can think of many worthy and remarkable poets who do not, and many who never will, have Twitter (now X) accounts. Many of these presently grace the planet with their work, but a greater number from a plethora of times and traditions have departed the twittering world entirely, and the preeminent among them quite some time ago. What does it mean for poets to have their range of admiration so narrowed during a time when access to longstanding models of practice, and various traditions, has never been so enrichingly immediate? What does the trend toward contemporaneity and the potential impermeability of poetic communities—if these are trends—mean for poetic practice? How might it impact the role of the audience, or rather the poet's conception of audience, in the making of a poem?

I raise these questions fully aware of Robert Graves's chastening caveat: "Never use the word 'audience.' The very idea of a public, unless the poet is writing for money, is wrong. Poets don't have an 'audience.' They're talking to a single person all the time."[2] Fair enough. I extend all of my esteem to the purity of Graves's intention, as well as his farsighted and sardonic assessment of poets who prize popularity over artistry, among whom Rupi Kauer and Amanda Gorman, as well as bevies of Insta-poets, are the latest iterations. On the other hand, the aforementioned student—a poet not uncharacteristic of her generation—appears almost singularly conscious of her prospective audience in the most literal incarnation. Given the zeitgeist in the proverbial poetry business, it is not surprising. A recent colloquium at one prominent venue for poets addressed the issue head on in its title: "How to Grow Your Audience." Earlier in the twenty-first century, another venue offered a podcast entitled "The Poetry of the Future," in which three poets discussed among other things the idea of audience. Each highlighted an issue that seems relevant to my inquiry here. One stated what appears to be obvious: relative to other arts, poets constitute their own "little world" and, mostly, constitute the audience for their art. Another underscored the incontestable fact that the very idea of poetry in America has expanded to include formerly marginalized poets whose race, sex, and class, as well as gender identification, affirm a more expansive practice in the art. The final panelist stated more narrowly and simply that poets had to see to it themselves to make themselves heard. Along such lines, in 2006, the redoubtable though more recently mercurial Poetry Foundation pursued a wide-ranging study on the audience for poetry, scientifically conceived, and replete with all kinds of data configured into all manner of detailed tables and charts. The findings now appear dated.

One might delve back further to trace the roots of the poetic audience during the rise of modernity: Pope's courtly trepidation and rise, Wordsworth's assumption of a universal audience grounded in nature, Byron's transgressive popularity, Shelley's desire for popularity and his failure to obtain it, Tennyson's social and cultural good fortune, Yeats's alchemy of the ideal and the actual, as well as the modernist penchant for "difficulty" and rarified reception.[3] All things considered, this brief foray appears to give the lie, alas, to Graves's spare though lofty ideal. Perhaps nothing can be more emphatically the case in view of the predominance of today's social media world than that poets must "make ourselves heard" or potentially have their work gain relevance only to the very few, though hopefully fit, to carry forward Milton's and Pound's shared dictum; or to have it ignored, or drift sadly away like the fictional Hugh Selwyn Mauberley into ever-widening Sargassos of ephemera. Still, at the other extreme, when one astute contemporary poet and Net-surfer took consideration of the question "Who do I write for?" the individual responded to his own momentous rhetoric with the acutest perspicacity and laudable honesty: "Fuck if I know."

COURT AND FLAME

Yet, the circumstance of not knowing who one is writing for is not necessarily the same as having no idea of an audience. It does, however, suggest an open-endedness that naturally gravitates to a further conception of audience, one which appears consonant with a certain leveling and broadening of reach. My student would take this condition as the given habitat of poetry in the currently twittering, X-enamored world, and for the foreseeable future. This open-ended, seemingly egalitarian reach finds resonance with Bonnie Costello's considerations in *The Plural of Us,* her study of the "first-person plural" pronoun in poetry, where she claims optimistically that "poetry's first-person plural suggests how the genre may propose or project open, reflective, splayed community, and create a sense of potential in 'us' that is not predicated on consensus, domination, or the mentality of the crowd."[4] In view, however, of the tactics and attitudes of contemporary cancel culture and its penchant for scorched-earth censorship of a perceived offender—the individual's failure to align with prevailing ideological codes—any unreflective embrace of such a "splay community" appears, well, imagined. Imagining an idealized reality isn't hard to do, as John Lennon continues to remind us, but in the case of the intersection of audience and social media one feels, inevitably, the need for caution. De Tocqueville's "tyranny of the majority" comes to mind, for example. In view of, or in spite of, all such legitimate apprehensions, there is validity in seeing the audience in "Twitter world" as wholly prefabricated. One enters the portal, and one then has to wonder how subtly the twittering audience influences one's work, and perhaps deforms its deeper and purer intentions, assuming of course the poet cares. A poet should care, of course, really must care, for the poet's idea of an audience inevitably shapes the work, and does so to the point of reflecting one's idea of the world, indeed one's idea of what is real in any ultimate sense.

While there are numerous poets who conformed their lives and work to the prospects of "the court," whether literally or merely the court of Po-Biz, there have been poets whose idea of audience had little to do with any social currency. As such, the technical currency of their work exhibited an uncommonly pure commitment to their art. "This is my letter to the World / that never wrote to me," Emily Dickinson wrote, at once giving voice to her sense of painful separateness and to her allegiance to "Nature" whose "Message," she hopes will be judged tenderly by Hands she cannot see. The paradox of Dickinson's poem rests in an essential ambiguity: the poet has no audience, though there is also an audience *in potentia* in the Hands that will judge. Or are those Hands, like Nature itself, suggestive of a greater presiding Audience? Such an Audience, while open-ended, insinuates a valuation more comprehensive and necessary than her time. Likewise, Dickinson's estimation of fame was similarly complex. Fame has, as one of her poems tells us, both a sting and a wing and, as another witnesses, fame is fickle. Obviously, fame requires audience, though in what I take to be her greatest poem on the subject, this most equally imperative and reticent of poets, cuts to the quick:

> Fame is the one that does not stay –
> Its occupant must die
> Or out of sight of estimate
> Ascend incessantly –
> Or be that most insolvent thing
> A Lightning in the Germ –
> Electrical the embryo
> But we demand the Flame

That the poem begins with the recognition of fame's inconstancy quickly elides to the still more essential recognition of the ephemerality of life. What transports the poem into the essential brilliance of its insight is its claim that the real ascent is "out of sight of estimate." And that is the same original and originating vitality that both creates the embryo and, still more imperatively for the poet, urges one to demand the pure source of being, the Flame, itself. At this junction, the one has become many, *we*. It is Costello's "plural singular" made incarnate, but its community, the poem's self's audience, its "we," allies itself with a reality more real than death and life, and certainly more real than any social and aesthetic estimate. In the end, Dickinson's poem is nothing other than a petition to the Flame, the Flame that is all at once ascent and embryo and inexhaustible end.

One could hardly imagine Emily Dickinson, by herself at the Hermitage in Amherst, delicately crimping her fascicles digitally for promotion on the internet, though it might make for a witty skit. Nor could one imagine the same of Gerard Manley Hopkins, whose true and almost only audience was God:

> Not, I'll not, carrion comfort, Despair, not feast on thee;
> Not untwist – slack they may be – these last strands of man
> In me or, most weary, cry *I can no more*. I can;
> Can something, hope, wish day come, not choose not to be.

Here, surely, we find Graves's single listener to whom the poet speaks, though because Hopkins is a devout Catholic his single listener is simultaneously and paradoxically a community of Three Persons in one God. "Oh, which one, is it each one" the poet exclaims near the poem's end, such that the heaven-handling hero, Christ, and the agonized soul become nearly con/fused with the poem's wrenching *Imitatio Christi*. If Hopkins's guiding idea of audience is simply God, then it is this rarified Audience that most forges the work and opens it to the world—a world that is decidedly not twittering.

Like Hopkins, Lorine Niedecker wrote poems against the backdrop of social limitation, in her case a life of mostly menial labor and a remove from any substantive center of literary community. Though Niedecker's idea of audience is not Hopkins's God, nor Dickinson's Flame burning within and before the essence of things, it is shaped by her economic circumstances as well as her relative solitude in Fort Atkinson, Wisconsin. One might say, it was her correspondence with Cid Corman and a few others that enabled and enhanced the natural "condensery" of her poetry, as she characterized it in her poem "Poet's Work." There, she describes writing as an arbitrary trade engaged in at the behest of her grandfather, one that offers no "lay-off" though, one suspects, it does offer a dedicated engagement with the world. The final section of her poem "Tradition" addresses the heart of that matter:

> Time to garden
>> before I
>> die—
> to meet
>> my compost maker
>> the caretaker
> of the cemetery

Neither the natural goings of the earth at which there appears to be no germinating flame, nor genuinely caring caretaker, nor any reverence for the shaping literary influences, appear here to inform Niedecker's grasp of the real. What does inform Niedecker's work is, I believe, the idea that the audience must be as linguistically parsimonious as she is. Unlike Dickinson or Hopkins, I can imagine Niedecker time-phased belatedly into the twittering, X-ing world of the twenty-first century, though I cannot imagine the work adapted one wit in its mode of being to all of the biz or buzz. What I do see in admittedly contrasting terms is a poet whose work is guided by an impassible limit, one that forces all questions of audience to face something that Dickinson might have called the ultimate silence beyond all estimate.

What characterizes my three exemplars in relief of a Poetry World that appears driven to estimations of immediate regard and praise is the notable absence of any "enigmatic impulse that does not allow one to settle down in the achieved, the finished."[5] Czeslaw Milosz takes this impulse as part and parcel of a poet's "quest for reality." His view prompts a further guiding principle: that "the whole fabric of causes and effects, whether we call it nature or history, points toward . . . another, hidden reality, impenetrable, though exerting a powerful attraction that is the central driving force of all art and science."[6] When one establishes the making of poems against the backdrop of this impenetrable but powerfully attractive reality, it seems one must alter one's assumptions about who the ultimate audience is for one's work—however one may wish or actively seek to have one's work gain purchase on the time one inhabits, or the literary history one aspires to make. In view of this, a third principle inevitably announces itself: "those who are alive receive a mandate from those who are silent forever."[7] Who do I write for, asks the poet considering all such issues? I write for the dead.

SECRET WAY OR MIDDLE PATH

The proposition that a poet should desire principally to write for an audience that by definition is not present in any material or temporal way, and can only be tangibly unresponsive to the poet's efforts, appears on its face to be an absurdity. There is something more readily assuring in James Wright's conception of the ideal audience as the intelligent reader of good-will. It is less potentially delusional as well. Wright's definition appears to cover all of the bases, and saves the poet from the sin of overreaching. In his Preface to *Lyrical Ballads,* Wordsworth claimed that "in spite of difference to soil and climate . . . the Poet binds together by passion and knowledge the vast empire of human society, as it is spread over the whole earth, and over all time." Despite the visionary aspirations of Wordsworth's conception of audience, his claim assumes "enormous potential for solipsism and self-aggrandizement."[8] Wordsworth's application of the word "empire" in his formulation infuses an incontestably political significance to his claim. From the vantage of our own historical moment Wordsworth's idea of an audience feels blinkered, dangerous, or ironic in its metaphorical employment of "empire." Likewise, Whitman's manifest notion that great poets need great audiences is irretrievably linked to an arguably univocally democratic vista that would define the destiny of an entire continent. Both conceptions give ample credence to the notion that the poet's idea of audience dovetails with the poet's cultural role and shapes the poetry."[9] It's little wonder that, fearful of this vital fusion and the poet's twice remove from the ideal World of Forms, Plato argued the poet should be banished from his quintessential Republic.

Of course, across many different "soils and climates," throughout diverse and numerous cultural histories, the poet has assumed a central and essential role. In ancient Ireland, the *file* ranked as living repositories of the identifying cultural narrative. They were also something like lawyers and ambassadors as well as poets and pre-internet memory-storage Clouds rolled into one. Professional in a manner that might rankle Robert Graves, their audience was their society, its chieftains "their court," and their poetry assumed its status in that context. At the same time, the world of the *file* existed on the geographical fringe of Europe, and so was more traditionally "native," despite its being subject to progressive and expanding waves of Western empire-building—though the implications of empire building and cultural take-over surely are not limited to Europe and the West. Track the human path out of Africa (now evidently in multiple iterations from Neanderthal to Sapiens) and one encounters a vista of adaptive and evolutive success married to and marred by competitive and local devastation. Collectively, we owe our very existence to the dead and, for that matter, not just the dead of our particular species.

The proclivity of humanity to overwhelm the competition genetically, tribally, and globally does not diminish the incalculable natural and cultural losses over the turbulent course of our "stewardship" of the planet. Nor does it provide a gainsay for oppression and genocide at this new dawn of what we have come to call the Anthropocene. If anything, at this stage of our collective life, the idea that something might direct the poet's soul in Joyce's phrase "to that region where dwell the vast hosts of the dead" should not seem so out of step with the virtual impress of the dead-as-audience on the poet's work. Aoghan O'Rathaille's deathbed poem, written to a friend at the time when Alexander Pope's work presided at court, stands as a less theoretical illustration of what I am trying to get at. Faced with the collapse of his language and his society, the last Irish bard bequeaths his last song:

> Out of the vast ruins of ancients from whom I come
> A mighty crashing rush ploughs through my every thought
> As from pure springs born from the crests of Kerry's Reeks,
> Shed with the Blackwater's into the tidal flats of Youghal.

I'm done now, picked clean, now that death's cliff is on me.
Since the dragon warriors of Laune, and Leane, and Lee
Have been cast down, I go to my beloved heroes in the grave,
The good lords who've fostered me from before Christ's death.[10]

The rage that laces across and through O'Rathaille's poem invests it with a tragic and brutal resignation, and it surely resonates with poems by modern and contemporary poets who faced, and face, the trauma of cultural loss. "How many homelands / play cards in the air / as the refugee passes through the mystery," Nelly Sachs asks. It is as if her poem "Flight and Metamorphosis" positioned itself at the exact fulcrum of consciousness where the dead reveal their witness to the living:

Who dies
here last
will carry the grain of sun
between his lips
will thundercrack the night
in death-throe rot.

Sachs continues her probing later in the poem in a manner that explicitly links death's ultimacy with the beginning of life:

Child
child
in the whirlwind of departure
pushing your toes' white flaming foam
against the burning ring of the horizon
seeking death's secret way out.

What startles in the juxtaposition of these sections is the poet's interplay of meditation and address—how permeable the poem's voice has become to the presence and petitioning of the death world. Here, the apparent foreclosure of being opens to a further secret, a transcendent horizon. At this most perplexing juncture, the dead listen first and the living overhear.

The question of whether one can and should write for the dead in the way a poet might presume to compose poems for any audience begs the question of the long-heralded death of poetry itself. O'Rathaille's social and linguistic world collapsed with colonization and penal laws intending to uproot a culture. Sachs survived the Holocaust, as did Celan, only to contend with the necrotized undersurface of language tooled to the machinations of genocide. One commentator on modernism saw the movement as a "right wing coup."[11] Pound's championing of Mussolini notwithstanding (nor Yeats's songs for the Blue Shirts, nor Eliot's condemnation of "strange gods" other than his own), the oft-lamented tribulations of poetry after modernism inevitably constellate around the problem of difficulty. In *After the Death of Poetry*, Vernon Shetley observes "today poetry itself, any poetry, has become difficult for even the more ambitious reader as the habits of thought and communication inculcated by contemporary life have grown to be increasingly at variance with those demanded for the reading of poetry."[12] Conversely, Robert von Hallberg in *American Poetry and Culture, 1945–1980* makes the point that, in fact, poetry found a steadier audience in the middle years of the twentieth century. For him, "the tone of the center" informed much of the canonical work of the time.[13] Since then, the by now deflated salvos between the Language Poets and the New Formalists exemplified the problem Shetley initially outlined. Neither movement achieved "the tone of the center" envisioned by von Hallberg. If anything, Language Poetry embraced difficulty through its alignment with academic theory and its investment in the doctrine that words refer only to words, and not "to a reality that must be described as faithfully as possible."[14] The New Formalists advocated what they saw as a return to poetry's lost populism, or at least to reclaim some of the territory annexed by prose. Neither school succeeded in resuscitating the corpse of poetry, assuming there was a corpse to begin with, in view of von Hallberg's counter-assessment of poetry's midcentury audience.

Were one to articulate a middle path between these contending aesthetic and ideological ramparts, one way forward that might redress the purported death of poetry is to increase the comprehensive engagement of the readership by making the difficulty of poetry worthwhile beyond the truncated expectations of our entertainment culture. The separation between poet and audience is not the fault of poets, contended W. Y. Tindall in 1945, but of society.[15] Some forty years later in his Norton Lectures, Milosz contended that "citizens in a modern state, no longer mere dwellers in their village and district, know how to read and write but are unprepared to receive nourishment of a higher intellectual order. They are sustained artificially on a lower level by television, films, and illustrated magazines."[16] What would the Nobel laureate say about electronic gaming, Twitter, X, Tik Tok, and Instagram? Both Tindall's and Milosz's uncomfortable assessments hold true today, despite the reinvigoration of poetry's popularity and the visible rise of communities of poetry and audiences for poetry over the first two decades of the twenty-first century. Poetry now by most accounts has risen from the dead, and among other virtues is acutely responsive to the social pressures of the time. Still, in a present that continues to exhibit "a dizzying proliferation of styles and almost no commonality of taste,"[17] where does the poet turn for perspective, and under what auspices? After the death of the death of poetry, how can writing for the dead nourish the depth, aspiration, and breadth of poets seeking to align their art with "a higher intellectual order?"

A CHOICE, A CALLING

Perhaps the central lament in Milosz's *The Witness of Poetry* is his admission that the poetry of the twentieth century "testifies to serious disturbances in the perception of the world."[18] He formulates his steely judgment as someone who experienced dislocation at an early age during the First World War, lived proximate to the Holocaust, and found himself caught between the dual horrors of Nazism and Stalinism. He lived in exile for very nearly the remainder of his life. It is no surprise that he believed the word "disintegration" best characterized what he experienced firsthand during his lifetime. In our twenty-first century, technologically speaking, while the world is more integrated than ever before, we still have no shortage of seismic political and social disturbances, though thankfully (as yet) no world wars. We also experience subtler and indeed more insidious forms of disintegration in the way in which we live, some arising from those very technological advances that appear to link us as never before with an inescapable connectivity.

The most emphatic of these disintegrations pertains to our experience of community and identity, which has evolved along with the rise and cultural leavening of nominalist and positivist modes of thinking, as well as with the marginalization of viable models of the transcendent. The source of this marginalization of the transcendent might be called fundamentalist materialism. The contrary fundamentalisms of religion have no answer to the former, for the very reason that they have themselves grown out of the cultural breakage barring them from the rich veins of theological and philosophical thought out of which Western science itself evolved. Despite all of our connectivity, we have become fragmented into what Bonnie Costello calls "speech communities." In turn, she contends, poetic rhetoric "is shaped by the kind of speech communities it imagines and imitates."[19] Given these conditions, the influence of so-called "identity poetics" finds the source of its vitality in such inherently nominalist social dynamics. In view of such reflections, for Costello, the poet's relation to any reader is always potential not actual;[20] though the inverse—the narrowly settled presumption of a poet's actual audience—is just what might be becoming additionally atomizing for poetry.

Needless to say, this is thorny subject matter. My aim is not to promulgate traditionally established modes of "poetic rhetoric" over and against traditionally marginalized "speech communities" and their histories, but only to underscore the fact that no history or artful practice is entirely cut off from any other, nor should be. The gathered throngs condemning what they identify as appropriation need to consider the fact that great art comes, if it comes, out of complex and extensive conversations across differences. There is also the biological fact that we are all inextricably linked with each other and to the universe that has given rise, for a time, to us. As our collective history as nations and as a species confronts the potential fracturing of any shared common identity embraced across legitimate and often painfully realized differences, it appears urgently necessary for poets, like everyone, to eschew the predominant "remorseless binary thinking" in favor of seeking actively to discover "commonalities across groups."[21] Or, as George Oppen wrote with an acuity that precedes the present circumstance:

Obsessed, bewildered

By the shipwreck
Of the singular

We have chosen the meaning
Of being numerous.

Despite the well-established harbingers of institutional nominalism broadcast everywhere like a barely heard background score, the singular understood as something distinct unto itself will always be shipwrecked. The poet's job is to explore in the solitary work of making poems the verity of our being numerous. That is the nature of the human family to which poetry should offer its unequivocal assent.

On the subject of being numerous the dead are nonpareil, for the dead are nothing if not ever-more numerous, the most encompassing, inclusive, and diverse of audiences of which each of us will one day be a part. "But now go the bells, and we are ready," John Crowe Ransom's great elegy begins. Do not ask for whom they toll for beyond John Whiteside's daughter, for "gold-engrove" as Hopkins's grieving Margaret knows "un-leaves" for all of us. For poets to seek to bring their work consciously into earshot of the dead is to place the highest and most responsible demand on the art. For the dead, in the pregnancy of their silence, require of the poet the most conscientious and comprehensive practice.

Natasha Trethewey is one contemporary poet whose body of work is self-consciously and concertedly pitched to an audience of the dead—the slaves and ex-slaves whose lives have been submerged under oppressive tides of history, Bellocq's photographer's model the Storyville prostitute Ophelia, Trethewey's grandmother who was a long-time domestic servant, and especially Trethewey's mother who was murdered by her stepfather. In *Native Guard,* the poet's Pulitzer prize-winning sequence that interleaves her mother's murder with the history of the Corps Afrique who guarded white soldiers during the Civil War, Trethewey sonorously and ruefully gives voice to the dead. The "ghost of history," as she observes in one poem, lies down beside her, "rolls over," and "pins her with a heavy arm." Yet it is precisely the apparently unbearable heaviness of history, a history of the forgotten and neglected dead, that so enables the poet to lift the voice of witness.

Consistent with this voice of witness, Trethewey's crown of sonnets, "Native Guard," begins with her anonymous ex-slave giving testament to memory and the truth that often eludes the history books:

Truth be told, I do not want to forget
anything of my former life: the landscape's
song of bondage . . .

In sinuous detail, Trethewey's sequence embodies simultaneously the self-circling form of eternity and the self-consumingly recurrent pattern of trauma. "Death makes equals of us all," the poem's memoirist reflects ironically, "a fair master." Nonetheless, "there are things that must be accounted for." The urgency of that double vision—what needs to be brought to the visible and auditory life of witness among the living, the truth that widens beyond apprehension with the dead—obtains an almost palpable currency, pervasive and incontestable, somehow hovering between absence and presence:

Beneath battlefields, green again,
the dead molder—a scaffolding of bone
we tread upon, forgetting. Truth be told.

Truth, of course, is the crux of the matter, the truth of the irreducible witness of the dead that commands the poet to speak on their behalf. It infuses "Native Guard" with a kind of spiritual necessity, a sense of urgency further underscored by a pattern of allusion—to crucifixion, to the Parish of Ascension—resonant with the poet's own age, her "Jesus year," alluded to in another of the book's poems. It is a sacred duty, as these lines from "Invocation, 1926" in *Congregation* insist:

Bless the laborers
whose faces we do not see—like the girl
my grandmother was, walking the rails home:

bless us that we remember.

Still more insistently, what Trethewey's commitment to her art embodies is nothing less than the consciousness of a vocation. I mean "vocation" (from *vocare,* "to call") in the most religious understanding of that term. She is "bound fast" to the work and vision of the poems. The crowded audience of the silenced dead has lifted her work far above the twittering of merely professional notice, though obviously her work has garnered considerable regard:

Three weeks gone, my mother came to me

In a dream, her body whole again but for
one perfect wound, the singular articulation

of all of them: a hole, center of her forehead,
the size of a wafer—light pouring from it.

How then could I not answer her life
with mine, she who saved me with hers?

And how could I not—bathed in the light
of her wound—find my calling there?

What could be more movingly revealing than this vision of Trethewey's murdered mother as a figure reminiscent of the imitation of Christ, who now sanctifies the poet's calling? It is as if the dead were not only the truest audience for the poet's work, but its sanctifying and redemptive muse.

LAND OF SHADOWS

In one of his prose reflections in *Unattainable Earth,* Czeslaw Milosz reminisces about his early life as he pores over a photograph of a village he knew on the border of Poland and Lithuania. "All the people who once walked there are dead by now," he considers. Everything about them, "era, fashions, mores," has lost its original meaning in "that densely populated land of shadows" that allows us "to imagine that the dead of all places and centuries, made equal" and communicating "with each other."[22] Milosz's observation goes to the heart of the matter, and dovetails perfectly with the historical, moral, and imaginative terrain of Trethewey's poems. The felt presence of the dead as audience discovered within one poet's particularly fraught personal and social history, as in Milosz's more broadly metaphysical musings, enlarges the frame by magnitudes. Both take to task implicitly if not explicitly his lament that "the language of literature in the twentieth century has been steeped in unbelief."[23] Through her own deliberative aesthetic lens, Trethewey greatly widens and clarifies the aperture of her poetry. Milosz also understands memory to be crucial to the poet's art. Though we have only momentary access to what he calls "interior memory," the fact that such memory exists beyond the limits of consciousness undermines "the belief that, with death" a person perishes forever. Such a view, he affirms, "implies that the oversensitive tape" of memory "is recorded for nobody," though likewise such an essentially absurd fate appears "improbable" to Milosz. Here again, the dead-as-audience petitions the poet to pursue the most urgent and aesthetically demanding of encounters.

Nowhere is the directive to write for the dead more vitally explicit than in elegy. Nonetheless, like all poems, elegies assume a double audience. On the one hand, there is what Costello calls "the exquisite, transparent meeting of two solitudes"; on the other, the "expansive congregation" of the literary audience in its more social aspect.[24] This latter, she avers, while not wholly separable from the former, involves implied or overt metaphors of performance and theatricality. In short, poems to one degree or another presume a "dramatization of consciousness." In its socially turned aspect, poems bring about "a hypothetical, untethered community, as it forms a network known to itself and unlinked to identity."[25] Costello's assertions strike me as incontestable, but what elegy calls for is a farther congregational horizon. Elegies are, according to Eavan Boland and Mark Strand, essentially public poems of lament, and therefore comprise "a crucial formal link with the history of public poetry," so much so that "elegy is one of the forms that can be said to be co-authored by its community."[26] Peter Sacks underscores this same idea when he envisions elegy having "roots in a dense matrix of rites and ceremonies."[27] The very word "elegy" comes from the double pipe "aulos" that would accompany its recitation, the elegy following as it does "the basic passage through grief or darkness to consolation and renewal" even "immortality."[28] Jahan Ramazani, in turn, reframes the modern elegy around the idea that "for many of us religious rituals are no longer adequate to the complexities of mourning for the dead."[29] As such, he sees the modern elegy as a poem that must "hold up the acid suspicions of our own moment," while remaining a poem that nonetheless affirms "though God may have died . . . the dead have turned to gods for many modern poets."[30]

Indeed, whether viewed as poems to gods in Ramazani's sense, or more traditional memorials of loss and mourning, elegies are inevitably tethered to the dead who, because they are the inextricable subject, confer upon the poet crucially urgent and culturally vital demands for poetic performance. Though examples of elegy are legion and tonally varied from Milton's "Lycidas" to Whitman's "When Lilacs Last in the Dooryard Bloom'd," from Jonson's lyrical "On My First Son" and Donne's meditational "Elegies," from Dickinson's projective self-elegies to Lowell's monumental "The Quaker Graveyard in Nantucket," elegies constitute the purest and most needful linkage between poet and audience, particularly given their incontestable cultural origins in ritual and ceremony.

Geoffrey Hill's "In Memory of Jane Fraser" illustrates the point. The first two quatrains in both the elegance of their formalism and the vivid immediacy of their imagery establish the wintry precedence of impending death. In a brilliant inversion of expectation, it is the dying woman who broods over death "like a strong bird of prey," rather than succumb submissively to the inevitable. In this, Jane Fraser's relationship to her own death obtains exemplary stature:

Damp curtains glued against the pane
Sealed time away. Her body froze
As if to freeze us all, and chain
Creation to a stunned repose.

All deaths are embodied in the death of this one person, as is indeed the death of creation itself through the chain of being that binds all to all. When in the final quatrain the poet projects the hopeful stirring of spring alders, the promise of new life redounds to the poet, the reader, and to all creation and not only to the newly dead. Though the poem is addressed to Jane Fraser ("she kept the siege"), as a link in creation's chain, she is at once singularity and plurality. All things are connected by that chain, and to the repose of death. Her individual mortality binds her to all perishing things. She cannot help but be, therefore, especially in death, a part of the audience. She listens, as it were, like Seamus Heaney in his elegiac sonnet sequence for his mother, "Clearances," "beyond silence listened for."

Something similar if less hopeful obtains in William Matthews's elegy for Charles Mingus, the extraordinary jazz pianist who died of ALS. In "Mingus in Shadow," the poet evocating the extremity of the disease has no qualms describing "how much / stark work it took to fend death off and fail." In keeping with the metaphorical work of elegies, beached whales in Baja signal nature's own investment in the poet's lament:

> Great nature grieved
> for him, the story means, but it was great
>
> nature that skewed his cells and siphoned
> his force and melted his fat like tallow
> and beached him in a wheelchair under
> a sombrero.

What Matthews's poem ultimately celebrates, however, is "human nature, tiny nature." It is tiny human nature that seeks to redress the stark diminishment of death with art, which is itself a paean to Mingus's own artistry. The poet aims for the precision of the photographer. Even where no alder cones stir the poet's imagination toward renewal—the lamented "is all the light there is"—it is the dead's presence in their very absence that paradoxically completes the congregation of poem and subject, living and dead.

In keeping with the demands of elegy, Hill's "In Memory of Jane Fraser" and Matthews's "Mingus in Shadow" assume the heavy responsibility, the gravity in every sense, of writing for the dead. The urgent demands of elegy become ever more intimately fashioned when the poem makes direct address to the one who has died—or, in the case of Betty Adcock's "No Encore," everyone who has ever died or ever will die. "I'm just an assistant in the Vanishing Act," Adcock's wry but devasting poem begins, "my spangled wand points out the disappeared." The wand, of course, is nothing other than the poem itself, "a poor thing made of words" that "lacks / the illusive power to light the darkling year." What Adcock's poem owns is the impotence of elegy to redress the pervasive inevitability of death, and not only for the dead but for all: "the thing that's gone is never coming back." At the same time, her theatrical conceit is nothing less than transfiguring, for her extended metaphor is exactly the vehicle which gives the poem its power and its unflinching truthfulness. In the face of death and the dead, seen now as an infinite multitude, the poet's work appears almost ridiculous, however precise the illusion:

> For now, I wear a costume and dance obliquely.
> The applause you hear is not for me, its rabid sound
> like angry rain—as one by one the known forms cease to be:
> childhood, the farm, the river, forested ground;
> the tiger and the condor, the whale, the honeybee;
> the village, the book, the lantern. Then you. Then me.

Adcock's infinitely expanding catalogue of loss evolves from the constituencies of selfhood and personal circumstance to the natural and global, and finally envelops everything. The "everything" brought to "nowhere" is no summary collective, but rather "you" and "me," for each death involves the loss of each singular being and every relationship, the one and the many brought to cessation throughout time. "No Encore," in effect, might be called a self-consuming elegy, or as the poem declares "not prophecy, not elegy, but fact." Were one to ferret out the slightest hope inside Adcock's limit condition for the genre, it might be the extent of "the known forms" to which she alludes. What might live beyond those forms the poem cannot tell us since, to borrow from Wallace Stevens, whatever might transcend the known metaphysically extends beyond "the palm at the end of the mind." It therefore eludes representation, for the limit of death precludes it. What the poet has is language, metaphor—"the known forms."

As elegy, Adcock's "No Encore" is ruthlessly encompassing, though in another poem to her late husband in the same volume, *Rough Fugue,* she reflects "all words contain a tree, / language a rooted branching / on the paths of breath."[31] One might even say, in this vein, that the tree seeded in every word has its roots in the complex branching of life itself, its weave of connection despite, or perhaps through, the seemingly impassible fact of death. Stanley Kunitz's proto-ecopoem of the Anthropocene, "The Wellfleet Whale," explores this theme with astonishing perspicacity and formal complexity, and with a meditative grandeur that blends the apparently conflicting aspirations of the elegy and the ode:

You have your language too,
     an eerie medley of clicks
        and hoots and trills,
location-notes and love calls,
     whistles and grunts. Occasionally,
        it's like furniture being smashed,
or the creaking of a mossy door,
     sounds that all melt into a liquid
        song with endless variations,
as if to compensate
     for the vast loneliness of the sea.
        Sometimes a disembodied voice
breaks in as if from distant reefs,
     and it's as much as one can bear
        to listen to its long mournful cry,
a sorrow without name, both more
     and less than human. It drags
        across the ear like a record
running down.

In Kunitz's take on whale life—an evocative presence in both Matthews's and Adcock's poems as well—language is the bearer of a common, creaturely relation between the nonhuman and the human, both of whom are united in their existence within a "vast loneliness" that is not only the literal sea but the still vaster ocean of being. The whale's "long mournful cry" is "a sorrow without a name," which is the same nameless sorrow to which the poet is called to give a name.

The poet's naming of reality is always provisional precisely because what is ultimate eludes representation in language, and what is ultimate in Kunitz's poem is nothing less than a profound metaphysical loneliness running through the whole of creation. Yet, there is vision in the provisional, and it is Kunitz's description of the whale: at first an "advent" before which the human world waits in anticipation, then an occasion of "awe and wonder," and then the brutalized magnet for voyeurism and souvenirs that nonetheless embodies the witness's own "terror and recognition." Finally, in the poem's last section, the poet restores and celebrates the whale's monumental, parallel existence to human evolution and human history by remythologizing the dying and abused creature—only to once again demythologize it by delivering the creature, the fellow creature, ironically, to "the mercy of time" in which the whale becomes "like us, / disgraced and mortal." In Kunitz's "The Wellfleet Whale," the directive to write for the dead at once transcends the frangible condition of the human species and binds it existentially to an encompassing myth of creaturely relation, such that in our very mortality and disgrace we find commonweal—not with the human alone but with the nonhuman as well, and by extension with the planet and the cosmos. It is a vision to which the final lines of Nâzim Hikmet's great poem "On Living" likewise bear incontestable witness:

This earth will grow cold,
a star among stars
          and one of the smallest,
a gilded mote on blue velvet—
          I mean *this*, our great earth.
This earth will grow cold one day,
not like a block of ice
or a dead cloud even
but like an empty walnut it will roll along
          in pitch-black space . . .
You must grieve for this right now
—you have to feel this sorrow now—
for the world must be loved this much
          if you're going to say "I lived."

In elegy, writing for the dead constitutes the poem's subject, its incontrovertible occasion. Beyond that obvious fact, what I am interested in is the idea of the dead as audience, indeed the dead as the unavoidable and most necessary audience. Again, Bonnie Costello sees audience and therefore the poem as "part of the constellation of relations that projects the idea of community."[32] In turn, the reach of community and therefore of audience can be extensive, though it is also always "horizontal." Audience merely widens in this view; it doesn't deepen or elevate. For all of the idealism attendant upon linking the idea of audience to a potentially evolving community with all of its social implications, such a view elides what Milosz called "the vertical orientation."[33] For Milosz, the vertical orientation, when the human being "turned its eyes toward Heaven, has gradually been replaced . . . during the last few centuries by a horizontal longing." In turn, "the always spatial human imagination has replaced 'above' with 'ahead.'" The very idea of transcendence itself has undergone, in essence, a reversal where transcendence envisioned "ahead" has displaced any transcendence directed "above." We should take that old idea of "above" figuratively or analogically rather than literally, for this vertical metaphor stands for the redeeming amplitude beyond our finite conceptions and apprehensions of immediate reality, beyond all of the known forms of our knowing. We see, now, through a glass darkly, which is nothing other than a figure for the figural, an analogue for the analogical, a metaphor the infinite tenor of which inevitably exceeds the vehicle's finitude.

If one takes the reanimated orientation of vertical transcendence seriously, then the poet's aspiration to write for the dead invites a dual summons. On the one hand, one must write in such a way as to aim for the fullest embodiment of truth. On the other, one must take beauty as an axiomatic goal. From a somewhat different vantage, poetry must "trouble the culture" and "resist incorporation into the degraded language of public discourse or into the idioms of the dominant intellectual skepticisms,[34] as Vernon Shetley reflected more than a quarter-century ago. It does not take an extended survey of the current state of the art, however, to see that the aforementioned resistance to the degraded language of public discourse has not been widely achieved. On the contrary, if Milosz is right in claiming that "the fate of poetry depends on whether such a work as Schiller's and Beethoven's "'Ode to Joy' is possible," then if anything poetry's fate appears bound to the erosion, not of standards, but of the very idea of standards. The "universals" a critical lover of poetry like Bonnie Costello believes can be affirmed through "horizontal" community— *e pluribus unum*—can only find their secure grounding in a re-affirmed instantiation of "vertical" regard.

This kind of "vertical" orientation to writing for the dead that I am advocating finds expression in Mark Doty's "Atlantis," written as an elegiac sequence for a friend who died of AIDS. In the title section the poet confesses "I thought your illness a kind of solvent / dissolving the future a little at a time." Doty's initial orientation is strictly "ahead," and this horizontal perspective positions the mind toward death's inevitability. Though as the speaker considers two herons "plying their town trades of study and desire," not unlike the poet and his friend, the poem repositions itself movingly and dramatically in view of the "above":

> I've seen
> two white emissaries unfold
>
> like heaven's linen, untouched,
> enormous, a fluid exhalation. . . .
>
> but there in the air was white tulip,
>
> marvel, triumph of all flowering, the soul
> lifted up, if we could still believe
>
> in the soul, after so much diminishment . . .

At this moment, Doty's diction signals a tonal change that pivots expressly to the spiritual. The herons now are "emissaries" and unfold before the poet "like heaven's linen," a marvel simultaneously of hyperbole and understatement, and a stunning figure. The vision of the lifted soul, conditional as it is, nonetheless embodies the longing for transcendence all the more powerfully because of Doty's admission of worldly diminishment. The same figural dynamic orchestrates Alan Shapiro's marvelous proto-elegy, "On Hearing of a Friend's Illness," where a shaping vase on a potter's wheel embodies the interfusing, indeed the esemplastic communion of above and below, inside and outside:

> Unevenly on the wheel
> in a weather front
> of thumb and finger,
> nail, palm, and knuckle,

the damp clay spins
and rises to so soft so
continuous a shaping
that the shape is both
emerging up from
inside out and down
from outside in
unravelling like rough
petals from the empty
center of the absent
flowers that it now
for a moment holds and is.

The vase in Shapiro's poem is at once figuratively merely a vase, the coming into being of a single momentary life, and by implication the created space of the universe entire, not to mention the shape of the poem itself. As both "Atlantis" and "On Hearing of a Friend's Illness" prove, to write for the dead or the soon-to-be dead with the conviction that one is really writing for the dead, however figuratively one may conceive the idea, is surely a profoundly compelling way to keep faith with the art of poetry, and with life, even when the direct appeal to religious belief is not doctrinally present.

"All reality is hierarchical," Milosz declares, "simply because human need and the dangers threatening people are arranged on a scale."[35] It could be bread or the word, he reflects, or it could be death itself or slavery. What is incontestable in our own time is the preponderant desire to level seemingly all hierarchies. Nevertheless, Milosz continues, "anyone who accepts the existence of such a scale behaves differently than someone who denies it."[36] Certainly one *writes* differently. In any case, "the poetic act changes with the amount of background reality embraced by the poet's consciousness."[37] Death is always at the very least in the background, and eventually death always comes to the foreground. Witness again Doty's "Atlantis," and Shapiro's "On a Friend's Illness." One might just as easily invoke "The Shield of Achilles," where the figural shield in Auden's handling of Homer's myth is emblematic not of a single death—hard enough—but of the historical atrocities of the mid-twentieth century:

A plain without a feature, bare and brown,
    No blade of grass, no sign of neighborhood,
Nothing to eat and nowhere to sit down,
    Yet, congregated on that blankness, stood
    An unintelligible multitude,
A million eyes, a million boots, in line,
Without expression, waiting for a sign.

Auden's "unintelligible multitude" might just as easily be witnessed by any-one with access to a twenty-first-century news outlet. Foregrounded in "The Shield of Achilles" is the prospect of man-made mass death, a reality that had become all too real in Auden's time, and our own. To take a cue from Kunitz's "The Wellfleet Whale," one might consider the rapidly increasing depletion of species from the planet. In any case, Auden's allusion to the "darkling plain" of Matthew Arnold's prescient "Dover Beach" only bolsters and intensifies the later poet's confrontation with unthinkable loss.

The theme of loss and its magnitudes is not unfamiliar to our own more recent history and our present. At the cusp of the twenty-first century and drawing from an array of cultural traditions—Urdu, Hindu, Arabic, European, American—the late Agha Shahid Ali carries over the genuine form of the Per-sian "ghazal" into the English of his poetry and in doing so adds to the sum of the language's poetic practice. One of his great subjects, in addition to love, is loss—of friends, family, and culture. Ali is not unaware of colonial history, and his imaginative riposte is a combination of rueful protest and formal redress:

The only language of loss left in the world is Arabic—
These words were said to me in a language not Arabic.

Ancestors, you've left me a plot in the family graveyard—
Why must I look, in your eyes, for prayers in Arabic?

The ghazal demands a formal "teasing into disunity,"[38] to use Ali's own words, insofar as each couplet from the matla (the first) onward carries no narra-tive import and appears discontinuous. At the same time, the compositional demands of the *radif* (refrain word or phrase) and the *quaafiya* (pattern of rhyme) insist on the form's associative connectivity. In the case of this particular ghazal, the form enables Ali to affiliate a variety of diverse literary and cultural allusions from Arabic history, fable, the Bible and Melville, the Palestinian poet Mahmoud Darwish, Kashmiri art and textiles, the Koran, Lorca, and Yehuda Amichai, among other references. It is, in fact, the very "disunity" of the form that occasions the poem's more encompassing unity.

Building upon hundreds of years of tradition in Urdu, Persian, and Arabic, the ghazal in Ali's hands becomes a formal medium for difference orchestrated into unity—unity-in-difference—in which the tensive adjoining of various allusions resolves into a vitally animated equilibrium. Obviously, the dead, Ali's ancestors invoked early in the poem, stand as audience. He addresses them and writes for them. Yet, the other dead of the poem, the fabled Majnoon and real-life Lorca among others, likewise stand with the living as hearers of Ali's words. As the ghazal nears its end, crucially it is the forgotten dead that loom most powerfully, those Palestinian men, women, and children, massacred in Palestine's Deir Yassein by Zionist paramilitary in 1948:

> Where there were homes in Deir Yassein, you'll see dense forests—
> That village was razed. There's no sign of Arabic.
>
> I too, O Amichai, saw the dresses of beautiful women
> And everything else, just as you, in Death, Hebrew, and Arabic.
>
> They ask me to tell them what *Shahid* means—
> Listen: it means "The Beloved" in Persian, "Witness" in Arabic.

The juxtaposition of Deir Yassin and the Israeli poet Yehuda Amichai intends to assert Ali's claims to witness for the dead as well as to affirm his artistic claims with reference to a great poet he himself respects. Brilliantly, the *maqta,* the final couplet in which the poet's name must appear, inscribes Ali's double take on reality. The name Shahid's meaning in Urdu, "The Beloved," suggests the traditional figure for God's union with the soul. The second meaning, "witness" in Arabic, links the poet to history, and to the dead of history. Ali's doubletake on his own name amounts to a double vision that links the poet simultaneously to eternity and time. In effect, Agha Shahid Ali's "Ghazal" commands a redoubling of Milosz's impress upon the poet of one's background reality: the first, the "Beloved," one might say is vertically inflected; the second, "Witness," is horizontally pitched. Transcendence and immanence find their tensive communion in the poet's invocation of his own name.

Though more discursive in form than Ali's ghazal, Auden's "In Praise of Limestone" likewise elaborates an extended metaphor that renders the poem's "background reality" obsessively present as the ultimate purpose of existence. In the poem's final movement, Auden's conceptual framework of anagogical completion asserts itself powerfully into the imaginative foreground of the poem:

> In so far as we have to look forward
> To death as a fact, no doubt we are right: But if
> Sins can be forgiven, if bodies rise from the dead,
> These modifications of matter into
> Innocent athletes and gesticulating fountains,
> Made solely for pleasure, make a further point:
> The blessed will not care what angle they are regarded from,
> Having nothing to hide. Dear, I know nothing of
> Either, but when I try to imagine a faultless love
> Or the life to come, what I hear is the murmur
> Of underground streams, what I see is a limestone landscape.

In essence, Auden's "In Praise of Limestone" highlights three crucial and defining attributes of writing for the dead. The first is the eschatological nature of the endeavor. The inevitable incursion of "last things" upon the mind of the poet is nothing more than the refusal to turn from what has been self-evident to human consciousness from the earliest cave paintings and tombs. What Milosz again identifies as the traditional longing of poets "to visualize an order located somewhere else" reveals itself in "The Shield of Achilles" to be resident in the poem's extended metaphor-as-eschatology.[39] All great poems are formally as well as subjectively owing to the incontestable truth of "death as a fact." The poet's aesthetic striving to achieve the utmost—to place the poem in conversation with the greatest that has been done by those who have gone before—is therefore nothing less than an effort of practical eschatology.

The second attribute is analogical. The underground murmur of Auden's limestone landscape announces metaphor as the figural medium by which the poet negotiates and creatively enacts language's relation to the inhabited world. The "unity-in-difference" Costello envisions as constitutive of "the plurality of us" is rendered credible antecedently through the fact of the world's existence as an infinite network of analogical relations. The ultimate analogy is the analogy of being. The final attribute of the poet's directive to write for the dead, to posit the dead as the ideal audience, is its foundation in the anagogical—the "faultless love" of "the life to come" in which the dead become "blessed," naked before and within the all-in-all, the surpassing fullness of a faultless love. The paradox at this uttermost juncture is that the ultimate end is nothing other than never-ending. Auden's "faultless love," because he is Christian, resides in the unity of relation among Three Persons—a plurality of One. Such is the symbol of the Trinity. It is for this reason that in Auden's metaphorical grasp of ultimate reality, a limestone landscape—a landscape animated and defined by fault upon fault, its creational fallenness—is simultaneously the embodiment of the One Love that is, paradoxically, perfectly faultless.

AFTER THE KNOWN FORMS

"Will the Marlin speak human when we meet Him face to face?" That was the question posed by a friend's mother on her deathbed, her final words or thereabouts. From the standpoint of someone disinclined to discern anything more than the pure product of a final delirium in the question, the stirring vision of a magnificent fish metonymically standing in for God would have little currency, though that is precisely the stuff of poetry, its spiritually freighted magic. And the woman's final interrogation, undoubtedly framed and configured around her life as a daughter of Cuban exiles with an abiding connection to the sea, is poetry. It is also as bracing a theological question as any posed by a professional theologian, for it goes straight to the anagogical heart of the matter. What is the relationship between this life and what comes next after all the "known forms" fall away? That potent phrase, the denial of death, amplifies resonantly, though its compelling subversion of all our imaginative, cultural, social, and historical strategies of avoiding the prospect of the absence of any encore tends to devolve to the glibness of a slogan before the actual face querying one last time into the final conundrum—"the center of the absent" as Alan Shapiro's poem has it.

To write with this eschatological vantage in mind, with the dead in mind, enforces a much more serious conception of audience than what the twittering, X-haunted world requires of the poet. Such a view does not preclude a poet's presence in the fluid and mercurial world of social media; it does, however, suggest the caveat that major poets are never merely reactive to their time, but exhibit the kind of unity of purpose that underwrites an effort to achieve or embrace some comprehensive vision of reality. Finally, it might even place a demand on the poet to revise one's understanding of being in the world and, as such, what one seeks to accomplish with the task of making poems. Charles Wright's "Homage to Paul Cezanne" announces this re-envisagement in no uncertain terms, painterly terms—the impossible possibility of the dead present comprehensively in their absence: "The dead are a cadmium blue. / We spread them with palette knives in broad blocks and planes. / We layer them stroke by stroke / In steps and ascending mass, in verticals raised from the earth. . . . The dead understand all this, and keep in touch . . . The dead are a cadmium blue, and they understand." To accept the dead as audience in every sense is to accept that one has to make art in such a way as to live up to the wholly transfigured mindfulness of the dead, what Auden called their blessedness, what Wright calls their understanding—impossible as that may appear to be from any finite vantage. But that is what the poem, like any great work of art, ultimately calls for.

LAMENTATION, POETRY, AND THE DOUBLE LIFE

SOJOURNER

For I am a passing guest,
  a sojourner like all my fathers. . . .
    —PSALM 39:12

Noon, the low winter sun at its pinnacle, beginning of the afternoon visiting hour in Lutheran Medical intensive care, where my father continues to hold onto his life after nearly a week of capitulations and rallies, his cardiac function enumerated like a stock-ticker on the machine beside his bed, and I'm still forty blocks away in front of Sally's Luncheonette waiting for my wife and mother-in-law to drive me to his bedside. I wait five more minutes, run inside to call car service, only to find them waiting outside in the car, frantic themselves. They'd hit traffic on the Belt Parkway coming into Brooklyn from Floral Park, where my mother-in-law moved shortly before my wife's father passed away two years ago. From my old childhood apartment, it's about ten minutes to the hospital if you catch the lights along Third, or cut down to Ridge Boulevard to avoid the buses and double-parkers, the new construction on the 67th Street Bridge. I don't bother to cancel the car service, but hop in, still feeling anxious as we pull out and head down the avenue. I try to calm myself, remembering that yesterday the guard let me stay at my father's bedside a little after the end of visiting hour.

I've been at the hospital morning, afternoon, and evening, every day since I discovered my father slumped in the foyer chair when I returned six days earlier from teaching at the January residency of the Warren Wilson MFA Program for Writers, my plane delayed because of fog caused by the unseasonable warmth. Reaching the four-room walk-up where my father lived with my mother for fifty years, I noticed the door was unlocked and slightly ajar so I could see the jamb, the dulled gold paint-streaked tin-gray from where it used to stick, year after year, during my childhood. It still does. The apartment was dark, though to the right of the door I could see my father's friend, John Gogarty, look up at me from his niche just inside the kitchen.

"What's wrong?"

"He can't walk. He's been like this all day."

"Why didn't you call BRAVO?"

Never one to confuse Bay Ridge Ambulance Volunteer Organization with what was then a cable television Arts and Culture channel, my father always bristled at the code name, as though merely mentioning it might bring its necessity. Feet splayed, his head bent as though he were looking at something lost inside himself, traces of his red hair still noticeable in his Navy issue crew-cut, my father mustered his predictable two cents, his voice slackened but still resonant with his years as a longshoreman on the Brooklyn docks after the War, as a bartender weekends at the American Legion.

"What's the matter? How are you feeling?"

"Lousy. Lousy."

John broke in:

"I found him in the bathroom when I came up with the coffee this morning around ten. All day he wouldn't let me call. 'Wait till Danny gets home,' he said. So, what could I do? It's all day, Danny, all day."

He was always stubborn about going to the doctor, about the best route out of the city (always over the Narrows Bridge, never through Manhattan), about not leaving Brooklyn since my mother died, though my brother and I both urged him to move near one of us. He wanted to make sure he was still in control, even if it meant killing himself, the way he'd always push each medical crisis almost beyond remedy—his collapse from a bleeding ulcer when I was ten, this past summer's heart failure at the family reunion. Then there's the more extensive history: sixty years of hard drinking and smoking despite his heart attack the year after I was born; despite the scalding as a child by his own alcoholic father; despite being abandoned at fifteen when his mother died, his father on the streets or in the drunk-tank on Riker's; despite the series of car crashes driving home late nights from the bars; despite years of high blood pressure and emphysema, pills and patches, and in the last two years, blood-thinners that should never be mixed with alcohol. All day he was sitting in this chair, waiting for me, or death, whoever came first.

There was blood all over the bathroom floor, John told me, and told me how he carried him out to the foyer, and still again how they'd been waiting for me all day to come home. John was a stocky bull of a man, seven years older than my father, who had been smoking cigars and drinking since before Ireland became a republic in 1948. He was a good friend over the years, and an indispensable friend to my father since my mother died two years before.

"We thought you'd be earlier, Danny. It's been all day."

John's Northern brogue was undaunted by over fifty years in Brooklyn.

"The plane was delayed. Fog. I'm calling BRAVO," I said urgently.

"Danny, wait . . ." my father interjected, raising his head a little. It was as if my father's stubborn mantra were a painter's chisel scraping the veneer off my professorial calm, and I found myself screaming at him.

"What are you nuts? This is serious. You can't walk."

I paused for a second at the phone, mastering the dutiful son inside myself who would wait and wait, anything his father wanted, then dialed the number of the neighborhood emergency corps to rush my father to Lutheran.

"Wait, wait, wait, wait, wait."

My father's voice sounded weak and disgusted, though more almost at my refusal to acquiesce to his demand than at his own condition. John had his hand on my father's shoulder and was talking to him soothingly.

"Danny's here now, Jerry, he knows what to do. They'll take care of you. You'll be alright now."

By the time I'm hung up the phone, I could hear my father muttering disgustedly to himself: "Oh, shit, oh shit," his speech slurred as though he'd been drinking, and shaking his head while his chest heaved to force air into his wasted lungs. I rubbed his shoulders—"They'll be here soon. We'll hear the siren."

When they wheeled him out that night, his blood pressure was ninety over fifty, though he stayed awake in the ambulance, and in the emergency room all that evening until he told me to go home and get some sleep. Now it is nearly noon and I'm walking as fast as I can without running, down the hallway toward intensive care, Christine and her mother having dropped me off before they looked for a parking space. My father is in the far-right room where they moved him two days ago from another part of the wing, but the first door nearest his room is locked. So I go through the next entry, walking intently across the room, only to find there is no bed where my father's bed was. It feels as if a trap door has just opened in my stomach. I look at the on-duty nurse who recognizes me, then points toward the door I was unable to enter: "There he goes." There is my father in his bed, still hooked up to his machines, the image of a marionette stretched out after its performance, my father—bed and all—wheeled along by nurses. "We're taking him to critical care," one of the nurses says. "It's an improvement." Now I feel like the marionette, moved by invisible strings, dumbfounded at how my father has managed all his life to cheat death while courting it like a mistress.

I follow them to my father's new room, not far but on the other side of the building, but they stop me from coming in. "We have to set him up. Dr. Zak is waiting for you over there." I had met Dr. Zak earlier in the week—no nonsense but, I decided, not without compassion. I knew he was doing the best for my father under difficult circumstances. Still recuperating from last summer's open-heart surgery, my father continued to smoke and drink despite taking coumadin, a blood thinner that could become lethal when mixed with alcohol. That was my father's problem now, coumadin toxicity leading to internal bleeding, complicated by his emphysema and the additional stress on his heart. It was Dr. Zak who had called last night to tell me that my father was in respiratory distress, that he could die unless they inserted the breathing tube again, though my father had adamantly refused another intubation. "No way," he managed, despite the trauma to his vocal cords. Dr. Zak wanted my permission to overrule the Do-Not-Intubate order. "Oh God," I'd blurted into the phone, "What do I do?" not of the doctor, nor of myself, but of some other—an Absence hard as a fist. My whole body shook. Then I heeded my father's wish.

As I approach Dr. Zak he begins to explain, "We've finally managed to stop the bleeding in the digestive track. Also, he seems now to be able to breathe on the mask. So, we have moved him to critical care, a little better than where he was. Not out of the woods, but better."

As Dr. Zak speaks, I glance toward my father's new room and notice more nurses going in, some now standing in the doorway. Now, one nurse walks over to where we are talking.

"Dr. Zak, I need you in Room 323."

"Is it important?"

Dr. Zak signals with raised index finger that he'll be back shortly. Again, a wry smile moves across my mouth as I think about phoning my brother who returned two days earlier to his family in Northampton. "He's amazing," I'm going to tell him with honest pride, despite my father's self-destructiveness, "an amazing man." And my brother will agree. As if on cue, Christine and her mother are walking down the hall.

"We had trouble finding you," my wife says.

"I bet. He's improved so they moved him here from intensive care. Can you believe it? He's amazing."

Now Dr. Li walks over to us, whom I met six days ago in the ER. Very competent, I felt at the time, very much in charge but warm, capable of dealing with frightened patients and anxious loved-ones. And I remembered my mother, hospitalized here with pneumonia, in delirium, convinced that people were trying to kidnap her: "Danny, you have to get me out of here. They're going to take me to China." "Very embarrassing," my father remarked stoically, "those Chinese doctors can be very good." And my mother afterwards saying, "I must have been hallucinating." That was three years ago, nine months before my mother died. I hadn't seen Dr. Li for the past few days, and now here she is at my side.

"Has anybody told you?"

"No."

"Your father has expired."

BREATH, SONG

For all our days pass away under thy wrath,
　our years come to an end like a sigh. . . .
　　　　　　　　and we fly away.
　—PSALM 90:9-11

Expire, from the Latin *exspirere* means "to breathe out," the word itself born out of the body, yet rooted there as we are rooted in earth, though in everyday use it seems to have lost its connection to bodily life: *expired,* like a subscription to the newspaper, or a car insurance policy, or that witty, but macabre grave that a friend told me about with its memorial sprouting a parking meter, its red flag reading EXPIRED. So, too, Dr. Li's "Your father has expired," the mechanized clock of the body run out, no coins to pay, no switch to turn to resume the time, another fifteen minutes, another hour, year, another lifetime. Twenty-five years ago, my mother's mother, Nora, "expired." "Expired" is the word, it seems, doctors are taught to use at such moments, accurate but somehow sterilized of its origin in metaphor, at the same time almost too metaphorically precise—"to breathe out for the last time." To turn to the Psalms, however, is to enter a world in which the final breathing out of death enjoins another, more encompassing expiration—*ruach,* meaning "spirit, breath, wind," the creative power of YHWH. It is YHWH's breath that moves across the face of the waters in Genesis, bringing life, that can reanimate a desert of dry bones in Ecclesiastes, and it is that same *ruach* in Psalm 103 that makes "springs gush forth in the valleys," makes "the moon to mark the seasons," makes "wine to gladden the heart of man, oil to make his face shine." It is the breath, the wind, of God's creative imagination, the historical source of Romantic poetry's "correspondent breeze," the theism of ancient Israel morphing into the panentheism of Wordsworth through the complex undercurrents of Western culture. In this same Psalm, however, YHWH also reveals his decreative side:

As for man, his days are like grass;
  he flourishes like a flower of the field;
  for the wind passes over it and it is gone.

Of all the many moods of the Psalms—grateful, ecstatic, laudatory, bitter, fiercely angry—it is this tone of lamentation I find supremely moving and compelling. Perhaps that is because by so vividly voicing his lament in the face of death the psalmist has managed to bespeak something universal in this most personal experience of loss. At the same time, most biblical scholars believe that in the Psalms we come closest to the thinking of ordinary Israelites: their exuberance at the harvest, joy at the deliverance from enemies, their pleasure in daily and seasonal rituals, but also their longing for redress, their exasperation and cries at feeling abandoned by their God, their sufferings and ultimately their need to reconcile death. In those passages when the human consciousness of death becomes dramatized, the Psalms achieve a transcendence that surpasses both the critical gaze of scholarly historical method and the untempered approbation of the true believer. Like all great poetry of suffering and mutability, the psalms of lament ground themselves in the physical details of life in order to express and ultimately dramatize an encounter with life's insignificance before forces that exceed our control—"the passivities of diminishment" Teilhard de Chardin called them—but I'm thinking still more of Job, of Oedipus, of Lear standing before Cordelia's lifeless body: "She's dead as earth," he cries out, and then he dies, too, in the moment dreaming vainly that she still breathes.

Nevertheless, over the course of the twentieth century, amidst spectacles of brutality barely imaginable even to the psalmist, we have managed to efface the consciousness of our inherent passivity with a veneer of heroism. This is what the French-Jewish phenomenologist Emmanuel Levinas found insidious in existentialist thought, and particularly in Heidegger's elucidation of *Dasein*—of human being as a kind of existence defined by the consciousness of death. For Heidegger, the fact of death permits a vista to open in which the human Will may act in the face of death's unsurpassable limit with freedom and virility. Levinas, in contrast, refuses the lure of Heidegger's idealism, and shifts the guiding metaphor of his philosophy from a sublime but isolated gaze to one of relationship. For Levinas, life calls each of us to stand face to face before one another and enter into dialogue. And so, ultimately, the primary relation between the human being and the world manifests itself as eros—lovers facing each other as equals—rather than the hero's solitary going forth into the unknown. "The Other," as Levinas calls all that lies outside us, finally eludes all of our efforts at understanding. So Levinas at once deepens our solitude and calls us to go out from it—an exodus at the heart of being. So, likewise, suffering is not a test that makes us stronger, nor can death be conquered by the Will. Instead, as he observes in *Time and the Other,* "in suffering there is an absence of all refuge. It is the fact of being directly exposed to being. It is made up of the impossibility of fleeing or retreating. The whole acuity of suffering lies in this impossibility of retreat."[1] To be fully exposed to being, of course, is to be fully exposed to death. In Levinas's subversion of Western idealist philosophy, I cannot help but hear an echo of the psalmist's cry, a desperate calling out toward YHWH who is the absolutely Other, the divine I AM who is at once the sufferer's personal God and beyond any human conception of personality:

> Hear my prayer, O Lord,
>   let my cry come unto thee!
> Do not hide thy face from me
>   in the day of my distress!
> Incline thy ear to me;
>   answer me speedily in the day when I call!
>
> For my days pass away like smoke,
>   and my bones burn like a furnace.
> My heart is smitten like grass, and withered;
>   I forget to eat my bread.
> Because of my loud groaning
>   my bones cleave to my flesh.
> I am like a vulture of the wilderness,
>   like an owl of the waste places;
> I lie awake,
>   I am like a lonely bird on the housetop.
> All the day my enemies taunt me,
>   those who deride me make use of my name for a curse.
> For I eat ashes like bread,
>   and mingle tears with my drink,
> because of thy indignation and anger;
>   for thou hast taken me up and thrown me away.
> My days are like an evening shadow;
>   I wither away like grass. (Psalm 102:1–11)

In justifying his exclusion of the World War I poets, Siegfried Sassoon, Isaac Rosenberg, Wilfred Owen, and the like, from the *Oxford Anthology of English Verse,* William Butler Yeats—a poet whose work I love as much as anyone's—remarked that passive suffering was not an acceptable theme for poetry. Obviously, he had not been reading the Psalms. By then, however,

Yeats had already long assumed the mask of the heroic, a stance that inclined him toward nostalgic ideas about the Irish race as well as arch-conservative politics. If Yeats flirted with totalitarianism in his support of Colonel William Duffy and the Blue Shirts, then Ezra Pound became its whore in his delusions about Mussolini and in his embrace of fascism as a heroic purgative to the mire he believed civilization had become. What affronts is not Pound's elitism, but a hero worship that amounts to complicity with genocide: "The yidd is a stimulant and the goyim are cattle / in gt/proportion and to salable slaughter / with the maximum docility," Pound wrote in one of his expurgated *Cantos.* In our time, such dangerously misplaced desires for the transcendent—what we once called idolatry—have rendered the idea of transcendence itself suspect, even in some theological circles. "Immanentist theology" it's called, an effort over the latter part of the last century to shake post-Nietzschean Christianity loose of its supernaturalism. Likewise, according to the dominant theoretical template in academic circles, all talk of poetry must be "historicized" and "politicized." In such views, the longing for transcendence is a dangerous longing, at best nostalgic, at worst intellectually and even spiritually bankrupt.

Yet, the desire for transcendence reveals itself differently in the Psalms. Rather than otherworldly longing, or an obeisance before the god, which is nothing other than the hero's alter-ego or attendant lord, the psalmist's voice is the voice of justifiable complaint, of passionate speech driven to expression by a personal, historical, and ontological urgency:

> How long, O Lord? wilt thou forget me forever?
>   How long wilt thou hide thy face from me?
> How long must I bear pain in my soul,
>   and have sorrow in my heart all the day?
> How long shall my enemy be exalted over me?
> Consider and answer me, O Lord, my God. . . . (Psalm 13:1–3)

Far from bowing down before some transcendent power, the speaker of Psalm 13 not only pleads but petitions to be heard, and requires a justification for God's absence, for his own apparent abandonment by God. As such, the psalm at once subverts the dialogical structure of transcendence on which it is based—the speaker *has* been abandoned by YHWH whose name is I AM and who therefore is unconditioned Being—even as it sustains that expectation by establishing a future, the only future imaginable, in which the speaker *is* answered. The desire for transcendence, brought on by acute suffering, becomes manifest as a call to relationship with God conceived of as radically other. The trajectory, however, is "downward" rather than otherworldly, for YHWH is petitioned to respond in history, so transcendence becomes manifest as a relationship experienced in time. Rather than a denial of history, transcendence becomes realized within history as a longing cry. We hear that cry again in Psalm 6:

> O Lord, rebuke me not in thy anger,
>   nor chasten me in thy wrath.
> Be gracious to me, O Lord, for I am languishing;
>   O lord heal me, for my bones are sorely troubled.
> But thou, O Lord, how long?

For me, this double-speak of petitioning God against his own absence is no Freudian delusion but constitutes the very essence of consciousness—of thought seeking an answer to its solitude, of thought seeking to establish a welcome for itself in Being through the act of speech. Philosophically speaking, this double-speak requires a double vision for, though God is never seen, he is conceived of as being at once utterly transcendent and immanent through his Word, his inspiring breath. The God called out to by the psalmist is therefore also really Other, not merely the image of the speaker's desire, and therefore not wholly accountable to those desires. What does the psalmist ultimately desire? That God still breathes, that he exists, creates, and shapes history. What fear is implicit in the psalmist's cry? Incredible as it sounds, beyond any punitive action that God might take against the psalmist's presumptuous questions, he fears that God may have willed Himself out of existence, or perhaps out of His existence as God. He fears that God has expired. The psalmist's speech, his song, is his effort to sing God back into Being since, for the time being, God has become mute, an absence, ineluctable, an emptiness at the heart of glory. The dialogical expectation of the psalm requires an eschatological answer, for God is both the primordial Poet and the ultimate Audience on which both the psalmist's being and God's Being depend:

> Turn, O Lord, save my life;
>   deliver me for the sake of thy steadfast love.
> For in death there is no remembrance of thee;
>   in Sheol who can give thee praise? (Psalm 6:4–5)

Sheol, the land of the dead: a state akin to an eternal coma in which consciousness has all but expired: "What man can live and never see death? Who can deliver his soul from the power of Sheol?" (Psalm 90:48). And so the psalmist holds up to God, holds up before God's absent face, the reality of death itself as a kind of ontological bribe: You need me to remember You, just as I need for You not to forget me. The psalmist's song is the immanent dwelling for this mutual remembrance, the word's anticipatory *templum*. In the end the psalmist declares his hope: "the Lord accepts my prayer." It's as though, as Robert Hass says in "Meditation at Lagunitas," "the little song *transcend, transcend* could actually get us anywhere." The psalmist's lament is the eschatological song of reciprocal acknowledgment, covenant, of call and response—YHWH calling on his people to be his people, the people calling on YHWH to be their God, and each awaiting the voice of the answerer. It is the same song uttered through the breath of being and called out Other to other, other to Other, without end, without expiration.

AFFLICTION

Why are you cast down, O my Soul,
  and why are you disquieted within me?
  —PSALM 42:5

All day the painters scraped the four sides of the house, chip after brittle chip, the layers raining down until bare wood showed through. Christine and I had been up since their early morning arrival, every now and then looking out a window at this father and son who worked in tandem on high, sliding ladders. Later on, we watched them outstretched on our unmown lawn eating lunch.

We heard the coarse rhythm of their tools along the old clapboards for hours as we worked inside on poems until, after small talk, fingers crossed for continued clear weather, they left in their truck. Maybe it was the small upheaval of this wanted change that wore us out, or the unrelenting heat, so that into the evening we flopped on the couch to watch TV. On the tube an aerial view of postwar Berlin, the bombed buildings flattened, jagged, unreeled in vividly obliterated presence on the bright square in front of us with the documentary voice-over of Marlene Dietrich saying: "Who can believe in life after death, those hundreds of thousands killed, gone? Do you really believe they are all flitting around up there?" Later, we sat entranced at the *Nova* special, "Runaway Universe," with its evidence of an accelerating expanding cosmos that reverses all expectations: no final cosmic implosion bringing everything back to the origin; no eternal return of big bangs, expansions, and contractions oscillating through futureless futures; instead, an infinite cosmic extension that made my wife and me think of Whitman:

All goes onward and outward, nothing collapses,
And to die is different from what anyone supposed, and luckier.

It's not luckier for one physicist interviewed, but his worst imagined end—whole galaxies spinning further and further apart, an unrelenting emptiness filling infinitely an infinite universe, the power of N raised to the neverending. Unimaginable loneliness. Though what of the radical evidence they spoke of: only 5 percent of the universe, bodies, planets, stars, nebulae, galaxies, is sensible matter; the rest is "dark matter" and the more elusive "dark energy"—Einstein's "cosmic constant" true, so it turns out—filling the void with itself in its own image, present everywhere, visible nowhere, establishing itself out of the known and unknown. Invisibility. Omnipresence. God? Though God would require omnipotence as well—forgiveness and wrath—a dimension of the personal whether to create or destroy.

CHRISTINE: "We live in Flatland. We live in three dimensions, while the universe exists in twelve, at least, so the physicists say. Who's to presume consciousness ends, since consciousness is energy, and energy can't be destroyed?"

DANIEL: "That sounds like *Star Trek*, the Traveler episode about the alien who transforms from matter to energy and back again because energy and matter and thought are really one."

CHRISTINE: "Right, maybe that's our destiny."

And when the body dies, is it liberated, not to Sheol, but to Nirvana? And was Ovid a proto-physicist, like Whitman, each metamorphosis a redistribution of energy from human to flower, from god to human, from human to god? And what of the resurrection, the risen body transfigured beyond death? Does the dark energy build from our deaths, whole universes within our own, everlasting, and beyond our ken only until we are called to them? Beyond the playful speculations of a tired couple watching a science special before bed, Giuseppe Ungaretti's great poem "Meditations on Death" in Stanley Kunitz's marvelous translation bears witness to the question of ultimacy that underlies a quiet evening's metaphysical insouciance:

> O sister of the shadow,
> blackest in strongest light,
> Death, you pursue me.

Here is death portrayed as a kind of dark energy, invisible, omnipresent, "blackest in strongest light," gaining like a fleet-footed god on the speaker, bringing the final metamorphosis. There is an inescapable hauntedness in Ungaretti's voice that resonates with the psalmist's when the horror of death overwhelms him: "O that I had wings like a dove! I would fly away and be at rest; / yea I would wander afar, I would lodge in the wilderness" (Psalm 55:6–7). To lodge, to dwell, in a state of being unassailable by death, that is what the psalmist desires, like the Italian poet. It is this very hope that seems absent from another great poem of death, Philip Larkin's "Aubade." Here is the first stanza:

> I work all day and get half-drunk at night.
> Waking at four to soundless dark, I stare.
> In time the curtain-edges will grow light.
> Till then I see what's really always there:
> Unresting death, a whole day nearer now,

Making all thought impossible but how
And where and when I shall myself die.
Arid interrogation: yet the dread
Of dying, and being dead,
Flashes afresh to hold and horrify.

In Larkin's poem, Ungaretti's relentless pursuit and the psalmist's longing for flight settle into a psychic steady-state, an *acedia* that cannot be reconciled or alleviated because here the psalmist's fear of metaphysical solitude has been realized. There is only the self, Descartes's personal pronoun thinking the ego into being and, confronted with "restless death," all it can do for the rest of the poem is remove thought's assuaging answers. In one of the great metaphors of the later twentieth century, religion itself becomes "a vast moth-eaten musical brocade / created to pretend we never die." Death is "a special way of being afraid," Larkin affirms, and by owning death so relentlessly and unflinchingly Larkin's speaker portrays a world utterly without transcendence; without even the secular transcendence of Matthew Arnold's lovers at the end of "Dover Beach." "Aubade" ends:

Slowly light strengthens, and the room takes shape.
It stands plain as a wardrobe, what we know,
Have always known, know that we can't escape,
Yet can't accept. One side will have to go.

At the end, there is no one for the speaker to be true to, there are only crouching telephones "getting ready to ring" and work that "has to be done" when the morning comes. The world is "intricate," but ultimately only "rented." Even the solaces of immanence—personal companionship, erotic love—have been curtailed to an almost pure isolation without prospect of appeal or appeasement, but for the postmen "like doctors" going from house to house. If we assume for a moment that the psalmist's longing exists perhaps unacknowledged in the poet's motivation to appeal to some "Other," if only in the unquestioned desire to make the poem, then God's healing answer—the living breath of the divine Word—here has been reduced to the hope of a word from a distant friend or relation, though what's left in the mailbox may be only a solicitation or a bill. Though at first it may appear coercive to find something of the psalmist's cry in Larkin's resolute refusal of transcendence, it seems to me obvious that poems like "High Windows," "Sad Steps," and "The Trees," to cite just a few examples from Larkins's work, demonstrate a longing for transcendence equal in urgency to the psalmist's but abbreviated from explicitly religious expression by the poet's resolute skepticism. It likewise seems self-evident to me that the act of making a poem is a gesture outward toward "the Other," even if the other is a wholly immanent audience. Of course, at the same time, language itself is other. The process of writing is a process of discovery—"no surprise in the writer, no surprise in the reader," Frost said—and so writing is nothing other than a process of "othering" oneself in the making of a poem. Beyond such theoretical considerations, however, Larkin's speaker and the psalmist find common ground in their tone of lamentation because each, even Larkin's bourgeois speaker, has confronted in his own *acedia* the reality of affliction.

The spiritual sense of affliction subsumes and ultimately absorbs the physical meaning associated with the word, though physical pain in its most extreme manifestation epitomizes and embodies the unspeakable loss of spiritual abandonment that affliction signifies. As Simone Weil defines it, affliction is "an uprooting of life, a more or less attenuated equivalent of death, made irresistibly present to the soul by the attack or immediate apprehension of physical pain."[2] Affliction, however, also entails the ego's ravaging before the felt prospect of its own nothingness, as well as the social degradation that attends this most diminished of states. Moreover, for Weil, affliction is "the great enigma of human life," for the allowance if not the agency that brings about affliction is finally God's. It is God's bargain with the devil to bring Job to utter desolation. As Weil observes, constrained by affliction, even Jesus cried out for consolation and believed himself "forsaken by the Father." A troublesome Jew, degraded and nailed in agony to the cross, he quotes Psalm 22:

> My God, my God, why hast thou forsaken me?
> Why art thou so far from helping me, from the words of my groaning?
> O my God, I cry by day, but thou dost not answer;
> and by night but find no rest. (Psalm 22:1–2)

By joining Jesus's own anguished cry to the psalmist's, the gospel writers sought to give what they saw as Christ's redemptive sacrifice cultural as well as spiritual amplitude. Though what is most haunting about the scene in spite of all the iconography is Jesus's anonymity. In the world's eyes he is just another criminal, just another slave. I have to travel back in memory to my childhood and the crucifix that hung on the wall over my parents' bed, and look at the anguished face turned downward, the crown of thorns, the gaunt body forever frozen in time like a figure on Keats's urn, to recall probably my first image of affliction. Then I have to look back darkly through the warped glass of my own perceptions to see my mother dead in the same bed, under the same cross, wasted by years nursing a childhood wound she could not heal, nursing a sadness that was for her unspeakable; and I have to go back to the room in Lutheran Medical and try again to make out my father's unintelligible rasps, then the mouthed silence after the breathing tube was removed, and then the slack zero of his mouth in death. On the cross above both these beds, Christ isn't saying anything. His pain is beyond speech. He is the Word-made-Flesh emptied into the body of flesh that has swallowed the Word.

Years ago, reading Elaine Scarry's *The Body in Pain: The Making and Unmaking of the World,* I recognized intellectually at least that affliction is an impassible path; it is the world brought to its limit as a world. "Physical pain," Scarry writes, "does not simply resist language but actively destroys it, bringing about an immediate reversion to a state anterior to language, to the sounds and cries a human being makes before language is learned."[3] Scarry's insight is one implicitly addressed in Ellen Bryant Voigt's "Song and Story." Weaving the Orpheus myth together with a story of a young girl strapped to a mechanical crib who in her affliction cannot cry out, Voigt's poem redefines the poet's work in the most compelling and urgent terms:

The one who can sing sings to the one who can't,
who waits in the pit, like Procne among the slaves,
as the gods decide how all such stories end. . . .

In Voigt's poem, the child's affliction "unmakes" the world. Pain unmakes the world even though it pervades the world we inhabit, a *terra incognita* always encountered anew. It is the raw silence for which the poet, the singer, nevertheless must find words. Though unlike Voigt's poem the Psalms at times understand affliction as the outgrowth of sin—as Psalm 3 says, "There is no soundness in my flesh because of thy indignation"—at the deepest level of affliction sin reveals itself to be a subordinate rationale, a deflection from an unthinkable abandonment. Affliction is the world's cipher and origin, a wound and a womb, where the world is made, or re-made, in the poet's own answering efforts of reversal, the reversal that would answer the world's unmaking even if it's only in the form of the soul's most despairing lament:

> O Lord, my God, I call for help by day;
>   I cry out in the night before thee.
> Let my prayer come before thee,
>   incline thy ear to my cry!
> For my soul is full of troubles,
>   and my life draws near to Sheol.
> I am reckoned among those who go down to the Pit;
>   I am a man who has no strength,
> like one forsaken among the dead,
>   like the slain that lie in the grave,
> like those whom thou dost remember no more,
>   for they are cut off from thy hand.
> Thou hast put me in the depths of the Pit,
>   in the regions of dark and deep.
> Thy wrath lies heavy upon me,
>   and thou dost overwhelm me with all thy waves.

> * * *

> Is thy steadfast love declared in the grave,
>   or thy faithfulness in Abaddon?
> Are thy wonders known in the darkness,
>   or thy saving help in the land of forgetfulness?

> * * *

Afflicted and close to death from my youth up,
  I suffer thy terrors; I am helpless.
Thy wrath has swept over me;
  thy dread assaults destroy me. (Psalm 88:1–7, 10–12, 15)

WITNESS

For a thousand years in thy sight
  are but as yesterday when it is past,
or as a watch in the night.
  —PSALM 90:4

Twenty years ago, I had the good fortune to be in the audience during Czeslaw Milosz's delivery of the Charles Eliot Norton Lectures at Harvard University. A graduate student in Religion and Culture at the time, I had only just earnestly begun seeking a life in poetry by taking classes and joining workshops. I had picked up *Bells in Winter* the year before, and still remember reading it on the "R" train from Brooklyn to my job as a clerk at the Doubleday Bookstore in Lower Manhattan—work I had sought against my parent's wishes that I begin a management training program at Merrill-Lynch. The second son of a blue-collar family, I was expected to find a well-paying job, preferably in business, though it was my mother's dream that I should become, of all things, a dentist. The priesthood would have been a worthy choice as well, and indeed for a time I contemplated that vocation, majoring in religion at Iona College—"that blue-collar Roman school," as one graduate professor described it. Now I sat in stately Memorial Hall Theater, a would-be doctor of theology and culture who would be lured away from that calling as well. Though proud that I attended Harvard, my parents would have preferred the "B" School and an MBA.

Nevertheless, there I was, listening to one of the great poets of the twentieth century expound not only on an art that despite its allure seemed impossibly beyond my birthright, but on religion, politics, European literature, the nature of Western culture across the axis of Rome and Byzantium, past and future, as well as on the unthinkably brutal history of the twentieth century told from the perspective of one who had witnessed it and survived. I knew then, however awkward I might have felt as "a blue-collar scholar," so one "Div" School friend called me, that I was by any reasonable account privileged both to be where I was at that moment and not to have been born into the cauldron of wholesale want and atrocity that composes much of the world. The following year, when *The Witness of Poetry* appeared in print, I underlined whole passages, emphasized still more urgent ideas with checks and stars and, occasionally, my own scrawled commentary. Here is one of Milosz's observations to which I continue to return: ". . . the twentieth century is a purgatory in which the imagination must manage without the relief that satisfies one of the essential needs of the human heart, the need for protection. Existence appears as ruled by necessity and chance, with no divine intervention: until recently God's hand used to bring help to pious rulers and to punish sinful rulers. But now even the idea of Progress, which was nothing else but Providence secularized, no longer provides any guarantee."[4]

Over forty years since I first read these words, Milosz's assessment of the situation of poetry strikes me as no less remarkably trenchant and germane for this next century. If faith in divine intervention against the often-cruel operations of history and blind fate retains any currency, it does so more often than not without the assurance of a rite that unequivocally galvanizes the soul. Indeed, when a particular *cultus* reaches such intensity, even within the circles of traditional religious practice, one begins to fear that Freud and Marx may have been right about the inherently delusive nature of religion. On the other hand, as Milosz's observation equally reminds us, the cult of Progress offers no appeasement, and smacks of an equally dubious determinism and triumphalism. And far from improving the plight of those left behind, the immense strides in technology that have shaped the world since I sat in that theater dedicated to sublime thought and expression have done nothing to change the sources of oppression and brutality in the human heart, the same heart that longs for protection—political, economic, metaphysical, or otherwise. Given this circumstance, and the degree of injustice and violence that manifests itself daily in our global village, it strikes me that one could understand Milosz as optimistic when he called our present state a purgatory. There is an end to purgatory, but there is no end to affliction.

From this perspective, the Psalms seem removed from us precisely because, however afflicted the speaker may be, the expectation of dialogue that pervades and underwrites the psalmist's lament negates YHWH's absence by calling on God's presence eschatologically: How long, O Lord? There will be protection; the suffering will end. Above all, the expectation of cosmic or divine protection requires a kind of metaphysical waiting. If one were to believe my old professor at Iona College, the long late Brother Mark Hunt, then despite the psalmist's intense affliction, it is God's *chesed*, His "steadfast love," that finally triumphs, and so faith can overcome even utter disintegration:

> By the waters of Babylon,
>   there we sat down and wept
> when we remembered Zion.
> On the willows there
>   we hung up our lyres.
> For there our captors
>   required of us songs,
> and our tormentors, mirth, saying
>   "Sing us one of the songs of Zion!"
>
> How shall we sing the Lord's song
>   in a foreign land?
> If I forget you O Jerusalem,
>   let my right hand wither!
> Let my tongue cleave to the roof of my mouth,
>   if I do not remember you,
> if I do not set Jerusalem
>   above my highest joy. (Psalm 137:1–6)

In the first stanza, one of the most beautiful and famous in all the Psalms, song is refused as an action efficacious of faith, for it has become a tool of irony alone, irony that bespeaks and intensifies Israel's disintegration not only as a community of tribes and a *cultus* but possibly as a civilization. Whether in protest against the jeers of their captors, or in response to a world-altering loss, Israel has been silenced in the most radical way. The second stanza, however, performs the redemptive reversal of that silence back into speech, into song, through the interpolation of the essential question—the question of existence. Song enacts itself in self-interrogation, and thereby enacts the psalmist's reversal of the negation of being, through a surpassing moment of self-witness. At this moment the psalm becomes something more than the lament of an individual caught in a historical atrocity, more than the collective voice of an oppressed people in shambles, more even than the human voice transmuted into a kind of exemplary subjectivity, a befitting emblem for all the lost-of-history. Beyond all of these, the psalmist's question manifests the voice of the eternal in search of its own infinitely assuaging being, for without song there is no divine audience and therefore no covenant, no call and response, no eternity at once transcending and subtending the primary relationship of Being to itself: I AM therefore YOU are, you ARE so therefore I MUST BE. This is the essential ontological logic of the Psalms, perhaps of all song, all making, and the indispensable presumption of language. Here, the song or word that creates, that "Lets Be," is a question not an imperative—not exactly Rilke's *Gesang ist Dasein,* "song is existence," where Orpheus's song emerges as a pure affirmation, the mythopoeic, creational naming of Genesis lodged in the mouth of the Greek god—but song that rises out of Being's negation by history, the very history perceived to be shaped by YHWH, the source of all being.

About the same time as I enrolled in Brother Hunt's class on the Psalms, I found myself listening occasionally to Don McLean's benchmark album *American Pie.* One song on the flip-side from the album's classic track was a version of Psalm 137 sung *a cappella* by McLean, his voice velvety and resonant, lifting and diminishing beautifully with the psalm's moving lamentation and its desire for endurance even through momentous hardship. What McLean's version left out, what is often left out of an innocent reading of the Psalms, is the intensity of the retributive violence YHWH is called upon to inflict on behalf of the afflicted:

> Remember, O Lord, against the Edomites
>   the day of Jerusalem,
> how they said, "Raze it, raze it!
>   Down to its foundations!"
> O daughter of Babylon, you devastator!
>   Happy shall be he who requites you

with what you have done to us!
Happy shall he be who takes your little ones
and dashes them against the rock!

In Brother Hunt's class, such extreme calls for revenge were glossed over, and it's no surprise the same pop singer who crooned about "the devil laughing in the dark" when Buddy Holly died might elide Psalm 137's brutal crescendo. This is the God witnessed in Job's magisterial theophany, a God who exists outside human bounds and human morality, and who may act in history as He sees fit, whether to rally to avenge the tribal covenant or to vent His wrath on the chosen. It is a manifestation of absolute power that Simone Weil could not abide, despite her Jewish ancestry. It is this kind of divine portrayal that led Carl Jung in *Answer to Job* to conclude that evil must be seen as constitutive of the divine archetype itself. Let God "break the teeth in their mouth," Psalm 58 says of the wicked. In *Violence and the Sacred,* René Girard envisions humanity's urge to exact revenge and to displace its innate impulse toward violence in a scapegoat as the origin of all religion, indeed of civilization itself. For Girard, we need a version of malevolent transcendence so the violence that would destroy a community's social fabric might be sanctioned divinely and finally projected onto "the other." Against those who might see the call to violence in the Psalms as a subversion of their understanding of the sacred, and against those who on the contrary innocently gloss over this disturbing attribute of the psalmist's world, I would argue that the psalmist's voice achieves credibility by being so unguarded, by giving range to the most disturbing as well as to the most exalted of human impulses.

In Psalm 74, which is described in the Revised Standard Version of the Bible as a prayer for deliverance from national enemies, the psalmist petitions God to "have regard for thy covenant; for the dark places of the land are full of habitations of violence." Tempering an at times *Clockwork Orange* brand of divine "ultra-violence" in the Psalms is their call to social justice, a call that might be seen as a warning to God: "Help your people, or your people will perish." YHWH, to use a theological term, is a *mysterium tremendum*—a tremendous mystery, the other which is Absolutely Other: The Voice that addresses Moses on Sinai and Job in the whirlwind. But what happens when the acknowledged humanity of the Psalms—the longing for transcendence and justice as well as the nascent violence—confronts a world devoid of justice and constructed of false idols of transcendence? That is the world Milosz called to mind in his Norton lectures, the world of the Holocaust, another kind of *tremendum* as Jewish theologian Arthur Cohen defines it: the comprehensive model of brutality that ends in the total humiliation of human being. What place do the Psalms have in this world, or in the world that comes after? "After Auschwitz, no poetry," Theodore Adorno famously remarked. Yet, there is Paul Celan's "Psalm":

No one kneads us again
out of earth and clay,
no one breathes
back our dust.
       No one.

Praised be to you, No one.
For your sake
we shall blossom
brokenly to you.[5]

A survivor of the Holocaust, Celan lost his entire family to its ovens before producing some of the greatest poetry to have been written in the latter part of the twentieth century, and before he committed suicide in 1970. An admirer of Heidegger's philosophy despite Heidegger's silence regarding his own membership in the Nazi Party, Celan produced work that inhabits the ontological anti-world that came into being after the self-immolation of a prior Western idealism, the greatest poetic expression of which might be Rilke's "Duino Elegies": "Who, if I cried out would hear me among the angel's / hierarchies?" The answer after Auschwitz is, as Celan tells us, "No one." With its central metaphor derived from the tradition of Western love poetry stemming back to "The Song of Solomon" and carrying forward to Rilke, the negation of Celan's "Psalm" cannot be underestimated—the living are the "No one's Rose" the inversion of Dante's cosmic, incarnational theophany. The poem's voice, as if from the very nadir of cosmic affliction, rises out of "the Death-World," to use a term coined by Edith Wyschogrod in *Spirit in Ashes*.[6] In the Death-World, the wholesale extermination of persons has been accomplished by fiat, fine-tuned to a pristine technology and underwritten by a self-justifying myth born, as it were, out of the demonic perversion of the symbols that have shaped Western culture. The utopian paradise of Aryanism, like all brands of racial engineering, requires the apocalyptic eradication of the "scapegoated" other. So, in an utterly God-corrupted, God-forsaken universe, "Psalm" succeeds in speaking the unspeakable by singing the un-singable. It breathes out from the desolation of omnipotent being an answer to God's silence with its own "bloody word," evoked by Celan near the end of his poem, that aspires to transcendence beyond the expired image of God and in spite of an afflicted cosmos consumed by Malevolence and raised to the power of No-God at all.

DWELLING AND THE DOUBLE LIFE

God gives the desolate a home to dwell in. . . .
   —PSALM 68:6

That afternoon in late August five months before my father died, I strapped myself into the stiffly padded seat across from his stretcher in the ambulance hired to take him from Cooley-Dickinson Hospital in Northampton, Massachusetts, to Brigham and Women's Hospital in Boston. Since early July and his first attack at a family reunion in East Durham, New York, I had spent the better part of the summer living in hotels nearby hospitals where doctors tried to stabilize his condition. It was in Hudson Hospital that the doctor refused to send him home to his Brooklyn apartment—his heart so weak he could no longer make the stairs. Schooled, as he used to say, at "The College of Hard Knocks," my father wasn't prone to crying, though he cried that afternoon, holding onto my hand and my brother's as though we were all that kept him from falling off the edge of the world. We were.

Later that week, stabilized, an oxygen tank wheeled alongside of him with its translucent tube wrapped like a cheap Halloween mask around his ears, he climbed into my brother's mini-van to spend what he hoped would be two weeks recuperating outside Northampton while I took care of things in the Brooklyn apartment, and my wife waited for me back in Wisconsin. He looked forward to seeing his grandchildren, but looked forward even more to getting back to Brooklyn, to resuming the habits of his life—breakfast at Sally's Coffee Shoppe; Tuesday meetings at St. Anselm's Young at Heart; lunch at Pegasus or Hinsch's luncheonette; lighting candles at church; his afternoon scotch at Muse's Bar; then back to the lonely apartment to drink more, and smoke, and watch TV before going to bed. Even though my mother had died nearly a year earlier, he still hid the cigarettes and bottles out of habit. Habit was what kept my father going, and what was killing him. And he vowed to get back to Brooklyn, even after the second attack at my brother's house that brought another emergency call, and left him unconscious among my frantic brother and his wife, his screaming grandchildren, everyone waiting for the ambulance. Revived from the dead, kept alive by transfusions of plasma, fed intravenously, his heart monitored by radar, a respirator tube growing from his mouth like a plastic branch sprouting a long transparent vine, he jotted instructions to my brother and me, pad after pad reduced to a thin line of glue, his stubby pencils blunting with the words: *How are the kids? When is the tube coming out? When can I go back to Brooklyn?* And after they excavated the tube from his throat, and the doctor told him his one chance, he left for the sojourn of open-heart surgery, his head packed in ice as they re-routed his blood, replaced the collapsed valve, reconstructed the aorta; then days of living in Sheol, swollen, thrashing in bed, the heart stronger now but the consciousness in question; and then the waking, weeks of therapy; and then, refusing anything else, back to Brooklyn, to the old apartment two flights up now scaled one step at a time, or seated backwards, pushing himself up step by step with his arms—to the one place he believed he could be himself, to "the same four walls" he'd say when I'd call, the vow accomplished: back to his home.

It was after I'd left my hotel in Boston nearby the hospital, resumed my teaching position and the rhythm of the school year, after he had been rushed in trauma again to Lutheran Medical in Brooklyn, after the wake and the long ride following the hearse to Resurrection Cemetery, that I realized the judgment—"He's amazing"—referred most profoundly to my father's desire to dwell according to his own terms in the world; that whatever habits and compulsions he felt—even the destructive ones—were efforts at maintaining a world against the inevitability of loss. A great grandson of the Irish Famine who himself had witnessed and participated in the whirlwind of twentieth-century history, he lived during a period where physical pain had become, according to Czeslaw Milosz, "a most simple touchstone for reality." It is the unavoidable awareness of pain's pervasiveness, of affliction, that at once heightens our perceptions of the individual's solitude and prompts a renewed appreciation for the web of relationships that establish everyone, indeed everything, in being. Even the accoutrements of my father's illness—the tubes, the intravenous, the electrodes signaling invisibly to stations down the hall—made visible, made manifest, the web of dependencies that sustain us even in health. It is as though disease, horrible as it is, reveals the invisible patterns of affinity that enable each one of us to exist at all, and to which each one is called to participate according to one's chances, labors, and intents. Each one of us lives a double life, the life of one's sole self and the other invisible life we sometimes awaken to that binds us each to each, other to other, as if all things were held in relationship by some dark, some apophatic Energy transcending our knowledge and our mastery to name it.

In the Jewish mystical book, *The Kabbalah*, this darkness at the heart of being is called Ayin, "nothingness," or "the Boundless," because it transcends every conception even as it pervades all existence—invisible, omnipresent, like the primordial energy the *Nova* scientists claimed filled all space, and which accelerates the expanding universe, though perhaps it's dangerous to confuse spiritual and physical categories even through a simile, as if the contemporary mind considering such issues were hopelessly split? One wants to retreat from the vexatious confusions and trumped-up political agendas of "creation science," also from the coldly mechanical cosmos of scientific positivism, to avert one's eyes from the bumper-sticker in the shape of a fish that reads JESUS, from the bumper-sticker in the shape of the same fish that reads DARWIN. What has speculation of this kind to do with lamentation, pain, affliction, the causes of which beg for answers more assuaging than grandiose abstractions or New Age flakiness? "The one who can sing sings to the one who can't," Ellen Bryant Voigt's poem reminds us, and so she sings *for* the one who can't. Just so, Celan's "Psalm" sings as if in the impossible voice of the obliterated. Both poems predicate their singing on the assumption that a bridge can be made across the gulf that exists between the fragile nature of our materiality and the object of a longing that, however despaired of, nonetheless would offer an appeasement that surpasses the laws of materialist necessity. Voigt's gods in "Song and

Story" are as capricious as chaos itself; and Celan's paradoxically transcendent "No One" signifies a vacuum in the heart of omnipotence. Still, both presume the steadfast dialogue underlying the psalmist's spiritual urgency:

> As a hart longs
> for flowing streams,
> so longs my soul
> for thee, O God!
> My soul thirsts for God,
> for the living God.
> When shall I come and behold
> the face of God?
> My tears have been my food
> day and night
> while men say to me continually,
> "Where is your God?" (Psalm 42:1–3)

These lines from Psalm 42 constitute the perfect evocation of longing not merely as a profound emotion but as an act of metaphysical construction. God is not present, otherwise there would be no affliction as well as no song. The spiritual architecture of longing involves making a bridge between the immanent realm of the singer and the transcendent realm in which the singer's longing presumably will be satisfied. It begins in analogy, in metaphor: "As a hart longs for flowing streams. . . ." Though it would extend to an order of reality that eludes metaphor even though metaphor is all we have to describe its existence: "the face of God." No one can see the face of God and live, and so the sweep of longing extends from the created to the uncreated. It is a bridge across the gulf of being to a boundless Emptiness, and yet it is that boundless Emptiness that paradoxically secures the psalmist's song.

As Wallace Stevens observed in *The Necessary Angel,* where he invokes none other than Simone Weil, poetry in our time entails decreation, the act of making something pass from the created into the uncreated. Another way of stating this is to say that, because poetry is liminal, partaking of the senses and effacing them at the same time, it stands in for or anticipates an order to life consonant with an abiding and infinite Regard, and does so without denying the world's fragility and finitude. Poetry, as a witness to worldliness and a longing for what might assuage it, embodies the double life of our common human circumstance as beings in between the dust that we are and the divinity to which we would aspire. The poetry of longing would therefore inscribe a formal arc outward from the lived life into the uncreated. If the poet's song could wholly satisfy its longing and attain its desire it would transform itself into the "foreign song" of Stevens's "Of Mere Being," the bird alive beyond its visible fire-fangled feathers in an order of reality that transcends human meaning and human feeling—but not because that greater reality is inhuman. To adapt Dante's pivotal verb, to satisfy longing of this kind would be to "trans-humanize" song according to the heavenly registers. Instead, we are left with a formal arc that returns us to the sole self and its mere intimations of greater life. We follow the ecstatic course of consciousness exemplified in Keats's "Ode to a Nightingale": first solitude and heartache, then the desire to dissolve consciousness through a Bacchic disordering of the senses, then the flight of art with its delusion of union ("Already with Thee!"), then the plummet back to earth and darkness to confront the reality of pain and death with the solitary mind's desire for death as an answer to solitude, then finally, inevitably, the mind's return back to the "sole self" now disoriented from its inner sojourn, its would-be journey beyond its solitude. And it's not that Keats wishes to leave the flesh behind in favor of the golden realms of spirit. The desire is to transfigure flesh and spirit—that double life at the core of human consciousness—into a more rarified and subtle incarnation. Both Stevens's semi-transcendent bird and Keats's nightingale point us toward those scales of being that are at once resistant to human language and demanding of embodiment in human terms, in human words, in human art.

"Be still before the Lord, and wait patiently for him," Psalm 37 advises with its Zen-like sense of equanimity, so different from the psalms of lamentation with their acute awareness of affliction. Here, too, however there is longing; though now the agitated ecstasy exemplified in Keats's "Ode to a Nightingale" has been quelled to the selfless acceptance and transparency of being and its passing that we find in "To Autumn." It is the most fully realized instance of Keats's "negative capability"—the ideal poet's aptitude for waiting in doubt without anxiety, without the anxious grasping after more which Augustine defined as concupiscence, his phenomenological proof of original sin. At the same time, lest it devolve into quietism, waiting requires contention. These antithetical moods are present everywhere in the Psalms and at times they mingle, as in the poetry of Gerard Manley Hopkins's:

> Thou art indeed just, Lord, if I contend
> With thee; but, sir, so what I plead is just.
> Why do sinners' ways prosper? and why must
> Disappointment all I endeavor end?

Echoing the Psalms, Hopkins's "terrible sonnet" asks for nothing less than a biblical theodicy, God's own self-justifying revelation before the creaturely self. Regardless of the reader's own faith in an answer, Hopkins's longing is the reader's insofar as he articulates the ultimacy of such questions for human beings and not just for himself. It seems to me that the secular portrayal of what is at stake in Hopkins's poem may be found in Elizabeth Bishop's "In the Waiting Room." Here, the account of the child Elizabeth's waiting for her Aunt Consuelo in the dentist's office unfolds without reference to any vertical axis of faith whatsoever. It is February 1918. We are placed entirely within the horizontal timeline of history. The world of Bishop's dentist office is a world devoid of transcendence in any traditional sense. It is a wholly immanent spot of time. Nevertheless, the little girl's inner journey beyond the self by which she will realize her particular selfhood is spurred by a sudden, albeit restrained, revelation of suffering:

> Suddenly, from inside,
> came an *oh!* of pain
> —Aunt Consuelo's voice—
> not very loud or long.
> I wasn't at all surprised;
> even then I knew she was
> a foolish timid woman.
> I might have been embarrassed,
> but wasn't. What took me
> completely by surprise
> was that it was *me*

my voice, in my mouth.
Without thinking at all
I was my foolish aunt,
I—we—were falling, falling,
our eyes glued to the cover
of the *National Geographic,*
February, 1918.

The sudden vertigo the child experiences attends upon the obliteration of
the illusion of individual selfhood. It is as if the invisible strings that connect
us all had suddenly manifested themselves in a supreme moment of identification. As in "Ode to a Nightingale," the experience of self-surpassing is both
abrupt and ephemeral, and occasioned by the recognition of pain and mortality. While it does not make reference to anything outside the purely temporal
or appeal to the eternal I AM, "In the Waiting Room" does prompt the signature
question of ultimate concern, the question of existence itself: "Why should I
be my aunt / or me, or anyone?" In this essential respect Bishop's waiting room
becomes the world, the world in which longing defines the human circumstance and where we endure in waiting either with or without hope.

CODA: AN AFTERLIFE

Six months to the day after my father died, I received a letter informing me
of the poet Tom Andrews's death of a blood disease, *Thrombotic thrombocyto-
penic purpura.* He was only forty, and a poet of delicately capacious sensibility
whose work has since received insufficient regard. I had met Tom during the
January Residency at Warren Wilson, though I had read his poems years earlier and had been impressed by their spare beauty, as well as their wise and
compassionate sense of life. I knew of his hemophilia, as well as his passion for
racing motorcycles, from reading his memoir, *Codeine Diary*—hemophilia and
motorcycle racing: a combination of facts that still seems to me to a defiant
fusion of chance and intention, a marvelous affirmation of life in the face of
affliction. Though I didn't know him well enough to call myself a friend, we hit
it off over the course of the week, and I felt comfortable with his soft-spoken
nature, his friendly and generous demeanor, as well as his wicked sense of

humor. Near the end of the residency, we collaboratively led a workshop that afterwards we both agreed was among the best either of us had experienced in our teaching lives. Though Tom had recently given up his position at Purdue University and moved to Greece, we looked forward to meeting again.

Three months earlier, after my father's death and before Tom's, I received word that another friend lost his four-year-old daughter to a sudden illness. Then a colleague's college-age daughter died. Prior to these losses, but within the relatively short span of the past two years, I could add many others to the list: my father-in-law, my mother, a cousin's husband, a string of colleagues. Beyond them the numbers re-double, and re-double again into infinity. As well as being personal, death is nothing if not exponential. How, then, can poetry stand up to such loss. Or to quote Milosz again: "What is poetry that does not save nations, or people?" Yes, or the lost, or the forgotten, or the daily extinctions, or the dwindling environment? The universe is accelerating, expanding onward and outward, though all around us we perceive things collapsing. To the naked eye gazing from the naked self, it doesn't seem luckier as Whitman said. If God Is, we may have to abandon the idea of God's omnipotence, to embrace a God apparently as weak or weaker than ourselves, and still greater in that weakness if one can take seriously the Greek word *kenosis*, signifying the self-emptying of the divine into the cosmos: is, the very mode of creation ex nihilo.[7] God's ecstasy is the creation. Perhaps our ecstasy is to embody our own inevitable self-emptying in ways the most vital of our poetry strives to imagine. For this there is longing, and the dead talking back to us in our own secret voices, like Tom Andrews in his poem "At Burt Lake"—the dead in their afterlife of lives in-dwelling, to which I must give the last word:

> To disappear into the right words
> and to be their meanings . . .
>
> October dusk.
> Pink scraps of clouds, a plum-colored sky.
> The sycamore tree spills a few leaves.
> The cold focuses like a lens . . .
>
> Now night falls, its hair
> caught in the lake's eye.

Such clarity of things. Already
I've said too much . . .

                    Lord,
language must happen to you
the way this black pane of water,
chipped and blistered with stars,
happens to me.

Acknowledgments

"'Hello, I Must Be Going': The Poetry of Farewell" first appeared in *The Writer's Chronicle* 46.6 (May/Summer 2014).

"The Odeon, Or, Singing and Sensibility," first appeared in *The Writer's Chronicle* 50.2 (October/November 2017).

"John Donne and the Odeon" first appeared in *Berfrois* (April 17, 2014).

"What's Donne Isn't Done" first appeared in *Berfrois* (March 15, 2021).

"Writing for the Dead" first appeared in *Berfrois* (December 14, 2022).

"Ancient Salt, American Grains," first appeared in *The Marlboro Review* 12 (Summer/Fall 2001): 19–39. Reprinted in *Irish Pages* (Spring 2002): 120–37, and *Poet's Work, Poet's Play: Essays on the Practice and the Art*, ed. Daniel Tobin and Pimone Triplett (Ann Arbor: University of Michigan Press, 2007).

"One Arc Synoptic: Plot, Poetry, and the Span of Consciousness" first appeared in *The Contemporary Narrative Poem: Critical Crosscurrents*, ed. Steven P. Schneider (Iowa City: University of Iowa Press, 2012).

An early version of "Forms after Forms: On Metamorphosis and Improvisation" was given at the 2023 conference of the Association of Literary Scholars, Critics, and Writers, and later as a lecture at the Program for Writers at Warren Wilson College.

"Lamentation, Poetry, and the Double Life" first appeared in *Poets on the Psalms*, ed. Lynn Domina (San Antonio: Trinity University Press, 2008).

"At Burt Lake" from *Random Symmetries*. Copyright 2002 by Tom Andrews. Reprinted with permission of Oberlin College Press.

Jericho Brown, "Duplex (a poem is a gesture toward home)" from *The Tradition*. Copyright 2019 by Jericho Brown. Reprinted with the permission of The Permissions Company, LLC on behalf of Copper Canyon Press, coppercanyonpress.org.

"Unholy Sonnet 13" from *Bone Fires: New and Selected Poems*. Copyright 2011 by Mark Jarman. Reprinted with permission of the author and Sarabande Books.

"Millie and Christine McKoy" from *Olio*. Copyright 2016 by Tyehimba Jess. Reprinted with permission of the author and Wave Books.

"Mother Quiet" reprinted from *Mother Quiet,* by Martha Rhodes. By permission of the University of Nebraska Press. Copyright 2004 by Martha Rhodes.

"Rambling" from *The Plum Flower Dance: Poems, 1985–2005*. Copyright 2007 by Afaa Michael Weaver. Reprinted by permission of the University of Pittsburgh Press.

I also want to underscore my thanks, my deep appreciation, to the editors noted above, as well as to Alan Shapiro for his close early reading of the manuscript, and to Lee Sioles for her expertly judicious and wise editorship as *The Odeon* moved toward publication.

This book was supported in part by a grant from the Emerson College Hub Fund for Advancing Research.

Notes

THE ODEON, OR, SINGING AND SENSIBILITY

1. Mark Edmundson, "Poetry Slam: Or, The Decline of American Verse," *Harper's Magazine* (July 2013), 64.

2. Ibid., 62.

3. Seamus Heaney, *Stepping Stones: Interviews with Seamus Heaney*, ed. Dennis O'Driscoll (New York: Farrar, Straus, and Giroux, 2008), 457.

4. William Lynch, *Christ and Apollo: Dimensions of the Literary Imagination* (New York: Intercollegiate Studies, 2003), 176.

5. Ibid., 148.

6. Heinrich Päs, *The One* (New York: Basic Books, 2023), 1, 289.

7. Christian Wiman, "An Idea of Order," in *After New Formalism*, ed. Annie Finch (Ashland, OR: Story Line Press, 1999), 204ff.

8. Heaney, *Stepping Stones*, 470.

9. Frank Kermode, *The Sense of an Ending: Studies in the Theory of Fiction* (London: Oxford University Press, 1968), 3ff.

JOHN DONNE AND THE ODEON

1. John Heath Stubbs, *John Donne: The Reformed Soul* (New York: Norton, 2006), 207.

2. Ibid.

3. Owen Barfield, *Saving the Appearances* (Middletown, CT: Wesleyan University, 1988), 79.

4. T. S. Eliot, *The Use of Poetry and the Use of Criticism* (London: Faber and Faber, 1933), 124.

5. Marilynne Robinson, *Absence of Mind* (New Haven, CT: Yale University Press, 2010), 8.

6. Owen Barfield, *The Rediscovery of Meaning* (Oxford: Barfield Press, 2013), 13ff.

7. Heaney, *Stepping Stones*, 470.

8. T. S. Eliot, *Selected Prose of T. S. Eliot*, ed. Frank Kermode (New York: Harcourt, Brace, Jovanovich, 1975), 64.

9. Ibid.

10. William Lynch, *Christ and Apollo*, 176.

11. Robinson, *Absence of Mind*, 23.

12. George Steiner, *After Babel: Aspects of Language and Translation* (Oxford: Oxford University Press, 1975), xiii.

13. Stubbs, *John Donne,* 44–45.

14. Eliot, *Selected Prose,* 64.

15. Wallace Stevens, *The Necessary Angel: Essays on Reality and the Imagination* (New York: Vintage, 1951), 22.

16. Ibid.

17. Ibid., 36.

18. Stubbs, *John Donne,* 174.

19. Quoted in Louis Martz, *The Poem of the Mind: Essays on Poetry English and American* (New York: Oxford, 1966), 44–45.

20. Stevens, *The Necessary Angel,* 31.

21. W. B. Yeats, *Essays and Introductions* (New York: Collier Books, 1961), 162–63.

22. Stubbs, *John Donne,* 95.

23. Louis Martz, *The Poetry of Meditation: A Study of English Literature of the Seventeenth Century* (New Haven, CT: Yale University Press, 1954), 33.

24. Stubbs, *John Donne,* 92.

25. Martz, *Poem of the Mind,* 35.

26. Ibid., 39.

27. Lynch, *Christ and Apollo,* 252.

28. Ibid., 148.

29. David Tracy, *The Analogical Imagination* (New York: Crossroads, 1986), 408.

30. Stephen Fields, *Analogies of Transcendence* (Washington, DC: Catholic University of America Press, 2016), 28.

31. John T. Shawcross, *John Donne's Religious Imagination* (Conway: University of Central Arkansas Press, 1995), 183.

32. Matthew Guite, *Faith, Hope and Poetry: Theology and the Poetic Imagination* (Farnham, Eng.: Ashgate, 2012), 103.

33. Lynch, *Christ and Apollo,* 195.

34. Stevens, *Necessary Angel,* 22.

35. Barfield, *Saving the Appearances,* 58ff.

36. Lynch, *Christ and Apollo,* 155ff.

37. Simone Weil, *Gravity and Grace* (London: Routledge, 1952), 3.

38. Ron Silliman, "Postmodernism: Sign for a Struggle, Struggle for a Sign," in *Conversant Essays: Contemporary Poets on Poetry,* ed. James McCorkle (Detroit: Wayne State University Press, 1990), 79ff.

39. Ibid., 95.

40. Ibid., 93.

41. Charles Bernstein, "Time Out of Motion: Looking Ahead to See Backward," in *Conversant Essays: Contemporary Poets on Poetry,* 421.

42. John Barth, *Further Fridays: Essays, Lectures, and Other Nonfiction, 1984–1994* (Boston: Back Bay Books, 1996), 332.

43. Lynch, *Christ and Apollo,* 228.

44. Stubbs, *John Donne,* 329.

45. Lynch, *Christ and Apollo,* 60.

46. Stubbs, *John Donne,* 286.

47. Bernstein, "Time Out of Motion," 421.

48. Carl Phillips, *Coin of the Realm: Essays on the Life and Art of Poetry* (St. Paul, MN: Graywolf, 2007), 112.

WHAT'S DONNE ISN'T DONE

1. David Bentley Hart, *The Experience of God* (New Haven, CT: Yale University Press, 2013).

2. See David Bentley Hart, *The Beauty of the Infinite* (Grand Rapids, MI: Eerdmans, 2003), 179ff

3. See Daniel Tobin, *On Serious Earth: Poetry and Transcendence* (Asheville, NC: Orison Books, 2019).

4. Freeman Dyson, *Infinite in All Directions* (New York: Perennial, 2004), 119.

5. Lynch, *Christ and Apollo,* 259–60.

6. Albert-Lázló Barabási, "The Physics of the Web," *Physics World* (July 2001), 33.

7. Ibid., 34.

8. Ibid.

9. Denise Levertov, "Some Notes on Organic Form," in *The Poet's Work: 29 Poets on the Origins and Practice of Their Art,* ed. Reginald Gibbons (Boston: Houghton-Mifflin, 1979), 255.

10. See Guite, *Faith, Hope and Poetry,* 169.

11. Robert Hayden, *Collected Prose* (Ann Arbor: University of Michigan Press, 1984), 84.

ANCIENT SALT, AMERICAN GRAINS

1. Calvin Bedient, "Five Notes on American Poetry," *Metre* 7–8 (Fall 2000), 26–27.

2. Michael Donaghy, "The Exile's Accent," *Metre* 7–8 (Fall 2000), 183–88.

3. Robert Mezy, "On Form," *Metre* 7–8 (Fall 2000), 65–66.

4. Ibid.

5. Robert Hass, *Twentieth Century Pleasures* (New York: Ecco Press, 1984), 116.

6. Ibid.

7. Timothy Steele, *Missing Measures: Modern Poetry and the Revolt against Meter* (Fayetteville: University of Arkansas Press, 1990), 62.

8. Ibid.

9. W. B. Yeats, *Essays and Introductions,* 502.

10. Ibid., 509.

11. Ibid., 521.

12. Robert Frost, *Robert Frost: Complete Poems, Prose, and Plays* (New York: Library of America, 1995), 675.

13. Hass, *Twentieth Century Pleasures,* 57.

14. Ibid., 65.

15. Samuel Taylor Coleridge, *Selected Prose* (New York: Random House, 1951), 173.

16. Hass, *Twentieth Century Pleasures,* 70.

17. Steele, *Missing Measures,* 283.

18. Ibid., 59–60.

19. Hass, *Twentieth Century Pleasures,* 67.

20. William Carlos Williams, *Selected Prose* (New York: New Directions, 1969), 281.

21. Charles Olson, "Projective Verse" in *Collected Prose* (Berkeley: University of California Press, 1997), 239.

22. Ibid., 245.

23. Ibid., 242.

24. Ibid., 241.

25. Ibid., 245.

26. David Perkins, *A History of Modern Poetry: Modernism and After* (Cambridge, MA: Harvard University Press, 1987), 519.

27. Ellen Bryant Voigt, *The Flexible Lyric* (Athens: University of Georgia Press, 1999), 124–25.

28. Ibid., 150.

ONE ARC SYNOPTIC

1. Robert Scholes and Robert Kellogg, *The Nature of Narrative* (New York: Oxford University Press, 1966), 207.

2. Thomas Leitch, *What Stories Are: Narrative Theory and Interpretation* (University Park: Pennsylvania State University Press, 1986), 130.

3. Virginia Woolf, "The Novel of Consciousness," in *The Modern Tradition,* ed. Richard Ellmann and Charles Feidelson, Jr. (New York: Oxford University Press, 1965), 123.

4. Scholes and Kellogg, *The Nature of Narrative,* 13–14.

5. Ibid., 276.

6. Leitch, *What Stories Are,* 139–43.

7. Paul Ricoeur, *Time and Narrative* (Chicago: University of Chicago Press, 1984), 1:33.

8. Leitch, *What Stories Are,* 131.

9. Ricoeur, *Time and Narrative,* 2:156.

10. Ibid., 1:33.

11. Ibid., 1:ix.

12. Wallace Martin, *Recent Theories of Narrative* (Cornell, NY: Cornell University Press, 1986), 86.

13. Colin McGinn, *The Mysterious Flame* (New York: Basic Books, 2000), 163.

14. Ricoeur, *Time and Narrative,* 2:9–10.

15. Ibid., 3:19.

16. Frank Kermode, *The Sense of an Ending,* 47.

17. Stephen Dobyns, *Best Words, Best Order* (New York: St. Martin's, 1996), 140.

18. Ricoeur, *Time and Narrative*, 1:20.

19. Alan Shapiro, "In Praise of the Impure: Narrative Consciousness and Poetry," *Triquarterly* 81 (Spring/Summer 1991), 13.

20. Scholes and Kellogg, *The Nature of Narrative*, 223.

21. Ibid.

22. Leitch, *What Stories Are*, 84ff.

23. Dana Gioia, "The Dilemma of the Long Poem," in *The New Expansive Poetry*, ed. R. S. Gwynn (Ashland, OR: Story Line Press, 1999), 206.

24. Dick Allen, "The Forest for the Trees: Preliminary Thoughts on Evaluating the Long Poem," in *New Expansive Poetry*, 200.

25. Ibid.

26. Hart Crane, *The Bridge* (New York: Liveright, 1992), 2.

27. Hart Crane, *Complete Poems and Selected Letters* (Washington, D.C.: Library of America, 2006), 349.

28. Richard Poirier, *Robert Frost: The Work of Knowing* (Stanford: Stanford University Press, 1977), 279.

29. Shapiro, "In Praise of the Impure," 14ff.

30. Tony Hoagland, *Real Sofistikashun* (St. Paul, MN: Graywolf, 2006), 174.

31. Ricoeur, *Time and Narrative*, 1:77–78.

32. Ibid., 1:78.

33. Ibid.

34. Shapiro, "In Praise of the Impure," 14.

35. Frost, *Collected Poems, Prose, and Plays*, 664.

36. Ibid., 665.

37. Ibid., 675.

38. Bernstein, "Time Out of Motion," 426.

39. Poirier, *Robert Frost*, 267.

40. Frost, *Collected Poems, Prose, and Plays*, 892–93.

41. Ibid., 777.

42. Barth, *Further Fridays*, 340–41.

43. Ibid., 341.

44. Ibid., 332.

45. Ibid.

46. Marjorie Perloff, *Poetics of Indeterminacy* (Princeton, NJ: Princeton University Press, 1981), 3ff.

47. Christian Wiman, "An Idea of Order," in *After New Formalism*, ed. Annie Finch (Ashland, OR: Story Line Press, 1999), 205.

48. Ibid.

49. Sven Birkerts, *The Electric Life: Essays on Modern Poetry* (New York: William Morrow, 1989), 235ff.

50. Hoagland, *Real Sofistikashun,* 173.

51. Ibid., 186.

52. Ibid., 177.

53. Ibid., 179.

54. Ibid., 187.

55. Ibid.

56. Ricoeur, *Time and Narrative,* 1:75.

57. Ibid.

FORMS AFTER FORMS

1. Agha Shahid Ali, "In Defense of the Canon, or, A Darkly Defense of Dead White Males" in *Poet's Work, Poet's Play: Essays on the Practice and the Art,* ed. Daniel Tobin and Pimone Triplett (Ann Arbor: University of Michigan Press, 2007), 153.

2. Ibid., 153.

3. Ibid., 159.

4. Ibid., 150.

5. Afaa Michael Weaver, "Afaa Michael Weaver with Nicolette Reim." Interview. https://www.theartsection.com/afaa-weaver.

6. Jericho Brown, "Gutting the Sonnet: A conversation with Jericho Brown," *The Rumpus.* https://therumpus.net/2019/04/01/the-rumpus-interview-with-jericho-brown/

7. Agha Shahid Ali, "To Be Teased into Disunity," in *An Exaltation of Forms: Contemporary Poets Celebrate the Diversity of Their Art,* ed. Annie Finch and Kathrine Varnes (Ann Arbor: University of Michigan Press, 2002), 210.

8. Ibid.

9. Quoted in Ralph Patterson, "Blues," in *An Exaltation of Forms,* 187–92.

10. Tyehimba Jess, "An Interview with Tyehimba Jess," *Frontier Poetry* (April 21, 2017). https://www.frontierpoetry.com/2017/04/21/interview-tyehimba-jess/.

11. Ibid.

12. Patterson, "Blues," 188.

13. For a more complete discussion see Daniel Tobin, *On Serious Earth: Poetry and Transcendence* (Ashville, NC: Orison Books, 2019).

14. Eliot, "Tradition and the Individual Talent," *Selected Prose,* 38.

15. Ibid.

16. Ali, "Darkly," 155.

17. Eliot, "Tradition and the Individual Talent," *Selected Prose,* 39.

18. Ali, "In Defense of the Canon," 154.

19. Ibid., 146.

20. Ibid., 152.

21. Ibid., 150.

"HELLO, I MUST BE GOING"

1. Brian Green, *The Elegant Universe* (New York: Vintage, 1999), 208.
2. Kermode, *The Sense of an Ending*, 3ff.
3. Hans-Georg Gadamer, *Truth and Method* (New York: Crossroad, 1985), 167ff.
4. Mikel Dufresne, *The Phenomenology of Aesthetic Experience*, trans Edward S. Casey (Evanston, IL: Northwestern University Press, 1973), 229.

WRITING FOR THE DEAD

1. The phrase is from Michael Donaghy's poem "The Years": *penetrar el espejo, Conjure* (London: Picador, 2000), 38.
2. Robert Graves, "The Art of Poetry, No. 11." *Paris Review* 47 (Summer 1969).
3. See Ian Jack, *The Poet and His Audience: English Literature, 1700–1830* (Cambridge: Cambridge University Press, 1984), 3ff.
4. Bonnie Costello, *The Plural of Us: Poetry and Community in Auden and Others* (Princeton, NJ: Princeton University Press, 2017), 225.
5. Czeslaw Milosz, *Nobel Lecture* (New York: Farrar, Straus, and Giroux, 1980), 6.
6. Ibid., 20.
7. Ibid., 22.
8. Michael Ryan, "Poetry and the Audience," in *Poets Teaching Poets,* ed. Gregory Orr and Ellen Bryant Voigt (Ann Arbor: University of Michigan Press, 1996), 171.
9. Ibid., 163.
10. My translation.
11. Ibid., 165.
12. Vernon Shetley, *After the Death of Poetry* (Raleigh, NC: Duke University Press, 1993), 3.
13. Robert von Hallberg, *American Poetry and Culture, 1945–1980* (Cambridge, MA: Harvard University Press, 1985), 13, 35.
14. Ibid.
15. W. Y. Tindall, "Exiles: Rimbaud to Joyce," *American Scholar* 14.3 (Summer 1945), 351–55. Quoted in Shetley.
16. Czeslaw Milosz, *The Witness of Poetry* (Cambridge, MA: Harvard University Press, 1983), 109.
17. Ryan, "Poetry and the Audience," 181.
18. Milosz, *Witness,* 17.
19. Costello, *The Plural of Us,* 126.
20. Ibid., 26.
21. Ibid., 94.
22. Czeslaw Milosz, *Unattainable Earth* (New York: Ecco Press, 1986), 56.
23. Ibid.
24. Costello, *The Plural of Us,* 120.

25. Ibid., 121.

26. Eavan Boland and Mark Strand, *The Making of a Poem* (New York: Norton, 201), 167.

27. Peter Sacks, *The English Elegy* (Baltimore: Johns Hopkins University Press, 1985), 2.

28. Ibid., 20, 27.

29. Jahan Ramazani, *Poetry of Mourning* (Chicago: University of Chicago Press, 1994), ix.

30. Ibid., x, 1.

31. Betty Adcock, *Rough Fugue: Poems* (Baton Rouge: Louisiana State University Press, 2017), 5.

32. Costello, *The Plural of Us*, 138.

33. Milosz, *Witness*, 15.

34. Shetley, *After the Death of Poetry*, 191.

35. Milosz, *Witness*, 96.

36. Ibid., 97.

37. Ibid.

38. Ali, "The Ghazal: To Be Teased into Disunity," in *An Exaltation of Forms*, 210.

39. Milosz, *Witness*, 107.

LAMENTATION, POETRY, AND THE DOUBLE LIFE

1. Emmanuel Levinas, *Time and the Other* (Pittsburgh, PA: Duquesne University Press, 1990), 69.

2. Simone Weil, *Simone Weil Reader* (New York: Meyer Bell, 2007), 445.

3. Elaine Scarry, *The Body in Pain: The Making and Unmaking of the World* (London: Oxford University Press, 1987), 4.

4. Milosz, *Witness*, 53.

5. Daniel Tobin, *The Stone in the Air: A Suite of Forty Poems from the German of Paul Celan* (Cliffs of Moher, Ireland: Salmon Press, 2018), 45.

6. Edith Wyschogrod, *Spirit in Ashes: Hegel, Heidegger, and Man-Made Mass Death* (New Haven, CT: Yale University Press, 1990), 14ff.

7. Jordan Daniel Wood, *The Whole Mystery of Christ: Creation as Incarnation in Maximus Confessor* (Notre Dame, IN: University of Notre Dame Press, 2022) 39.

Works Cited

Adcock, Betty. *Rough Fugue: Poems.* Baton Rouge: Louisiana State University Press, 2017.

Ali, Agha Shahid. "In Defense of the Canon: A Darkly Defense of Dead White Males." In *Poet's Work, Poet's Play, edited by* Daniel Tobin and Pimone Triplett, 144–60. Ann Arbor: University of Michigan Press, 2007.

———. *The Veiled Suite.* New York: Norton, 2009.

Ammons, A. R. *Collected Poems.* New York: Norton, 1972.

Andrews, Tom. *Random Symmetries.* Oberlin, OH: Oberlin College Press, 2002.

Ashbery, John. *Collected Poems, 1956–1987.* New York: Library of America, 2008.

Auden, W. H. *Collected Poems.* New York: Vintage, 1991.

Barabási, Albert-László. "The Physics of the Web." *Physics World* 14 (July 2001): 33–34.

Barfield, Owen. *The Rediscovery of Meaning.* Oxford: Barfield Press, 2013.

———. *Saving the Appearances: A Study in Idolatry.* Middletown, CT: Wesleyan University Press, 1988.

Barth, John. *Further Fridays.* Boston: Back Bay Books, 1996.

Beasley, Bruce. *Prayershreds.* Asheville, NC: Orison Books, 2024.

Bedient, Calvin. "Five Notes on American Poetry." *Metre* 7–8 (Fall 2000): 26–29.

Berryman, John. *The Dream Songs.* New York: Farrar, Straus, and Giroux, 2014.

Birkerts, Sven. *The Electric Life: Essays on Modern Poetry.* New York: William Morrow, 1989.

Bishop, Elizabeth. *The Complete Poems, 1927–1979.* New York: Farrar, Straus, and Giroux, 1984.

Brooks, Gwendolyn. *Blacks.* Chicago: Third World Press, 1994.

Brown, Jericho. "Gutting the Sonnet: A Conversation with Jericho Brown." *The Rumpus.* https://therumpus.net/2019/04/01/the-rumpus-interview-with-jericho-brown.

———. *The Tradition.* Port Townsend, WA: Copper Canyon Press, 2019.

Coleridge, Samuel Taylor. *Selected Prose.* New York: Random House, 1951.

Costello, Bonnie. *The Plural of Us: Poetry and Community in Auden and Others.* Princeton, NJ: Princeton University Press, 2017.

Crane, Hart. *The Bridge.* New York: Liveright, 1992.

———. *Complete Poems and Selected Letters.* Washington, D.C.: Library of America, 2006.

Dennett, Daniel C. *Consciousness Explained.* Boston: Back Bay Books, 1992.

Dickinson, Emily. *Complete Poems of Emily Dickinson.* Edited by Thomas H. Johnson. Boston: Little, Brown, 1960.

Dobyns, Stephen. *Best Words, Best Order.* New York: St. Martin's Press, 1996.

Donaghy, Michael. *Collected Poems.* London: Picador, 2009.

———. "The Exile's Accent." *Metre* 7–8 (Fall 2000): 183–88.

Donne, John. *The Complete English Poems.* New York: Penguin, 1977.

Doty, Mark. *Atlantis.* London: Jonathan Cape, 1996.

Dufresne, Mikel. *The Phenomenology of Aesthetic Experience.* Translated by Edward S. Casey. Evanston, IL: Northwestern University Press, 1973.

Dyson, Freeman. *Infinite in All Directions.* New York: Perennial, 2004.

Edmundson, Mark. "Poetry Slam: Or, The Decline of American Verse." *Harper's Magazine* (July 2013): 64–65.

Eliot, T. S. *The Complete Poems and Plays.* New York: Harcourt, Brace and World, 1973.

———. *Selected Prose of T. S. Eliot.* Edited by Frank Kermode. New York: Harcourt, Brace, Jovanovich, 1975.

———. *The Use of Poetry and the Use of Criticism.* London: Faber and Faber, 1933.

Ellmann, Richard, and Charles Feidelson, eds. *The Modern Tradition.* New York: Oxford University Press, 1965.

Fields, Stephen. *Analogies of Transcendence.* Washington, DC: Catholic University of America Press, 2016.

Finch, Annie, ed. *After New Formalism: Poets on Form, Narrative, and Tradition.* Ashland, OR: Story Line Press, 1999.

Finch, Annie, and Kathrine Varnes. *An Exaltation of Forms: Contemporary Poets Celebrate the Diversity of Their Art.* Ann Arbor: University of Michigan Press, 2002.

Frost, Robert. *Robert Frost: Complete Poems, Prose, and Plays.* New York: Library of America, 1995.

Gadamer, Hans-Georg. *Truth and Method.* New York: Crossroad, 1985.

Girard, René. *Violence and the Sacred.* Baltimore: Johns Hopkins University Press, 1979.

Glück, Louise. *The First Four Books of Poems.* New York: Ecco, 1995.

Greene, Brian. *The Elegant Universe.* New York: Vintage, 1999.

Gwynn, R. S., ed. *The New Expansive Poetry.* Ashland, OR: Story Line Press, 1999.

Hart, David Bentley. *The Beauty of the Infinite.* Grand Rapids, MI: Eerdmans, 2003.

———. *The Experience of God.* New Haven, CT: Yale University Press, 2013.

Hass, Robert. *Praise.* New York: Ecco Press, 1999.

———. *Twentieth Century Pleasures.* New York: Ecco Press, 1984.

Hayden, Robert. *Collected Poems.* New York: Liveright, 2013.

Hayes, Terrance. *American Sonnets for My Past and Future Assassin.* New York: Penguin, 2018.

Heaney, Seamus. *Stepping Stones: Interviews with Seamus Heaney.* Edited by Dennis O'Driscoll. New York: Farrar, Straus, and Giroux, 2008.

Hikmet, Nazim. *Poems of Nazim Hikmet.* Translated by Mutlu Konuk and Randy Blasing. New York: Persea, 2002.

Hill, Geoffrey. *Collected Poems.* Oxford: Oxford University Press, 1986.

Hoagland, Tony. *Real Sofistikashun.* St. Paul, MN: Graywolf, 2006.

Hopkins, Gerard Manley. *Poems and Prose.* London: Penguin, 1953.

Hudgins, Andrew. *After the Lost War.* Boston: Houghton-Mifflin, 1988.

———. *Ecstatic in the Poison.* New York: Overlook Press, 2003.

Jack, Ian. *The Poet and His Audience: English Literature, 1700–1830.* Cambridge: Cambridge University Press, 1984.

Jarman, Mark. *Bone Fires: New and Selected Poems.* Louisville, KY: Sarabande Books, 2011.

Jess, Tyehimba. "An Interview with Tyehimba Jess." *Frontier Poetry* (April 21, 2017). https://www.frontierpoetry.com/2017/04/21/interview-tyehimba-jess.

———. *Olio.* Seattle: Wave Books, 2016.

Joseph, Allison. "Sweetelle." In *Poetics and Ruminations,* a blog by Lewis Turco. https://lewisturco.typepad.com/poetics/2015/04/form-of-the-week-35-the-sweetelle.html.

Keats, John. *The Complete Poems.* Edited by Jack Stillinger. Cambridge, MA: Harvard University Press, 1982.

Kelly, Brigit Pegeen. *Song.* Syracuse, NY: BOA Editions, 1995.

Kermode, Frank. *The Sense of an Ending: Studies in the Theory of Fiction.* London: Oxford University Press, 1968.

Kocher, Ruth Ellen. *From the Fish House: An Audio Archive of Emerging Poets.* https://www.fishousepoems.org/the-gigans-xi.

Kunitz, Stanley. *The Collected Poems.* New York: Norton, 2000.

Larkin, Philip. *The Complete Poems.* New York: Farrar, Straus, and Giroux, 2012.

Leitch, Thomas. *What Stories Are: Narrative Theory and Interpretation.* University Park: Pennsylvania State University Press, 1986.

Levertov, Denise. "Some Notes on Organic Form." In *The Poet's Work: 29 Poets on the Origins and Practice of Their Art*, edited by Reginald Gibbons. Boston: Houghton Mifflin, 1979.

Levinas, Emmanuel. *Time and the Other.* Pittsburgh: Duquesne University Press, 1990.

Lynch, William. *Christ and Apollo: Dimensions of the Literary Imagination.* New York: Intercollegiate Studies, 2003.

Martin, Wallace. *Recent Theories of Narrative.* Cornell, NY: Cornell University Press, 1986.

Martz, Louis L. *The Poem of the Mind.* New York: Oxford University Press, 1966.

Matthews, William. *Search Party: Collected Poems.* Boston: Houghton Mifflin, 2004.

McCorkle, James, ed. *Conversant Essays.* Detroit: Wayne State University Press, 1990.

McGinn, Colin. *The Mysterious Flame.* New York: Basic Books, 2000.

Mezey, Robert. "On Form." *Metre* 7–8 (Fall 2000): 65–66.

Milosz, Czeslaw. *Nobel Lecture.* New York: Farrar, Straus, and Giroux, 1980.

———. *Unattainable Earth.* New York: Ecco Press, 1986.

———. *The Witness of Poetry.* Cambridge, MA: Harvard University Press, 1983.

Nelson, Marilyn. "Owning the Masters." In *After New Formalism: Poets on Form, Narrative, and Tradition.* Ashland, OR: Story Line Press, 1999.

Niedecker, Lorine. *Collected Works.* Berkeley: University of California Press, 2002.

Olson, Charles. *The Collected Poems of Charles Olson.* Berkeley: University of California Press, 1987.

———. *The Maximus Poems.* Berkeley: University of California Press, 1985.

———. "Projective Verse." In *Collected Prose.* Berkeley: University of California Press, 1997.

Oppen, George. *New Collected Poems.* New York: New Directions, 2008.

Ovid. *Metamorphoses: A New Translation.* Translated by Charles Martin. New York: Norton.

Päs, Heinrich. *The One.* New York: Basic Books, 2023.

Patterson, Raymond. "Blues." In *An Exaltation of Forms: Contemporary Poets Celebrate the Diversity of Their Art.*, edited by Annie Finch and Kathrine Varnes. Ann Arbor: University of Michigan Press, 2002.

Perkins, David. *A History of Modern Poetry—Modernism and After.* Cambridge, MA: Harvard University Press, 1987.

Perloff, Marjorie. *Poetics of Indeterminacy.* Princeton, NJ: Princeton University Press, 1981.

Phillips, Carl. *Coin of the Realm.* St. Paul, MN: Graywolf, 2007.

Poirier, Richard. *Robert Frost: The Work of Knowing.* Stanford, CA: Stanford University Press, 1977.

Rhodes, Martha. *Mother Quiet.* Omaha, NE: Zoo Press, 2004.

Ricoeur, Paul. *Time and Narrative.* Chicago: University of Chicago Press, 1984.

Rilke, Rainer Maria. *Sonnets to Orpheus.* Translated by Stephen Mitchell. New York: Touchstone, 1986.

Robinson, Marilynne. *Absence of Mind.* New Haven, CT: Yale University Press, 2010.

Scarry. Elaine. *The Body in Pain: The Making and Unmaking of the World.* London: Oxford University Press, 1987.

Scholes, Robert, and Robert Kellogg. *The Nature of Narrative.* New York: Oxford University Press, 1966.

Searle, John R. *The Mystery of Consciousness.* New York: New York Review of Books, 1997.

Shapiro, Alan. *By and By.* Chipping Norton: Oxfordshire, 2023.

———. "In Praise of the Impure: Narrative Consciousness and Poetry." *Triquarterly* 81 (Spring/Summer 1991): 13.

Shetley, Vernon. *After the Death of Poetry.* Raleigh, NC: Duke University Press, 1993.

Snyder, Gary. *The Real Work: Interviews & Talks, 1964–1979.* New York: New Directions, 1980.

Steele, Timothy. *Missing Measures: Modern Poetry and the Revolt against Meter.* Fayetteville: University of Arkansas Press, 1990.

Stevens, Wallace. *The Collected Poems.* New York: Knopf. 1971.

———. *The Necessary Angel: Essays on Reality and the Imagination.* New York: Vintage, 1951.

Strand, Mark. *Collected Poems.* New York: Knopf, 2016.

Stubbs, John Heath. *John Donne: The Reformed Soul.* New York: Norton, 2006.

Thomas, R. S. *Collected Poems, 1945–1990.* London: Phoenix, 1993.

Tobin, Daniel, and Pimone Triplett, eds. *Poets Teaching Poets.* Ann Arbor: University of Michigan Press, 1996.

———. *On Serious Earth: Poetry and Transcendence.* Ashville, NC: Orison Books, 2019.

———. *The Stone in the Air.* Cliffs of Moher, Ireland: Salmon Publishing, 2018.

Tracy, David. *The Analogical Imagination.* New York: Crossroads, 1986.

Trethewey, Natasha. *Monument: Poems New and Selected.* New York: Ecco, 2018.

Voigt, Ellen Bryant. *Collected Poems.* New York: Norton, 2023.

———. *The Flexible Lyric.* Athens: University of Georgia Press, 1999.

von Hallberg, Robert. *American Poetry and Culture, 1945–1980.* Cambridge, MA: Harvard University Press, 1985.

Weaver, Afaa Michael. "Afaa Michael Weaver with Nicolette Reim." Interview. https://www.theartsection.com/afaa-weaver.

———. *The Plum Flower Dance: Poems, 1985–2005.* Pittsburgh: University of Pittsburgh Press, 2007.

Weil, Simone. *Gravity and Grace.* London: Routledge, 1952.

———. *Simone Weil Reader.* New York: Meyer Bell, 2007.

Wenthe, William. *The Gentle Art.* Baton Rouge; Louisiana State University Press, 2023.

Williams, William Carlos. *Selected Prose.* New York: New Directions, 1969.

Wilson, Ryan. *The Stranger World.* Evansville, IN: Measure Press, 2017.

Wittgenstein, Ludwig. *Tractatus Logico-Philosophicus* (2d edition). London: Routledge, 2001.

Wood, Jordan Daniel. *The Whole Mystery of Christ: Creation as Incarnation in Maximus Confessor.* Notre Dame, IN: University of Notre Dame Press, 2022.

Wordsworth, William. *The Collected Poems of William Wordsworth.* London: Wordsworth Editions, 1998.

Wright, Charles. *Oblivion Banjo: The Poetry of Charles Wright.* New York: Farrar, Straus, and Giroux, 2019.

Wyschogrod, Edith. *Spirit in Ashes: Hegel, Heidegger, and Man-Made Mass Death.* New Haven, CT: Yale University Press, 1990.

Yeats, W. B. *The Collected Poems of W. B. Yeats.* New York: Macmillan, 1989.

———. *Essays and Introductions.* New York: Macmillan, 1961.

Index

acedia, 211–12

action, 10, 90–98, 113–15

Adcock, Betty, 186–88; "No Encore," 186–87; *Rough Fugue*, 187

Adorno, Theodore, 220

Aeneid (Virgil), 101

affliction, 212–15, 216–21, 223–25. *See also* suffering

After the Death of Poetry (Shetley), 178

After the Lost War (Hudgins), 108–10

Ali, Agha Shahid, 70, 131–32, 137, 143–45, 193–95; "Lenox Hill," 164–67

Allen, Dick, 100

allusions, 16, 26–27, 90, 99, 159, 182, 193–94

"The Altar" (Herbert), 76

amalgamation, 9–10, 21, 22, 37, 43

ambiguity, 112–13, 172

American poetry, 3–4, 12, 17, 65–71, 81, 95, 124–26, 170. *See also* blues

American Poetry and Culture, 1945–1980 (von Hallberg), 178

American Sonnets for My Past and Future Assassin (Hayes), 141

Amichai, Yehuda, 194

Ammons, A. R., 124; "Corson's Inlet," 7, 77–81, 84, 116; *Sphere*, 80

"Among School Children" (Yeats), 70

anagogic/anagogical, 4, 7, 11, 12, 13, 41, 51, 62, 195, 196

The Analogical Imagination (Tracy), 33

analogy/analogical, 33–35; analogical order, 5; Donne's Holy Sonnets, 41; and longing, 224; microcosm and macrocosm,

61; Milosz's vertical orientation, 190; and reality, 33–34; syntax of the metaphysical., 13; Thomas's "Emerging," 49; truth of human experience, 13; Voigt's "Song and Story," 15; writing for the dead, 195–96; Yeats's "Crazy Jane Talks with the Bishop," 55

anapests, 153

anaphora, 55–56, 71–72, 120

"An Anatomy of the World, The First Anniversary" (Donne), 19

Andrews, Tom, 227–29; "At Burt Lake," 228–29; *Codeine Diary*, 227–28

Animal Crackers (film), 149

Answer to Job (Jung), 219

Anthropocene, 176, 187

anthropomorphisms, 48–49

apophasis/apophatic, 55, 155–57, 162, 167, 223

aporia, 94

architecture, 4, 7, 9, 17, 35, 41, 51, 53–54, 93–94, 135

Aristotle, 68, 87–91, 116; *Poetics*, 91, 98

Arnold, Matthew: "Dover Beach," 193, 211

arrival and departure, 150–51. *See also* farewell, poems of; "Waving Adieu, Adieu, Adieu" (Stevens)

artificiality, 164–65

"An Arundel Tomb" (Larkin), 29–30, 50, 60

Ashbery, John, 116, 121–24; "Flow Chart," 121; "Litany," 121; "Scheherazade," 122–23; "Self-Portrait in a Convex Mirror," 122; "A Wave," 121

"As Kingfishers Catch Fire, Dragonflies
Draw Flame" (Hopkins), 32–33
associative poetry, 43–44, 119–21, 126
"At Burt Lake" (Andrews), 228–29
ateleological narrative, 117
"Atlantis" (Doty), 101–3, 107, 190–92
"At the Fishhouses" (Bishop), 81–84, 120
"Aubade" (Larkin), 30, 210–12
Auden, W. H., 29, 192–96, 197; "In Praise
of Limestone," 195–96; "The Shield of
Achilles," 192–93, 195
audience, 171–75; and modernity, 170–71;
poet's idea of, 175–76; writing for the
dead, 176, 178, 181–87, 189–92, 195–97
Auerbach, Eric: *Mimesis,* 155
Augustine, St., 22, 54–56, 225
avant-garde, 66, 76
"Ave Maria" (Crane), 102–3

Barfield, Owen, 20, 34–35; *Saving the
Appearances,* 35
Barth, John, 37–38, 116–17, 119, 120, 122–23;
"4 1/2 Lectures: Chaos Theory," 116
Beasley, Bruce: *Prayershreds,* 126
"Beauty" (Fairchild), 126
Bedient, Calvin, 65
Bells in Winter (Milosz), 215
Benveniste, Émile, 111–12
Bernstein, Charles, 37, 43–44, 112
Berryman, John, 135; *Dream Songs,* 76
The Big Smoke (Matejka), 126–27
Bingen, Hildegaard von, 11
Biographia Literaria (Coleridge), 52–54
Birkerts, Sven, 123–24
Bishop, Elizabeth, 81–85, 118–20, 123; "At
the Fishhouses," 81–84, 120; "The Filling
Station," 120; "In the Waiting Room,"
120, 226–27; "The Moose," 120; "Over
2,000 Illustrations and a Complete
Concordance," 84–85, 118–20; "The
Prodigal," 81

Blake, William, 99, 123
blank verse, 14, 71–72, 76, 100, 108, 131
"The Blue Buick" (Fairchild), 126
blues, 130, 135–39, 142–43
"Body and Soul" (Fairchild), 126
The Body in Pain (Scarry), 213
Boland, Eavan, 184
bop, 132–37, 139, 141, 142, 144–46
bouts-rimés (poetic game), 141
"Boy Breaking Glass" (Brooks), 8–10, 12–14, 17
The Bridge (Crane), 100–110
Brooks, Cleanth, 27
Brooks, Gwendolyn, 7–10, 105, 132, 141; "Boy
Breaking Glass," 8–10, 12–14, 17; "The
Sermon on the Warpland," 7–8
Brown, Jericho, 141; "Duplex," 139, 144–45;
The Tradition, 135–39
Bunting, Basil, 70
"burn" poems, 76
"Burnt Norton" (Eliot), 168–69

Cane (Toomer), 104–5
canonicity, 131–32, 143–44
"The Canonization" (Donne), 24–28, 29–33,
38, 50, 59–60
Cantos (Pound), 76, 90, 99–100, 206
canzones, 164–67
"Cape Hatteras" (Crane), 102–3, 106–7
causality, 94–95
Celan, Paul, 178; and affliction, 220–21; and
longing, 223–24; "No One," 224; "Psalm,"
220–21, 223
chaos theory, 110, 116, 130
Chardin, Teilhard de, 50, 204
Chaucer, Geoffrey, 131
Christ and Apollo (Lynch), 5, 22
"Christmas Tree" (Merrill), 76
circular structure/movement, 77, 80, 84,
106, 158–59
"Clearances" (Heaney), 185
closed form, 66, 70, 77

"closed verse," Olson, 80

closure, 67–68, 72, 75–77, 99–100, 110, 116–24

Codeine Diary (Andrews), 227–28

Cohen, Arthur, 220

Coleridge, Samuel Taylor, 73, 155–56; *Biographia Literaria,* 52–54; "The Rime of the Ancient Mariner," 12

colonial history, 131, 143–44, 193

Commedia (Dante), 116

composing on horseback, 42–43

"composition by field," Olson, 52

conceit-making, 49, 62, 163

concrete poems, 76

concupiscence, 225

confessional poem, 124

configuration, 108–10

Congregation (Trethewey), 182–83

connections/connectivity, 6, 11, 19–23, 51, 179–80

consciousness, 93–94; artistic commitment, 13; Ashbery's "Self- Portrait in a Convex Mirror," 122; of death, 204; as emergent phenomenon, 49–50; Keats's "Ode to a Nightingale," 225; Kelly's "Song," 10–11; Kunitz's "The Image-Maker," 156; Milosz's interior memory, 184; narrative poetry, 97–98, 124–27; and physics, 6; psalmist's cry, 207–8; Stevens's "Waving Adieu, Adieu, Adieu," 153; understanding of, 115; and Woolf, 87–89; writing for the dead, 195

contemplative tradition, 10, 30, 36, 38, 40, 55, 138, 155

contrapuntal form, 139–41

contraries, 9, 22, 41, 119, 154, 157–58

Corman, Cid, 174

"Corson's Inlet" (Ammons), 7, 77–80, 84, 116

Costello, Bonnie, 171–73, 180, 184, 189–90, 196; first-person plural pronoun in poetry, 171–73; *The Plural of Us,* 171

craft, 67–68, 75, 112, 121

Crane, Hart: "Ave Maria," 102–3; *The Bridge,* 100–110; "Cape Hatteras," 102–3, 106–7; "Cutty Sark," 101–2; "The Dance," 106; "The Harbor Dawn," 106; "Indiana," 100; "One Song," 101, 104; "Paradigm," 117; "Powhattan's Daughter," 100–106; "Proem: To Brooklyn Bridge," 101; "The River," 106; "Three Songs," 100; "The Tunnel," 101, 103, 106–7

"Crazy Jane Talks with the Bishop" (Yeats), 54–56

creation, 46, 51, 53, 128–30, 156, 185, 224–25, 228

Creeley, Robert, 72, 76

cultural losses, 176–77

cultus, 216–17

"Cutty Sark" (Crane), 101–2

cyclical time, 98–99, 103, 106–8

dactylic rhythm, 152–53

"The Dance" (Crane), 106

Dante, 16–17, 50, 102, 109, 120, 220, 225; *Commedia,* 116; *The Divine Comedy,* 97, 160; *Paradiso,* 4, 30, 54, 97, 98–99, 107

death: Adcock's "No Encore," 186–87; and affliction, 212–13; Auden's "The Shield of Achilles," 192–93; consciousness of, 204; death of poetry, 178–79; Doty's "Atlantis," 190–91; Hill's "In Memory of Jane Fraser," 185–86; Keats's "This Living Hand," 160–62; Larkin's "An Arundel Tomb," 29–30; Larkin's "Aubade," 210–11; Matthews's "Mingus in Shadow," 186; and memory, 184; O'Rathaille's poem, 176–78; in the Psalms, 203–4, 208; in Trethewey's *Native Guard,* 181–83; Ungaretti's "Meditations on Death," 210; writing for the dead, 176, 178, 181–87, 189–92, 195–97

decoherence, 6–7

decreation, 224–25
Deir Yassein, 194
Dennett, Daniel, 115
depth of field, 129, 134, 145
Descartes, René, 211
Devotions upon Emergent Occasions (Donne), 19
dialectical structure of the bop, 135
Dickinson, Emily, 31, 47–50, 65, 153–57, 162–63, 185; "Fame is the one that does not stay," 172–73; "My life closed twice before its close," 153–55, 159; "This World is not Conclusion," 47–50
"The Dilemma of the Long Poem" (Gioia), 99–100
DiPiero, W. S., 97–98
"Directive" (Frost), 71–72, 115
discourse, 111–12
discursivity, 97, 99–101, 108–9, 118–20
disintegrations, 179–80, 217–18. *See also* unlikeness
disorderliness, 37, 90, 96, 117, 124–25, 127, 130
dissimilarity, 4, 22, 58
dissociation of sensibility, 21–22
dissociations/dissociative, 5, 7, 20, 21–22, 30, 36, 38, 44, 124–25
The Divine Comedy (Dante), 97, 160
"Diving into the Wreck" (Rich), 21
Dobyns, Stephen, 96–97
Donaghy, Michael, 65, 169; "More Machines," 59–62
Donne, John, 18–21, 23–28, 29–32, 37–43, 46–50; "An Anatomy of the World, The First Anniversary," 19; "The Canonization," 24–28, 29–33, 38, 50, 59–60; *Devotions Upon Emergent Occasions,* 19; "The Ecstasy," 41–42, 46–48; "Elegies," 185; Holy Sonnets, 38–43, 59; knot in, 41–42, 57, 62; poetry of departures, 162–63; "The Progress of the Soul," 57; "Second Anniversary," 54; "A Valediction: Forbidding Mourning," 157–60, 163, 167
Doty, Mark, 190–92; "Atlantis," 101–3, 107, 190–92
Dove, Rita: *Sonata Mulattica,* 125–26; *Thomas and Beulah,* 125
"Dover Beach" (Arnold), 193, 211
dream songs, 135, 136
Dream Songs (Berryman), 76
Duffy, William, 206
"Duino Elegies" (Rilke), 220
Dumont, Margaret, 149
duplex, 135–39, 141, 142, 144–46
"Duplex" (Brown), 139, 144–45
Dyson, Freeman, 50–51

"Easter Wings" (Herbert), 76
"The Ecstasy" (Donne), 41–42, 46–48
Edmundson, Mark, 12–13; "Poetry Slam," 3–4
elegies, 29, 181, 184–92
"Elegies" (Donne), 185
Eliot, T. S.: arrival and departure, 150; art and religion, 29; Barth's directive, 37–38; "Burnt Norton," 168–69; and connectivity, 21–22; on Donne, 21, 23; experimental lineage, 65; *Four Quartets,* 36, 109, 150–51, 168–69; "historical sense," 143–45; "Little Gidding," 36, 62, 150; "The Metaphysical Poets," 20–21; poetic amalgamation, 9, 37; projective verse, 75; "twittering world," 168–69; "The Wasteland," 90, 95
Ellison, Ralph, 135, 138–39
emergence, 48–51, 54, 59, 122, 129–30
"Emerging" (Thomas), 48–50
Emerson, Ralph Waldo, 65, 110–12; "Nature," 110; "The Poet," 65
emotion, 38–39, 70. *See also* farewell, poems of; longing
empire, 101, 131, 175–76

emplotments, 94–95, 96, 97, 110, 119
emptiness, 22, 94, 155, 157, 168, 207, 209, 224
English sonnet, 91
enjambments, 39, 61, 70, 154, 164
enraged apostrophe, 24, 28, 38
entanglement, 6
envelope structure, 138–39
epic, 99–101
equivocal, 3, 5–6, 9, 13, 22, 35
"erasure" poems, 76
essential action, 87, 90–91, 94, 96, 107
etymologic English, 37
etymologic poetry, 43–44
evil, 104–5, 219
existence: analogical relations, 196; Auden's "In Praise of Limestone," 195–96; Bishop's "In the Waiting Room," 227; divine image, 54; human experience of time, 92; and longing, 223–24; song in the Psalms, 218; Stevens's "Waving Adieu, Adieu, Adieu," 152; and universality, 13; Voigt's "Song and Story," 15See also death
expansive poetry, 126

Fairchild, B. H.: "Beauty," 126; "The Blue Buick," 126; "Body and Soul," 126
Faith, Hope and Poetry (Guite), 33–34
"fallacy of imitative form," Winters, 117
fame, 172–73
"Fame is the one that does not stay" (Dickinson), 172–73
farewell, poems of, 155, 157, 160–63, 167
Faulkner, William, 88
"Fear of Narrative and the Skittery Poem of our Moment" (Hoagland), 111
Fields, Stephen, 33
figuration, 31–34, 38, 41–43, 106–7. See also transfigurations
"figure a poem makes," Frost, 114–15
file, 176
"The Filling Station" (Bishop), 120

"Final Soliloquy to the Interior Paramour" (Stevens), 152
first-person plural pronoun in poetry, 171–73
"The Flexible Lyric" (Voigt), 79
"Flight and Metamorphosis" (Sachs), 177
"Flow Chart" (Ashbery), 121
formal lyricism, 117–18, 139
form of the poem, 52–53, 72–81, 159, 163–65
"4 1/2 Lectures: Chaos Theory" (Barth), 116
Four Quartets (Eliot), 36, 109, 150–51, 168–69
free verse, 52, 66–68, 70–73, 76, 81, 84, 118, 162
Frost, Robert: and ambiguity, 112–13; American poetry's double inheritance, 65–66; "Directive," 71–72, 115; dramatic narratives, 95; and formalism, 117; "Home Burial," 113–14; meter and form, 65, 70, 76; "momentary stay against confusion," 21, 72, 96, 114, 117; process of writing, 212; "The Road Less Traveled By," 113; sentences/sentence sounds, 71, 112–15; "West-Running Brook," 92–94, 111, 164
function of language, 5, 35
futurist vision, 52, 65, 76

Gadamer, Hans-Georg, 158–59
The Gentle Art (Wenthe), 126
gesture, 137–38, 159–62, 212
ghazals, 70, 131, 135–39, 142, 193–95
gigan, 141–42
gig lamps, 88, 95, 115, 123
Gioia, Dana: "The Dilemma of the Long Poem," 99–100
Girard, René: Violence and the Sacred, 219
Glass, Philip, 105
Glück, Louise, 162; "Here Are My Black Clothes," 162
God: and affliction, 212–13; art and religion, 29; audience for Hopkins, 173; biblical theodicy, 226; Celan's "Psalm," 221; Donne's Holy Sonnets, 38–41; Donne's

God (*continued*)

"The Progress of the Soul," 42; Google search, 51; Hopkins's "As Kingfishers Catch Fire, Dragonflies Draw Flame," 33–34; incarnate, 27, 30; *kenosis* (self-emptying), 228; and longing, 224; poet's sensibility, 20; psalmist's cry, 206–8; in the Psalms, 203–8, 217, 219–20; Thomas's "Emerging," 48–50; and transcendence, 211–12; understanding of, 46

golden mean, 134–35

"golden shovel," Hayes, 141

Gorman, Amanda, 170

Graves, Robert, 170–71, 173, 176

Guite, Malcolm, 53–54; *Faith, Hope and Poetry*, 33–34

"The Harbor Dawn" (Crane), 106

Harrington, William, 23

Hart, David Bentley, 49

Hass, Robert, 72–73, 76; "Listening and Making," 66–67; "Meditation at Lagunitas," 208; "One Body: Some Notes on Form," 72

Hayden, Robert, 54, 58, 105, 132; "Middle Passage," 121; "Monet's Waterlilies," 46–48; "Those Winter Sundays," 91

Hayes, Terrance, 145; *American Sonnets for My Past and Future Assassin*, 141

Heaney, Seamus, 7, 20, 55; "Clearances," 185

Hecht, Anthony, 65, 70, 124

Heidegger, Martin, 204, 220

"Hello, I Must Be Going" (song), 150–55

Helms, Jesse, 57

Herbert, George, 31, 65; "The Altar," 76; "Easter Wings," 76

"The Hereafter" (Hudgins), 109

"Here Are My Black Clothes" (Glück), 162

hermeneutics, 94, 136, 154, 158

heroism, 86–87, 103, 204–6

"High Windows" (Larkin), 211

Hikmet, Nâzim: "On Living," 189

Hill, Geoffrey: "In Memory of Jane Fraser," 185–86

"historical sense," Eliot, 143–45

Hoagland, Tony, 124–25; "Fear of Narrative and the Skittery Poem of our Moment," 111

Hollander, John, 66; "Swan and Shadow," 76

Holy Sonnets (Donne), 38–43, 59

"Homage to Paul Cezanne" (Wright), 197

"Home Burial" (Frost), 113–14

"Home is So Sad" (Larkin), 163

homeostatic system, 116, 122–23

Homer, 98–100; *The Odyssey*, 99

Hopkins, Gerard Manley, 32–34, 173–74, 181, 226; "As Kingfishers Catch Fire, Dragonflies Draw Flame," 32–33

Howe, Susan, 75

Hudgins, Andrew, 116, 126; *After the Lost War*, 108–10; "The Hereafter," 109; "Piss Christ," 55–58

Hughes, Ted, 20

hyperboles, 25, 28, 61, 191

hypercatalexis, 154

"I, Maximus of Gloucester, to You" (Olson), 74–77

iambic(s), 25, 39, 54–55, 56, 67, 69–72, 77, 154, 159

ideal, 4, 21, 28, 46, 68–69

"The Idea of Order at Key West" (Stevens), 45, 80, 123

identity poetics, 180

Ignatius of Loyola (Saint): *Spiritual Exercises*, 31

"The Image-Maker" (Kunitz), 155–59

imagination, 5, 7, 13, 21, 23–27, 31–36, 53, 155–56

Imitatio Christi, 48, 173

immanence, 46, 49, 91, 99, 111, 195, 211

Immanentist theology, 206

immigrants, 37, 43

immortality, 155, 167, 184
imprisonment, 18–19, 40–42, 133–34
improvisation, 129–32, 135–36, 139–42
incarnation, 42, 57, 59
"incremental perturbations," Barth, 116, 120
"Indiana" (Crane), 100
"In Memory of Jane Fraser" (Hill), 185–86
"In Praise of Limestone" (Auden), 195–96
"In Praise of the Impure" (Shapiro), 91
Insta-poets, 170
intention(s), 3, 37–38, 94–95, 102, 111, 140–41, 144, 172, 227
"interior memory," Milosz, 184
Internet, 17, 21, 51
intertextual, poems as, 36
intertextual plot, 90
"In the Waiting Room" (Bishop), 120, 226–27
investitures, 37–40, 44, 116, 118
"Invocation, 1926" (Trethewey), 182–83
Iris (Jarman), 121, 126

Jarman, Mark: *Iris*, 121, 126; "Unholy Sonnet," 58–59
Jeffers, Robinson, 87, 120–21
Jess, Tyehimba: "Millie and Christine McKoy," 139–41, 144–45; *Olio*, 139–40
Jesus Christ, 30–36, 54–59
John Donne (Stubbs), 18, 23, 29
Johnson, Samuel, 27
Jones, David, 70
Jonson, Ben: "On My First Son," 185
Joseph, Allison, 141, 145
Joyce, James, 88, 176
Jung, Carl: *Answer to Job*, 219

The Kabbalah, 223
kairos/kairoi, 14, 17, 96, 97, 109
Kalmar, Bert, 150
Kauer, Rupi, 170
Keats, John, 42, 156, 162–63; "negative capability," 225–26; "Ode to a

Nightingale," 167, 225–27; "This Living Hand," 159–62; "To Autumn," 225
Kelly, Brigit Pegeen: "Song," 10–15, 17
kenosis (self-emptying), 57–59, 228
Kermode, Frank: *The Sense of an Ending*, 96, 151
known forms, 187, 190, 196–97
Kocher, Ruth Ellen, 142, 145
Koyaanisqatsi (film), 105
Kunitz, Stanley, 44, 162–63, 210; "The Image-Maker," 155–59; "The Long Boat," 156–57; "The Wellfleet Whale," 187–89, 193
Kyrie (Voigt), 126

labor, 40, 42, 46
lamentation, 184, 203–4, 212, 225
Land of Unlikeness, 4, 17, 22, 57–58
Langland, William: "Piers Ploughman," 145
language: analogical order, 33, 35; consciousness, understanding of, 115; dissociative model of reality, 22; encountered in the moment, 123–24; function of, 5; as known form, 187–88; ontological logic of the Psalms, 218; as other, 212; public discourse, 190; and reality, 32–33, 111–12; Thomas's "Emerging," 49; and typology, 31–32; and universality, 13*See also* metaphors
Language Poets, 178
Larkin, Philip, 29–30, 50, 60, 162–64; "An Arundel Tomb," 29–30, 50, 60; "Aubade," 30, 210–12; and death, 210–12; "High Windows," 211; "Home is So Sad," 163; "The Poetry of Departures," 163–64; "Sad Steps," 211; "The Trees," 211
Lawrence, D. H., 88
Leitch, Thomas, 87, 91, 99, 116
"Lenox Hill" (Ali), 164–67
Levertov, Denise, 52–53
Levinas, Emmanuel, 204–5; *Time and the Other*, 204

Life Studies (Lowell), 4
linear time, 98–99, 103, 106–8
lineation, 163
"Listening and Making" (Hass), 66–67
"Litany" (Ashbery), 121
"Little Gidding" (Eliot), 36, 62, 150
"little song," 139–41
logos, 13
"The Long Boat" (Kunitz), 156–57
longing, 223–27
long poems, 99–101
loss, theme of, 193
The Lotus Flowers (Voigt), 126
love, 46, 50, 58–62, 157–62, 196
Lowell, Robert, 3–4; *Life Studies*, 4; "The Quaker Graveyard in Nantucket," 185
"Lycidas" (Milton), 185
Lynch, William, 5–7, 22, 33, 35, 37–38; *Christ and Apollo*, 5, 22
lyric form, 89–91
lyric narratives, 126
lyric poetry, 98

mannerism, 77
marginalization, 180
Martin, Charles, 128
Martz, Louis, 30–31
Marx, Eden Hartford, 151
Marx, Groucho, 149–55
Matejka, Adrian: *The Big Smoke*, 126–27
Matthews, William, 186–88; "Mingus in Shadow," 186
Mauberley, Hugh Selwyn, 171
The Maximus Poems (Olson), 74–77, 100
McGinn, Colin: *The Mysterious Flame*, 93–94
McKay, Claude, 105
mechanisms, 6, 21, 50–53
meditation, 31, 138, 163, 177. *See also* contemplative tradition

"Meditation at Lagunitas" (Hass), 208
"Meditations on Death" (Ungaretti), 210
memory, 58–59, 74, 127, 137–38, 181–82, 184
Merrill, James: "Christmas Tree," 76
metamorphoses, 128–32; and death, 210; of inherited forms, 135–36, 139; and tradition, 145–46; traditional sonnet form, 141–42
Metamorphoses (Ovid), 128–30
metanarrative tradition, 88
"metaphoric means," Barth, 116–17, 119
metaphors: Adcock's "No Encore," 186–87; analogical order, 33; Auden's "In Praise of Limestone," 195–96; and Bishop, 84–85; Donaghy's "More Machines," 59–62; Donne's Holy Sonnets, 40–41; Donne's "The Canonization," 26–28; Donne's "Valediction," 158, 160; and elegies, 184; function of language, 5; and longing, 224; and metamorphoses, 129–32; metaphor-as-eschatology, 195; Milosz's vertical orientation, 190; theological metaphors in Donne, 59; Weaver's "Rambling," 134
"The Metaphysical Poets" (Eliot), 20–21
metaphysics/metaphysical: and the analogical, 13; and closure, 68; and death, 210–11; of dissimilarity, 4; and dissociations, 22; Donaghy's "More Machines," 59–62; Donne's "The Canonization," 26–28; and Dyson, 50–51; farewell, poems of, 167; God's presence, 217; Kunitz's "The Wellfleet Whale," 188; Larkin's "The Poetry of Departures," 163; and longing, 224; materialist worldview, 20; and metamorphoses, 128–29; subtending metaphysics, 22–23, 49; Teilhard's "Omega Point," 50*See also* meditation
metonymy, 162, 167, 196
Metre (journal), 65

metron, 66–69, 73, 80
Mezey, Robert, 65–66
microcosm and macrocosm, 20, 28, 61–62, 99
"Middle Passage" (Hayden), 121
"Millie and Christine McKoy" (Jess), 139–41, 144–45
Milosz, Czeslaw: assessment of the situation of poetry, 215–16, 228; and audience, 179; *Bells in Winter,* 215; Charles Eliot Norton Lectures, 179, 215–16, 220; "interior memory," 184; and pain, 223; and reality, 174–75, 192, 194–95; *Unattainable Earth,* 183–84; "vertical orientation," 190–91; *The Witness of Poetry,* 179, 216; world devoid of justice, 220; writing for the dead, 183–84
Milton, John, 99, 171; "Lycidas," 185
mimesis, 33, 88, 91–92
Mimesis (Auerbach), 155
mimetic fallacy, 7, 9
Mingus, Charles, 186
"Mingus in Shadow" (Matthews), 186
Missing Measures (Steele), 65
modernism, 88, 108, 110, 121, 178
"momentary stay against confusion," Frost, 21, 72, 96, 114, 117
"Monet's Waterlilies" (Hayden), 46–48
Montague, John: *The Rough Field,* 77
"The Moose" (Bishop), 120
More, Anne, 18–19, 24, 38
More, Sir George, 18
More, Sir Thomas, 23
"More Machines" (Donaghy), 59–62
"Mother, Quiet" (Rhodes), 161–62
motion-in-stillness, 160–61
musical orchestration of the sentence, 113–14
muthos: as an imitation of action, 98; in Ashbery, 122; and Barth, 116–17; and Bishop, 118–20; and consciousness, 94; Crane's *The Bridge,* 101, 106; and Dante, 97; defined, 87; and discursivity, 108–9; dynamic structure of a poem, 115; hotwired for, 93; mythic impulse, 99; and nostalgia, 125; and prose, 90–91; and reality, 88
"My life closed twice before its close" (Dickinson), 153–55, 159
The Mysterious Flame (McGinn), 93–94

narrative and ghazals, 137–38
narrative and plot, 110–13
narrative literature, 87, 98
narrative poetry, 87–95, 97–101, 107–10, 116–18, 121, 124–27
Native Guard (Trethewey), 126, 181–83
natura naturans and *natura naturata,* 53, 73
"Nature" (Emerson), 110
The Necessary Angel (Stevens), 224–25
"negative capability," Keats, 225–26
Nelson, Marilyn, 146
New Formalism, 73, 117, 126, 178
New Narrative poetry, 108, 117. *See also* Jarman, Mark
Niedecker, Lorine, 173–74; "Poet's Work," 174; "Tradition," 174
"No Encore" (Adcock), 186–87
nominalism, 5, 34–35, 111, 180–81
nonmetrical poetry, 66, 70
nonsequiturs, 124
"No One" (Celan), 224
nostalgia, 37, 66–68, 117, 124–26
"The Novel of Consciousness" (Woolf), 87–88

objectivity, 112
octava rima, 70, 76
odes, 187–88. *See also* elegies
"Ode to a Nightingale" (Keats), 167, 225–27
The Odyssey (Homer), 99
"Of Mere Being" (Stevens), 225

O'Hara, Frank, 124
Olio (Jess), 139–40
Olson, Charles, 65, 71, 74–77; "closed
    verse," 80; "composition by field," 52;
    "I, Maximus of Gloucester, to You,"
    74–77; The Maximus Poems, 74–77, 100;
    "Projective Verse," 74, 77, 84–85
"Omega Point," Teilhard, 50
The One (Päs), 6–7
"One Body: Some Notes on Form" (Hass), 72
"One Song" (Crane), 101, 104
"On Hearing of a Friend's Illness" (Shapiro),
    191–92
"On Living" (Hikmet), 189
"On My First Son" (Jonson), 185
open form, 66, 74, 77–81, 84
Oppen, George, 180–81
opposites, 27, 102–3, 107, 154
oral traditions, 76, 88
O'Rathaille, Aoghan, 176–78
order, 5, 21, 33, 95, 119, 195, 224–25. See also
    "rage for order," Stevens
organic form, 52–53, 72–73, 77–78, 80
"organizing mimesis," Ricoeur, 92
originality, 67–68, 77
Other, 204–8, 211–12
"Over 2,000 Illustrations and a Complete
    Concordance" (Bishop), 84–85, 118–20
overall, 80, 84
Ovid, 40, 210; Metamorphoses, 128–30
Owen, Wilfred, 205

pain, 223
pantoums, 70, 139, 142
"Paradigm" (Crane), 117
Paradiso (Dante), 4, 30, 54, 97, 98–99, 107
Paris Review (journal), 113
particulars, 4–5, 34–35
Päs, Heinrich: The One, 6–7
passionate speech and syntax, 40, 68–71,
    74, 206

Paterson (Williams), 76, 100
Patterson, Raymond R., 142–43
paynims, 119
Perkins, David, 77
Perloff, Marjorie, 117
Phillips, Carl, 44
physics, 6–7, 50–51, 59, 77, 116
"A Piece of the Storm" (Strand), 35–36
"Piers Ploughman" (Langland), 145
"Piss Christ" (Hudgins), 55–58
"Piss Christ" (Serrano), 55–57
Plato, 68–69, 176
plot: Ammon's "Corson's Inlet," 116; and
    Ashbery, 121–22; Barth's "4 1/2 Lectures:
    Chaos Theory," 116–17; and Bishop,
    118–19; Crane's "Powhattan's Daughter,"
    103; Crane's The Bridge, 100–101; Dante's
    The Divine Comedy, 97; and figuration,
    106; narrative poetry, 87–95, 107–10,
    124–27; polytropic principle, 99–100; and
    sentences, 113–15; and Shapiro, 98
The Plural of Us (Costello), 171
Poe, Edgar Allan, 103, 110
"The Poem as a Field of Action" (Williams),
    73–74
poesis, 90
"The Poet" (Emerson), 65
poetic rhetoric, 180
Poetics (Aristotle), 91, 98
Poetry Foundation, 170
"The Poetry of Departures" (Larkin), 163–64
"Poetry Slam" (Edmundson), 3–4
Poetry World, 174
poet's work, 7, 14, 17, 21–23, 33, 37, 53, 84,
    144–45, 176, 181–83
"Poet's Work" (Niedecker), 174
Poirier, Richard, 112
polyphonic orchestration, 101–2, 126–27
polysemous reality, 34, 37
"polytropic principle," Leitch, 99–100, 116
Pope, Alexander, 170, 176

popularity, 170–71

positivism and reductionism, 6, 21–22

postmodernism, 34–35, 108, 110–11, 121. *See also* projective verse

Pound, Ezra, 65; and audience, 171; *Cantos*, 76, 90, 99–100, 206; fascism of, 70–71, 143, 206; projective verse, 75; and rhythm, 73–74

"Powhattan's Daughter" (Crane), 100–106

Prayershreds (Beasley), 126

predictive typology, 31–32

"Preface to the *Lyrical Ballads*" (Wordsworth), 73, 175

"The Prelude" (Wordsworth), 32, 99

"pressure of reality," Stevens, 23–24, 26

prison. *See* imprisonment

"The Prodigal" (Bishop), 81

"Proem: To Brooklyn Bridge" (Crane), 101

profane, 14, 16, 27, 56, 57, 59, 90

"The Progress of the Soul" (Donne), 42, 57

projective verse, 74–78

"Projective Verse" (Olson), 74, 77, 84–85

"Psalm" (Celan), 220–21, 223

Psalms, 203–8, 210–15, 216–21, 223–26

"The Quaker Graveyard in Nantucket" (Lowell), 185

quantum world, 6, 11, 52–53

racism, 9, 104–5, 136

"rage for order," Stevens, 4, 21, 45, 67–68, 80, 95, 123–24

Ramazani, Jahan, 184–85

"Rambling" (Weaver), 133–35, 144–45

realism, 34

reality: Ali's "Ghazal," 194–95; analogical dimension of, 33–34; artistic commitment, 13; Auden's "In Praise of Limestone," 195–96; and connectivity, 21–22; and death, 29–30; dissociative model of, 22; Donaghy's

"More Machines," 60–61; Donne's Holy Sonnets, 41; Donne's "The Canonization," 24–28; and emergence, 49, 54; and God, 42; human place in the cosmos, 54–55; and the internet, 51; Kelly's "Song," 11; and language, 32–33; mechanistic view of, 52; Milosz on, 192; Milosz's quest for, 174–75; open poetics, 80; and plot, 89; poet's naming of, 188–89; polysemous reality, 37; "pressure of reality," Stevens, 23–24, 26; realistic novels, 88; and Saussure, 111–12; Strand's "A Piece of the Storm," 36; Teilhard's "Omega Point," 50; and unknowing, 55; vision of, 3–6, 17, 110–11; writing for the dead, 197

reconfiguration, 97, 105, 119, 139, 144

recurrences, 80, 138

religion/religious: art must assume the role of, 29–31; and Bishop, 83; Dickinson in "This World is not Conclusion," 47–48; and disintegrations, 180; faith in divine intervention, 216; Larkin's "Aubade," 211; likeness of things, 58; sermon, poem as, 7–8

renewal, 167, 184, 186

reordering of time, 91–93

repetition, 66–67, 137–38, 141–42, 152–53

restrictions, 72, 76

revelation, 226–27

Rhodes, Martha, 161–63; "Mother, Quiet," 161–62

rhyme schemes, 25, 54–55, 140–42, 154, 163–64

rhythm, 38–39, 67, 69, 73–74

Rich, Adrienne: "Diving into the Wreck," 21

Ricoeur, Paul, 91–95, 108, 111–12, 115, 125; *Time and Narrative*, 91

Rilke, Rainer Maria, 218; "Duino Elegies," 220; "Sonnets to Orpheus," 90–91

"The Rime of the Ancient Mariner" (Coleridge), 12

"The River" (Crane), 106
"The Road Less Traveled By" (Frost), 113
"The Road to the Contagious Hospital"
  (Williams), 91
Robinson, Edward Arlington, 87, 91
Robinson, Marilynne, 20, 65, 70
Romantics, 54, 72, 89, 203
Rosenberg, Isaac, 205
The Rough Field (Montague), 77
Rough Fugue (Adcock), 187
ruach, 203
Ruby, Harry, 150
The Rumpus (blog), 136

Sachs, Nelly, 177–78; "Flight and
  Metamorphosis," 177
Sacks, Peter, 184
sacred, 14, 16, 17, 48, 56, 59, 90, 219
sacred history, 119
"Sad Steps" (Larkin), 211
"Sailing to Byzantium" (Yeats), 69–70
Sassoon, Siegfried, 205
Saturday Night Fever (film), 86–87, 92
Saussure, Ferdinand de, 111–12, 115
Saving the Appearances (Barfield), 35
scale, 110–15
Scarry, Elaine: *The Body in Pain*, 213
Scheherazade, 117–18, 120, 121, 123–24, 126
"Scheherazade" (Ashbery), 122–23
Scholes, Robert, 87–89, 98
"The Schooner Flight" (Walcott), 145
"Searching for the Ox" (Simpson), 125
Searle, John R., 115
"Second Anniversary" (Donne), 54
"secular narrative," Scholes, 88
selfhood, 187, 226–27
"Self-Portrait in a Convex Mirror"
  (Ashbery), 122
"semantic slippages," Birkerts, 123–24
The Sense of an Ending (Kermode), 96, 151
sensibility, 4, 5–6, 20–23, 37, 45, 117, 169

sentences/sentence sounds, 71–72, 74, 79,
  112–15, 121
sermon, poem as, 7–8
"The Sermon on the Warpland" (Brooks), 7–8
Serrano, Andres: "Piss Christ," 55–57
sestinas, 70, 81, 165
sexual inuendo, 26–27
Shakespeare, William, 41, 67, 74, 140;
  Sonnet 116, 50, 60
shapelessness, 53, 76, 130
Shapiro, Alan, 97–98, 110, 112, 126; "In
  Praise of the Impure," 91; "On Hearing of
  a Friend's Illness," 191–92
Shetley, Vernon, 190; *After the Death of
  Poetry*, 178
"The Shield of Achilles" (Auden), 192–93, 195
signs, 111–13
Silliman, Ron, 37
Simpson, Louis: "Searching for the Ox," 125
singing place (Odeon), 3, 8, 10, 17
skepticism, 136
Snyder, Gary, 169
social justice/injustice, 10, 136, 144–45,
  219–20. *See also* violence
social media, 168, 171, 197
Socinus, 50
solitude, 204, 207, 211, 223, 225
"So Long" (Whitman), 167
Sonata Mulattica (Dove), 125–26
song, 9–17, 90–91, 217–18, 223–25
"Song" (Kelly), 10–15, 17
"Song and Story" (Voigt), 14–17, 213–14, 223–24
sonic textures, 82, 153
Sonnet 116 (Shakespeare), 50, 60
sonnets, 91, 134–42
"Sonnets to Orpheus" (Rilke), 90–91
soul, 38–41, 122, 212, 214
speech, 73–77
"speech communities," Costello, 180
Sphere (Ammons), 80
Spinoza, Baruch, 53

Spirit in Ashes (Wyschogrod), 221
Spiritual Exercises (Ignatius of Loyola), 31
splay community, 171
"spots of time," Wordsworth, 109
Steele, Timothy, 67, 73; *Missing Measures*, 65
Stevens, Wallace: art must assume the role of religion, 29; and decreation, 224–25; farewell, poems of, 162–63; "Final Soliloquy to the Interior Paramour," 152; "The Idea of Order at Key West," 45, 80, 123; *The Necessary Angel*, 224–25; "Of Mere Being," 225; pressure of reality, 23–24, 26; "rage for order," 4, 21, 45, 67–68, 80, 95, 123–24; and reality, 27; "Waving Adieu, Adieu, Adieu," 151–55, 159, 160
stewardship, 176
St. Paul's Letter to the Philippians, 57
Strand, Mark, 184; "A Piece of the Storm," 35–36
The Stranger World (Wilson), 126
Stubbs, John Heath: *John Donne*, 18, 23, 29
subjectivity, 122, 218
sublime, 80, 121, 204, 216
subtending metaphysics, 22–23, 49
suffering, 13, 16, 17, 125, 203–7, 217, 226–27. *See also* affliction
surpluses of meaning, 15, 28, 32, 37
"Swan and Shadow" (Hollander), 76
sweetelle, 141–42
"Symbol as Revelation" (Yeats), 29
symmetries, 110
syncopated sonnets, 139–42, 145–46
syntax, 68–71, 75, 79, 114, 115, 152–53, 159, 167

technology, 21, 75–76, 179, 216. *See also* connections/connectivity
teleology, 20, 40, 97, 99–101, 115, 123, 151
telos, 87, 99–100, 119
tercet, 135, 137, 142
theophany, 102, 219, 220
"This Living Hand" (Keats), 159–62

"This World is not Conclusion" (Dickinson), 47–50
Thomas, R. S., 45–46; "Emerging," 48–50
Thomas and Beulah (Dove), 125
Thomism, 50, 107, 116
"Those Winter Sundays" (Hayden), 91
"Three Songs" (Crane), 100
Tillich, Paul, 14
time, 14–16, 35–36, 50–51, 58–62, 82, 88–95, 96–99, 103–4, 112, 120–24, 155
Time and Narrative (Ricoeur), 91
Time and the Other (Levinas), 204
Tindall, W. Y., 178–79
"To Autumn" (Keats), 225
Tocqueville, Alexis de, 171–72
"tone of the center," von Hallberg, 178
tone(s), 14, 26, 38, 56, 61, 83, 101–2, 109, 123, 161–62, 163–64, 203, 212
Toomer, Jean: *Cane*, 104–5
To the Lighthouse (Woolf), 89–90, 92
Tractatus Logico-Philosophicus (Wittgenstein), 35
Tracy, David: *The Analogical Imagination*, 33
"Tradition" (Niedecker), 174
The Tradition (Brown), 135–39
traditional meter and form, 66–67, 70, 72–77
tradition(s), 68, 88–89, 136, 142–46
transcendence: and affliction, 219–21; Brooks's "Boy Breaking Glass," 9; in Dickinson, 154; Heaney's "impulse toward," 7–8; Larkin's "Aubade," 211–12; in the Psalms, 204–7; Thomas's "Emerging," 49; understanding of God, 46; writing for the dead, 190–91
transformations. *See* metamorphoses
"The Trees" (Larkin), 211
Trethewey, Natasha, 181–84; *Congregation*, 182–83; "Invocation, 1926," 182–83; *Native Guard*, 126, 181–83
triolet, 141
trochaic substitution, 39–40, 69, 154

"The Tunnel" (Crane), 101, 103, 106–7
"twittering world," Eliot, 168–69
typology, 31–32
Tzara, Tristan, 150

Unattainable Earth (Milosz), 183–84
Ungaretti, Giuseppe, 210–11; "Meditations on Death," 210
"Unholy Sonnet" (Jarman), 58–59
unity-in-difference, 51, 140, 194–96
unity of action, 97, 102, 106–7
universal(s), 5–6, 13, 34–36, 96, 110, 112, 164–65, 169, 190, 203
univocal, 5, 35, 108–9
unknowing, 12, 55, 154–55
unlikeness, 4–5, 22, 35–36. See also Land of Unlikeness

"A Valediction: Forbidding Mourning" (Donne), 157–60, 163, 167
Vaughan, Henry, 31
"vertical orientation," Milosz, 190–91
violence, 12, 24–28, 30, 40, 46, 133–34, 138, 218–20
Violence and the Sacred (Girard), 219
Virgil, 99; Aeneid, 101
vivid speech, 68, 74
vocation, 182–83. See poet's work
voice-over prose narrative, 102
voice(s), 3–4, 8, 10–11, 67, 74–76, 90, 101–4, 107–8, 113, 140, 177, 181, 206–8, 218–21
Voigt, Ellen Bryant, 79–80; "The Flexible Lyric," 79; Kyrie, 126; The Lotus Flowers, 126; "Song and Story," 14–17, 213–14, 223–24
volta, 59, 138, 142
von Hallberg, Robert: American Poetry and Culture, 1945–1980, 178

Wakoski, Diane, 66–67
Walcott, Derek: "The Schooner Flight," 145
"The Wasteland" (Eliot), 90, 95

"A Wave" (Ashbery), 121
"Waving Adieu, Adieu, Adieu" (Stevens), 151–55, 159, 160
Weaver, Afaa Michael, 132–36, 139, 141; "Rambling," 133–35, 144–45
Weil, Simone, 5, 35, 212, 219, 224–25
"The Wellfleet Whale" (Kunitz), 187–89, 193
Wenthe, William: The Gentle Art, 126
"West-Running Brook" (Frost), 92–94, 111, 164
"When Lilacs Last in the Dooryard Bloom'd" (Whitman), 185
Whitman, Walt, 65, 68, 102–3, 106, 209–10, 228; "So Long," 167; "When Lilacs Last in the Dooryard Bloom'd," 185
Wilbur, Richard, 65, 70, 124
Williams, William Carlos, 52, 65, 68, 73–76, 99, 169; Paterson, 76, 100; "The Poem as a Field of Action," 73–74; "The Road to the Contagious Hospital," 91
Wilner, Eleanor, 93, 125–26
Wilson, Ryan: The Stranger World, 126
Wiman, Christian, 117
Winters, Yvor, 117
The Witness of Poetry (Milosz), 179, 216
Wittgenstein, Ludwig: Tractatus Logico-Philosophicus, 35
Woolf, Virginia, 87–94, 98, 110, 115–16, 123; To the Lighthouse, 89–90, 92; "The Novel of Consciousness," 87–88
"wordness of language," Bernstein, 112
Wordsworth, William, 32, 68, 73, 99, 109, 150, 170, 203; "Preface to the Lyrical Ballads," 73, 175; "The Prelude," 32, 99
World of Forms, 176
World War I poets, 205–6
Wright, Charles: "Homage to Paul Cezanne," 197
Wright, James, 175
writing for the dead, 176, 178, 181–87, 189–92, 195–97. See also elegies
Wyschogrod, Edith: Spirit in Ashes, 221

Yeats, William Butler, 67–73; "Among School Children," 70; Auden's elegy for, 29; "Crazy Jane Talks with the Bishop," 54–56; exclusion of the World War I poets, 205–6; and Glück, 162; ideal and the actual, 171; meditative poem, 31; and modernism, 178; personal voice, 75; persona of the traditionally public poet, 4; poet's work, 21; and rhetoric, 66; "Sailing to Byzantium," 69–70; "Symbol as Revelation," 29; traditional meter and form, 76

Zeno, 110
Zukofsky, Louis, 52